Lord Krishna And His Essential Teachings

If God Were to Tell You the Truth About Life, This is It

By
Stephen Knapp

Dedicated to
My Spiritual Master, Srila A. C. Bhaktivedanta Swami,
Who gave me the knowledge and access to the realizations
about the ultimate goal of life.
This is also dedicated to all those who want to understand
the truth about what we are supposed to be doing here.

Copyright © 2014, by Stephen Knapp

All rights reserved. No part of this book may be reproduced without written permission from the copyright owner and publisher, except for brief quotations for review or educational purposes.

Published with the Support of
The World Relief Network,
Detroit, Michigan

ISBN-10: 1499655878
ISBN-13: 978-1499655872

Cover Photo: A miniature painting on marble of Lord Krishna carrying His flute, from the author's personal collection.

Numerous color prints of Lord Krishna and photographs of the various Vedic Divinities can be seen, downloaded or printed for your perusal, meditation or use from the author's websites.

You can find out more about Stephen Knapp
and his books, free ebooks, research,
and numerous articles and photos,
along with many other spiritual resources at his websites or blog:
www.stephen-knapp.com
http://stephenknapp.info
http://stephenknapp.wordpress.com

Other books by the author:
1. The Secret Teachings of the Vedas: The Eastern Answers to the Mysteries of Life
2. The Universal Path to Enlightenment
3. The Vedic Prophecies: A New Look into the Future
4. How the Universe was Created and Our Purpose In It
5. Toward World Peace: Seeing the Unity Between Us All
6. Facing Death: Welcoming the Afterlife
7. The Key to Real Happiness
8. Proof of Vedic Culture's Global Existence
9. The Heart of Hinduism: The Eastern Path to Freedom, Enlightenment and Illumination
10. The Power of the Dharma: An Introduction to Hinduism and Vedic Culture
11. Vedic Culture: The Difference it can Make in Your Life
12. Reincarnation & Karma: How They Really Affect Us
13. The Eleventh Commandment: The Next Step for Social Spiritual Development
14. Seeing Spiritual India: A Guide to Temples, Holy Sites, Festivals and Traditions
15. Crimes Against India: And the Need to Protect its Ancient Vedic Tradition
16. Destined for Infinity, a spiritual adventure in the Himalayas
17. Yoga and Meditation: Their Real Purpose and How to Get Started
18. Avatars, Gods and Goddesses of Vedic Culture: Understanding the Characteristics, Powers and Positions of the Hindu Divinities
19. The Soul: Understanding Our Real Identity
20. Prayers, Mantras and Gayatris: A Collection for Insights, Protection, Spiritual Growth, and Many Other Blessings
21. Krishna Deities and Their Miracles: How the Images of Lord Krishna Interact with Their Devotees.
22. Defending Vedic Dharma: Tackling the Issues to Make a Difference.
23. Advancements of the Ancient Vedic Culture.
24. Spreading Vedic Traditions Through Temples.
25. The Bhakti-Yoga Handbook

CONTENTS

PREFACE   1

INTRODUCTION: 3
    WHO IS SRI KRISHNA?
    What the Vedic Texts Say About Him * What Sri Krishna Says About Himself * The Mistake of Accepting Krishna as a Representation of Something Higher * Krishna as the Source of all Creation * Krishna as the Source of all Avatars of God * Why Lord Krishna Descends into this World * How Lord Krishna Took Birth in the Material World * Janmastami–Krishna's Birth Festival * Misunderstanding the Activities of Lord Krishna * The Beauty of Krishna * How to Understand God * The Result of Failing to Understand Krishna * Descriptions of Lord Krishna's Eternal Abode

CHAPTER ONE: 55
    WHAT IS REAL KNOWLEDGE
    What Lord Krishna Says to be the Most Important Knowledge * How This Vedic Knowledge is Descending Down Through Time

CHAPTER TWO: 62
    THE RARITY OF HUMAN BIRTH

CHAPTER THREE: 65
    THE TEMPORARY NATURE AND PURPOSE OF MATERIAL EXISTENCE * The Affects of Maya, The Illusory Energy * Finding Real Fulfillment

CHAPTER FOUR: 72
    OUR REAL IDENTITY AS SPIRITUAL BEINGS
    The Living Being in Material Existence * Seeing the Spiritual Unity Between Us

CHAPTER FIVE: 84
REINCARNATION AND THE IMMORTALITY OF THE SOUL

CHAPTER SIX: 90
THE WAYS OF SPIRITUAL DEVELOPMENT AND REAL FREEDOM
Jnana-yoga * How to Perform Karma-yoga

CHAPTER SEVEN: 102
HOW TO PRACTICE MYSTIC YOGA
Worshiping the Brahman: Lord Krishna's Impersonal Aspect * Lord Krishna's Instructions on Yoga * It Is Not Easy for One to Reach Spiritual Perfection in this Form of Yoga * The Essential Points in this Yoga System * Devotional Meditation Frees One From the Illusion * The Highest Levels of Spiritual Enlightenment * The Mystic Perfections Attained Through Yoga * The Way to Meditate * Leaving the Body Through Yoga: The Ultimate Perfection

CHAPTER EIGHT: 127
RECOGNIZING THE ENERGY OF GOD EVERYWHERE

CHAPTER NINE: 133
LORD KRISHNA AS THE SUPERSOUL

CHAPTER TEN: 136
REALIZING LORD KRISHNA AS BHAGAVAN, THE SUPREME BEING
The Process of Devotional Service--Bhakti-yoga * The Foundational Principles * The Essential Ways for Developing Love for Krishna * The Way to Worship the Deity Form of the Lord * In the End You go Back to Krishna * Why Lord Krishna Advises us to Engage in the Process of Bhakti-yoga * Those Who Render Devotional Service to Lord Krishna * Those Who

Do Not Take up Devotional Service * Bhakti-yoga Gives the Same Results as Mystic Yoga and More * How to Meditate or Think of Lord Krishna * Chanting Lord Krishna's Holy Names * The Bhakti Process Erases Past Karma * Even the Worst Sinners Can be Delivered and Reach Peace * The Conclusive Decision is Up to Us * The Need to Spread This Knowledge

CHAPTER ELEVEN: 167
THOSE WHO WILL REMAIN IN MATERIAL BONDAGE

CHAPTER TWELVE: 174
THOSE WHO ARE ELIGIBLE FOR LIBERATION

CHAPTER THIRTEEN: 180
REAL LIBERATION MEANS RETURNING TO LORD KRISHNA

CHAPTER FOURTEEN: 185
KRISHNA THE EVER-LOVING GOD

CHAPTER FIFTEEN: 194
ABOUT OTHER FORMS OF RELIGION AND ACTIVITIES
A Closer Look at the Effects of the Modes of Material Nature * Different Qualities in the Modes of Nature * Observing the Interactions of the Modes of Material Nature * Types of Knowledge in the Modes * Types of Foods in the Modes * Types of Actions in the Modes * Types of Residences in the Modes of Nature * Determination in the Modes * Happiness in the Modes * The Conclusion and Ultimate Purpose of the Vedic System--How to Become Free From the Modes of Material Nature

CHAPTER SIXTEEN: 207
   HOW TO BE A SPIRITUAL PERSON IN THIS MATERIAL
   WORLD
   Helpful Duties for Women * On Serving Parents * Criticizing
   Others * Duties of a Ruler

CONCLUSION 216

APPENDIX ONE: 217
   THE IMPORTANCE OF THE BHAGAVAD-GITA IN THIS
   DAY AND AGE

CHAPTER NOTES 227

REFERENCES 234

GLOSSARY 239

INDEX 250

ABOUT THE AUTHOR 254

PREFACE

If God were to tell you the truth about life, this is it, or as close to it as you can find. Often times we or others go through life and occasionally find ourselves confused about the purpose of life, or what our direction should be. That is normal when we are without proper knowledge or guidance. However, God is naturally the ultimate authority on spiritual topics and the purpose of His creation. Therefore, we should want to understand what God has to say about the purpose of life, how we got here, where we are going, and what we are supposed to do now that we are here. There are many teachings in many different religions that try to clarify these things, but there are more direct teachings that come directly from the instructions of God in the Vedic tradition, especially in His form as Lord Krishna, than can be found anywhere else.

Some of the most plentiful and prominent and clearly defined spiritual teachings of all are found in the Vedic tradition, and some of the most clear of these instructions are those that have been given to us by Sri Krishna Himself. These are found in such books as the *Bhagavad-gita, Bhagavata Purana, Vishnu Purana, Mahabharata,* and others. He has given some of the most elaborate, detailed, and direct of all spiritual knowledge that can be acquired by anyone. Therefore, this book uses numerous verses of Lord Krishna's directions, as found in these various texts, as the basis of what is provided herein. Furthermore, the explanations and purports to this knowledge have been given by some of the most realized saints and sages the world has known. These may be powerful *acharyas* of lines of disciples, or founders of particular schools of thought, or even western poets that were propelled to the deepest contemplations and realizations that were seeded by their reading of such teachings.

So it is to our benefit, luxury and blessings that we can still look deep into this spiritual understanding that can guide us toward the true purpose of life. Therefore, let us consider this profound spiritual knowledge that Lord Krishna has given to us. This knowledge should be studied repeatedly to attain additional clarity, insight and realization of its deeper meanings. It is known to be timeless, ever-fresh and ever-useful for anyone, regardless of their situation or background. This is because this knowledge is composed of the universal spiritual truths that are for anyone in any time in history, or place in the universe.

Remember, here in this volume is the heart or essential spiritual message of what Lord Krishna has given. We have assembled the most important and relevant teachings of God that can most quickly assist us in our understanding of life. This is not meant to include all of the many verses wherein He is quoted in the other Vedic texts. If that were the case, this book would be much longer than it is. So this is the essence of His teachings and explanations of spiritual truths, and only a small portion of the numerous references that contain the instructions of Lord Krishna or His incarnations, *avataras*, or expansions.

In this way, we can clearly understand the essence of spiritual knowledge and easily apply it in our lives. Many more of His instructions can be found in the *Bhagavad-gita, Srimad-Bhagavatam, Vishnu Purana, Mahabharata*, and other texts, which we encourage the reader to find and study for themselves.

However, there is much spiritual knowledge herein, and it cannot be taken in too quickly if you lose concentration. Therefore, the instructions and information included in this volume should be studied carefully and absorbed at one's own pace. So take your time and try to study it in a way that provides the best means for you to understand and imbibe it and become enlightened by it. Then, as planting a seed, it will grow as you begin to apply it in your life, which will make all the difference.

INTRODUCTION

Who is Sri Krishna?

WHAT THE VEDIC TEXTS SAY ABOUT HIM

It is the Vedic literature that most clearly reveals the nature and identity of the Absolute Truth or Supreme Personality. As with many of the Vedic texts, they begin to reveal this identity with hints that show how the Absolute is a person from which everything else originates. One such reference is the first and second verses of the *Vedanta Sutras*. The first verse states simply *Atato brahma jijnasa*, that "Now one should enquire into the Brahman." This means that now that you have attained a human body, you should use your intelligence to discover what is really spiritual and what is the Absolute Truth. Then the second verse begins to explain what is this Absolute Truth: "He from whom everything originates is the Absolute." Thus, as it refers to "He", the source of all that exists, the ultimate point of creation, is a person.

The *Katha Upanishad* (2.2.9) relates in like manner: "As with fire--the one original flame expands itself throughout the world by producing many more separate flames; similarly, the one Supreme Soul, who resides in every *jiva*, enters this cosmos and expands Himself in replica images known as *pratibimba*, or the *jivas*." Thus, herein we have further confirmation that the Lord exists outside of the created universe.

So who is this Being from whom all else is created? Much more information is supplied from numerous Vedic sources. For example, the early *Rig-veda* (1.22.20-21) relates that Lord Vishnu is that Supreme Being, the Absolute Truth whose lotus feet all the demigods are always eager to see. His most sublime region is only visible to those endowed with spiritual vision, accessed by ever-vigilant devotion.

The *Rig-veda* continues elsewhere (1.154.4-5): "Him whose three places are filled with sweetness and imperishable joy, who verily alone upholds the threefold, the earth, the heaven, and all living beings. May I attain to His well-loved mansion where men devoted to the Gods are happy. For there springs the well of honey [or Soma] in Vishnu's highest step."

The *Svetasvatara Upanishad* has similar verses that relate how no one is superior to Him, nothing is smaller or larger than Him. He is the one Supreme Being (purusha), who has created everything complete. On His planet, He is situated like a steadfast tree, emanating great effulgence.

As explained in the *Caitanya-caritamrita* (Adi. 2.106), Lord Krishna is the original primeval Lord, the source of all other expansions. All the revealed scriptures accept Sri Krishna as the Supreme Lord. Furthermore (*Cc*.Adi 2.24-26), it goes on to relate that Lord Krishna Himself is the one undivided Absolute Truth and ultimate reality. He manifests in three features, namely the Brahman, Paramatma and Bhagavan (the Supreme Personality).

The *Svetasvatara Upanishad* (5.4) also relates that the Supreme Being is worshipable by everyone, the one adorable God, repository of all goodness, ruler of all creatures, born from the womb [in His pastime of appearing as Sri Krishna in Vrindavana, India 5000 years ago], for He is eternally present in all living beings [as Supersoul]. Furthermore, it states (3.8), "I have realized this transcendental Personality of Godhead who shines most brilliantly like the sun beyond all darkness. Only by realizing Him one goes beyond the cycle of birth and deaths. Absolutely there is no other means to get God-realization."

The *Svetasvatara Upanishad* (5.6) further elaborates that Lord Krishna is the topmost of all the gods. "He is the most esoteric aspect hidden in the *Upanishads* which form the essence of the *Vedas*. Brahma knows Him as the source of himself as well as the *Vedas*. The gods like Shiva and the seers of the ancient, like

Vamadeva *rishi* realizing Him, ever became dovetailed in His service and therefore they naturally became immortal." And in (6.7) it continues: "Let us take our final resort at Him who is the Transcendent and the only adorable Lord of the universe, who is the highest Deity over all the deities, the Supreme Ruler of all rulers–Him let us know as the Paramount Divinity."

The *GopalaTapani Upanishad*, which is about Gopala or Krishna, is quite clear on this point, and naturally has numerous verses that explain the nature of the Absolute Truth and Lord Krishna. A few of such verses include the following: "Brahma with his full awareness emphatically said, 'Sri Krishna is the Supreme Divinity. (1.3) He who meditates on Sri Krishna, serves Him with unalloyed devotion and [makes His transcendental senses gratified by engaging one's own spiritual senses in] rendering service to Him–all of them become immortal and attain the summum bonum, or perfection of life. (1.10) Sri Krishna is that Supreme Divinity as the Paramount Eternal Reality among all other sentient beings and the Fountain-source of consciousness to all conscious beings. He is the only reality without a second but as a Supersoul dwelling in the cave of the hearts of all beings He rewards them in accordance with their respective actions in life. Those men of intuitive wisdom who serve Him with loving devotion surely attain the highest perfection of life. Whereas those who do not do so never gain this highest beatitude of their lives. (1.22) ... This Sri Krishna who is most dear to you all is the cause of all causes. He is the efficient cause of the creation of the universe as well as the superintending force for propelling the *jiva* souls. Therefore, although He is the enjoyer as well as the Lord of all sacrifices, He is ever *atmarama*, self-satisfied." (2.17)

So, summarily, as it is explained and concluded in a variety of Vedic texts, Lord Krishna is the Supreme Personality of Godhead. In other words, as it is said in Sanskrit, *krsnas tu bhagavan svayam (Bhagavata Purana* 1.3.28), Krishna is the source of all other incarnations and forms of God. He is the ultimate and end of all Truth and philosophical enquiry, the goal or

Krishna as Nand Kumar, standing in the groves of Vrindavana

end result of Vedanta. He is the all-attractive personality and source of all pleasure for which we are always hankering. He is the origin from which everything else manifests. He is the unlimited source of all power, wealth, fame, beauty, wisdom, and renunciation. Thus, no one is greater than Him. Since Krishna is the source of all living beings, He is also considered the Supreme Father and source of all worlds. He is shown with a blue or blackish complexion. This color represents absolute, pure consciousness, which also is unconditional love for all of His creation and all His devotees. Krishna is the embodiment of love. He is also *sat-chit-ananda vigraha*, which means the form of eternal knowledge and bliss.

The reason why the Lord is called "Krishna" is explained in a book known as the *Sri Caitanya Upanishad*, which is connected with the *Atharva-veda*. In verse twelve it is explained: "These three names of the Supreme Lord (Hari, Krishna and Rama) may be explained in the following way: (1) 'Hari' means 'He who unties [*harati*] the knot of material desire in the hearts of the living entities'; (2) 'Krishna' is divided into two syllables 'krish' and 'na'. 'Krish' means 'He who attracts the minds of all living entities', and 'na' means 'the supreme transcendental pleasure'. These two syllables combine to become the name 'Krishna'; and (3) 'Rama' means 'He who delights [*ramayati*] all living entities', and it also means 'He who is full of transcendental bliss'. The maha-mantra [the Hare Krishna mantra] consists of the repetition of these names of the Supreme Lord." In this way, Krishna's names represent His character and qualities, which, in this case, means the greatest and all attractive transcendental pleasure.

So, as we further our investigation of the identity of Sri Krishna in the Vedic literature, especially the *Bhagavad-gita*, *Srimad-Bhagavatam*, *Vishnu Purana*, *Brahma-samhita*, and many others, we find that they are full of descriptions of Lord Krishna as the Supreme Being. These actually can help us understand the nature of God regardless of which religion we may affiliate ourselves. So let us find out more about God from these descriptions.

The *Brihadaranyaka Upanishad* says, *purnam idam purnat purnam udachyate*: "Although He expands in many ways, He keeps His original personality. His original spiritual body remains as it is." Thus, we can understand that God can expand His energies in many ways, but is not affected or diminished in His potency. And His original form and personality remain the same.

The invocation mantra of the *Sri Ishopanishad* says the same thing:

> *Om purnam adah purnam idam*
> *purnat purnam udachyate*
> *purnasya purnam adaya*
> *purnam evavashishyate*

This means, in essence, that the Supreme Being is complete and perfect, and whatever is expanded from His energies is also complete and does not take away from His potencies in any way. He remains as He is, the complete whole and the complete balance.

The *Svetasvatara Upanishad* (6.6) also states: "The Supreme Personality of Godhead, the original person, has multifarious energies. He is the origin of material creation, and it is due to Him only that everything changes. He is the protector of religion and annihilator of all sinful activities. He is the master of all opulences." This verse specifically points out that only due to God's multi-potencies does the world continue to change and be maintained. He also protects religion, which could not be done if He were impersonal or without form. This is only logical since it takes a person to watch over, protect or maintain anything.

In the *Katha Upanishad* (2.2.13) there is the important verse; *nityo nityanam chetanas chetananam eko bahunam yo vidadhati kaman*: "He is the supreme eternally conscious person who maintains all other living entities." So, this Supreme Person is accepted by Vedic authority to be the Absolute Truth, as confirmed in the *Caitanya-caritamrita* (*Adi*.7.111): "According to direct understanding, the Absolute Truth is the Supreme Personality of Godhead, who has all spiritual opulences. No one can be equal to or greater than Him."

The *Svetasvatara Upanishad* (4.7-8) goes on to describe that, "The Supreme Lord is He who is referred to by the mantras of the *Rig-veda*, who resides in the topmost, eternal sky, and who elevates His saintly devotees to share that same position. One who has developed pure love for Him and realizes His uniqueness then appreciates His glories and is freed from sorrow. What further good can the *Rig* mantras bestow on one who knows that Supreme Lord? All who come to know Him achieve the supreme destination."

This is further corroborated in the *Katha Upanishad* (2.3.8-9) wherein it says: "Beyond the Brahmajyoti (*nirguna* or formless Brahman of the monist) there is the Great Purusha viz., Purushottama God who is all-pervading (as the Brahmajyoti) and without any empirical attributes, but having *sat-chit-ananda*--transcendental embodiment. He who realizes this Purushottama-tattva is finally liberated. Attaining a spiritual body he renders eternal service to the Purushottama [Supreme Being]. The Transcendental Personality of Godhead is beyond the purview of occult vision. But He can be apprehended through a pure transparent mind imbibed with intuitive wisdom born out of unalloyed devotional practices in the very core of one's own unstinted heart--those who have really got such a vision have gained final beatitude."

Additional references further describe how Lord Krishna exists beyond the impersonal Brahman effulgence, or great white light. The *Svetasvatara Upanishad* (6.7-8) relates that, "The Supreme Lord is the controller of all other controllers, and He is the greatest of all the diverse planetary leaders. Everyone is under His control. All entities are delegated with particular power only by the Supreme Lord; they are not supreme themselves. He is also worshipable by all demigods and is the supreme director of all directors. Therefore, He is transcendental to all kinds of material leaders and controllers and is worshipable by all. There is no one greater than Him, and He is the supreme cause of all causes. He does not possess a bodily form like that of an ordinary living entity. There is no difference between His body and His soul. He is absolute [pure consciousness]. All His senses are transcendental. Any one of His senses can perform the action of any other sense. Therefore, no one is greater than Him or equal to Him. His potencies are multifarious, and thus His deeds are automatically performed as a natural sequence."

The *Chandogya Upanishad* (3.17.6-7) goes on to relate the need to become aware and focused on the Supreme Being, Sri Krishna. "Ghora Angihasa *rishi* advised his disciple that he should invoke Bhagavan Sri Krishna, the Son of Devakidevi [*devakiputra*], by repeating this triad thinking as if death is sitting upon his shoulder: 'Thou art the Indestructible; Thou art the Unchangeable; Thou art the very Substratum that enlivens the entire universe.' On culturing this, he (the disciple) became free from desires. On this point there are two additional *Rig* verses. The light (Grace) that comes from the Primeval Fountain-Source dispels darkness of illusion like the morning sun dispelling the night darkness. [This is also found in *Rig-veda* 8.6.30] The Primeval Fountain-Source from Whom light (Grace) comes which dispels darkness viz., illusion of the soul like the morning sun dispels the darkness of the night and shines forth far beyond the universe. When we perceive that most Effulgent Highest Purusha (Supreme Person) dwelling in the world of Transcendent (*sarva loka urddham svah Bhagavat Lokam paripashantah*) and through unalloyed devotion when we attain Him, the most Effulgent One Who is the God of all gods. We in ecstatic joy proclaim, 'Yea, we have attained Him. Yea, we have attained the summum bonum of life--Yea, the final beatitude in life.'" [A similar point is also found in the *Rig-veda* 1.50.10, as well as at *Rig* 1.22.16-21.]

In the *Bhagavad-gita* (10.12-13), Arjuna also explains that Lord Krishna is the Supreme Brahman, the ultimate, the supreme

Introduction 11

Lord Krishna standing on the chariot, teaching Arjuna the Bhagavad-gita and showing His universal form in the background, while the armies ready themselves on the battlefield of Kurukshetra

abode and purifier, the Absolute Truth and the eternal divine person. He is the primal God, transcendental and original, the unborn and all-pervading beauty. All the great sages such as Narada, Asita, Devala, and Vyasa proclaim this.

He goes on to say that Krishna is the original Personality, the Godhead. He is the only sanctuary of the manifested material world. He knows everything and is all that is knowable. He is above the material modes. With limitless form, He pervades the whole cosmic manifestation. (*Bg*.11.38) Krishna is the father of the complete cosmic manifestation, the worshipable chief and spiritual master. No one is equal to Him, nor can anyone be one with Him. He is immeasurable. (*Bg*.11.43)

The receptivity of this nectarean knowledge about and from Lord Krishna depends on two things: one is the qualities of the receiver and how open or faithful the person is to such high thoughts and vibrations, and the other is whether the ecstasies within the message of the *Bhagavatam* get perverted or spoiled from the misinterpretation of a disbeliever or speculator who improperly writes or speaks the message.

It is like a light bulb being properly wired to the powerhouse. Unless the light bulb is appropriately wired and works favorably, there will not be light. Similarly, unless the speaker and receiver of the message of the *Bhagavatam* are both properly connected with favorable and unalloyed consciousness, the purity of the message will not manifest.

So, as we look further into the *Srimad-Bhagavatam*, we find that the very first verse summarizes Lord Krishna's position. "O my Lord, Sri Krishna, son of Vasudeva, O all-pervading Personality of Godhead, I offer my respectful obeisances unto You. I meditate on Lord Sri Krishna because He is the Absolute Truth and the primeval cause of all causes of the creation, sustenance and destruction of the manifested universes. He is directly and indirectly conscious of all manifestations, and He is independent because there is no other cause beyond Him. It is He only who first imparted the Vedic knowledge unto the heart of Brahmaji, the original living being. By Him even the great sages and demigods are placed into illusion... Only because of Him do the material universes, temporarily manifested by the reactions of the three modes of nature, appear factual, although they are unreal [because of being temporary]. I therefore meditate upon Him, Lord Sri Krishna, who is eternally existent in the transcendental abode, which is forever free from the illusory representations of the material world. I meditate upon Him, for He is the Absolute Truth."

Later, when Uddhava visits Vrindavana, he talks with Nanda Maharaja and explains things in a similar way: "Nothing can be said to exist independent of Lord Acyuta [Krishna]--nothing heard or seen, nothing in the past, present or future, nothing moving or unmoving, great or small. He indeed is everything, for He is the Supreme Soul." (*Bhag.*10.46.43)

So here, in summary, is the explanation of who is Sri Krishna. Therefore, we should be able to understand the importance of taking His instructions about life and its purpose seriously. However, there is more, especially regarding what Lord Krishna says about Himself.

WHAT SRI KRISHNA SAYS ABOUT HIMSELF

If we are expected to understand God, then who better to explain His qualities and characteristics than Himself? So in the *Bhagavad-gita*, Krishna provides the Self-revelatory truth about His position in His explanations to Arjuna. There are numerous verses in this regard, of which the following are but a few: "And when you have thus learned the truth, you will know that all living beings are but part of Me--and that they are in Me, and are Mine. (4.35) The sages, knowing Me to be the ultimate purpose of all sacrifices and austerities, the Supreme Lord of all planets and demigods, and the benefactor and well-wisher of all living entities, attain peace from the pangs of material miseries. (5.29) Of all that is material and all that is spiritual in this world, know for certain that I am both its origin and dissolution. (7.6) It is I who am the ritual, I the sacrifice, the offering to the ancestors, the healing herb, the transcendental chant... I am the father of this universe, the mother, the support, and the grandsire. I am the object of knowledge, the purifier and the syllable *om*. I am also the *Rig*, the *Sama*, and the *Yajur Vedas*. I am the goal, the sustainer, the master, the witness, the abode, the refuge and the most dear friend. I am the creation and the annihilation, the basis of everything, the resting place and the eternal seed. (*Bg*.9.16-18)

"I am the source of all spiritual and material worlds. Everything emanates from Me. The wise who perfectly know this engage in My devotional service and worship Me with all their hearts. (*Bg*.10:8)

"I am all devouring death, and I am the generator of all things yet to be. Among women I am fame, fortune, speech, memory, intelligence, faithfulness and patience. (*Bg*. 10.34) Because I am transcendental, beyond both the fallible and the infallible, and because I am the greatest, I am celebrated both in the world and in the *Vedas* as the Supreme Person." (*Bg*.15.18)

"Fools deride Me when I descend in the human form. They do not know My transcendental nature and My supreme dominion over all that be." (*Bg*.9.11)

"Unintelligent men, who know Me not, think that I have assumed this form and personality. Due to their small knowledge, they do not know My higher nature, which is changeless and supreme. I am never manifest to the foolish and unintelligent. For them I am covered by My eternal creative potency [*yoga-maya*]; and so the deluded world knows Me not, who am unborn and infallible. O Arjuna, as the Supreme Personality of Godhead, I know everything that has happened in the past, all that is happening in the present, and all things that are yet to come. I also know all living entities; but Me no one knows." (*Bg*.7.24-26)

Turning to the *Srimad-Bhagavatam*, Lord Krishna specifically explains that before, during, and after the creation, there is always Himself that exists.

"Brahma it is I, the Personality of Godhead, who was existing before the creation, when there was nothing but Myself. Nor was there the material nature, the cause of this creation. That which you see now is also I, the Personality of Godhead, and after annihilation what remains will also be I, the Supreme Lord." (*Bhag*.2.9.33)

"Gold alone is present before its manufacture into gold products, the gold alone remains after the products' destruction, and the gold alone is the essential reality while it is being utilized under various designations. Similarly, I alone exist before the creation of this universe, after its destruction and during its maintenance." (*Bhag*.11.28.19)

"Before the creation of this cosmic manifestation, I alone existed with My specific spiritual potencies. Consciousness was then unmanifested, just as one's consciousness is unmanifested during the time of sleep. I am the reservoir of unlimited potency, and therefore I am known as unlimited or all-pervading. From My material energy the cosmic manifestation appeared within Me, and in this universal manifestation appeared the chief being, Lord Brahma, who is your source and is not born of a material mother." (*Bhag*.6.4.47-48)

Lord Krishna also explains that He is the Supersoul of each and every living being, who exist only because of Him. He also establishes that He is the spiritual sound vibrations that can be chanted, as well as the forms of the deities that we can see. "All living beings, moving and nonmoving, are My expansions and are separate from Me. I am the Supersoul of all living beings, who exist because I manifest them. I am the form of the transcendental vibrations like *omkara* and Hare Krishna Hare Rama, and I am the Supreme Absolute Truth. These two forms of Mine--namely the transcendental sound and the eternally blissful spiritual form of the deity, are My eternal forms; they are not material." (*Bhag*.6.16.51)

"My dear Uddhava, I am the cause, protector and the Lord of all mystic perfections, of the yoga system, of analytical knowledge, of pure activity and of the community of learned Vedic teachers. Just as the same material elements exist within and outside of all material bodies, similarly, I cannot be covered by anything else. I exist within everything as the Supersoul and outside of everything in My all-pervading feature." (*Bhag*.11.15.35-36)

Lord Krishna goes on to explain how He is perceived by different people in different ways. "When there is agitation and interaction of the material modes of nature, the living entities then describe Me in various ways such as all-powerful time, the Self, Vedic knowledge, the universe, one's own nature, religious ceremonies and so on." (*Bhag*.11.10.34)

However, when a person reaches the vision of the Supreme by the process of Self-realization, which takes him or her above the influence of the material modes, the experience is one and the same, and on a higher level. Then there is no more confusion about what is or what is not the highest level of spiritual realization.

In conclusion Krishna explains, "Know that all opulent, beautiful and glorious creations spring from but a spark of My splendour. But what need is there, Arjuna, for all this detailed knowledge? With a single fragment of Myself I pervade and support this entire universe." (*Bg*.10:41-42)

THE MISTAKE OF ACCEPTING KRISHNA AS A REPRESENTATION OF SOMETHING HIGHER

Some people feel that Krishna is merely a representation of something higher, which is often mistaken for the impersonal Brahman. However, such texts as the *Taittiriya Upanishad* (2.1.2) explains, "One who realizes Brahman attains the summum bonum, highest goal of life. So who is Brahman? Who is to be known? What is the means to know Him? And what is the prospect? These

Lord Krishna, as the Supreme Being and Absolute Truth, the source of both the material and spiritual worlds.

are the four vital points in reference to which it has been declared: Brahman is eternally existent, source of all wisdom, and infinite or all-pervasive. One who realizes Brahman as such, he adores Him in the secret cavity of the heart which is converted into a transcendental plane, the replica of Vaikuntha, a resort of divine sports. Thereby he gets his objects fulfilled with the all-wisdom of Brahman i.e., he attains the summum bonum of life in rendering unalloyed devotion to Brahman, the Supreme Reality."

From this point, the above verse continues to explain how the various aspects of the material creation are manifested from the Brahman, directed by a Supreme Will. Yet, we can see in this verse that the Brahman is indicated to be a person whom we can render loving service, which is the means to reach the supreme goal of life. He is in the cavity of the heart as the localized expansion of the Supreme known as the Supersoul, Paramatma. Through this devotion the person will transform his heart and consciousness into the spiritual strata of Vaikuntha, the residence of the Supreme Being wherein spiritual activities are constantly taking place. Thus, the ultimate meaning of the Brahman is the Supreme Person from whom the Brahman emanates.

The *Brahma-samhita* (5.40) explains how the Brahman is but Sri Krishna's physical brilliance: "I worship Govinda, the primeval Lord who is endowed with great power. The glowing effulgence of His transcendental form is the impersonal Brahman, which is absolute, complete and unlimited, and which displays the varieties of countless planets with their different opulences in millions and millions of universes."

The *Isha Upanishad* (15) also confirms this: "O my Lord, sustainer of all that lives, Your real face is covered by Your dazzling effulgence. Kindly remove that covering and exhibit Yourself to Your pure devotee."

This Vedic evidence makes it clear that Krishna is not a mere representation for something that is higher or above Him, but He is the basis and foundation of the Brahman and all that is. The idea that the Supreme Personality or Bhagavan is merely a

Introduction

personified form or representational symbol for a higher abstract spiritual reality beyond Him is but the means to assign material attributes to what is inherently spiritual. It is a way of taking the Supreme and interpreting Him through our own limited understanding and misconceptions.

According to the Vaishnava understanding, Bhagavan is not merely a symbol of the Divine but is the essential nature of the Divine. A symbol would be like a national flag used as a representation of a nation, which is bigger and something different than the flag. So, to consider Krishna as a mere symbol created to make it easy for the mind to focus on what is spiritual is to say that Krishna Himself is but part of the material energy and only a representation of something else. This means that the Supreme Spiritual Reality must take assistance from *maya*, the material energy, in order to appear in this world, without which there is no possibility for it to have form. This is mayavada philosophy, along with the idea that any form of God, or His name, pastimes, or any demigod is but an equal symbol of what is a higher transcendent reality, like the Brahman. This means we are inflicting material qualities on what is essentially fully spiritual. But this is the wrong conclusion of those who do not understand the Absolute nature, energy, and power of the Supreme Person, Bhagavan. In this way, by forcing our own weaknesses and lack of depth on our attempt to understand what is beyond materialistic comprehension, the nature of the Supreme continues to escape us.

Therefore, we must understand from the Vedic evidence that is supplied herein, it is clear that Lord Krishna's name, form, pastimes, etc., exist eternally in the spiritual dimension and are never affected by even a tinge of the material energy. Thus, He can appear as often and whenever He likes as He is, or in any form He chooses within this material manifestation, and remain unaffected and no less spiritual. He is completely and totally spiritual for He is the Absolute Truth. As the *Vedanta Sutras* explain, the Absolute Truth is He from whom all else manifests. Thus, the Absolute Truth is the ultimate Person, as further explained.

KRISHNA AS THE SOURCE OF ALL CREATION

In the *Bhagavad-gita* (10.8) Krishna explains that He is the source of all spiritual and material worlds. "Everything emanates from Me. The wise who know this perfectly engage in My devotional service and worship Me with all their hearts."

Lord Krishna further relates that all other sages and creators also originate from Him: "The seven great sages and before them the four other great sages and the Manus [progenitors of mankind] are born out of My mind, and all creatures in these planets descend from them." (*Bg*.10.6)

Jambavan also says to Lord Krishna, "You are the ultimate creator of all creators of the universe, and of everything created, You are the underlying substance. You are the subduer of all subduers, the Supreme Lord and Supreme Soul of all souls." (*Bhag*.10.56.27)

When the demigods approached Lord Krishna to return to His abode and wind up His earthly pastimes, they also recognized that He was the supreme creator in their prayers: "You are the cause of the creation, maintenance and destruction of this universe. As time, You regulate the subtle and manifest states of material nature and control every living being. As the threefold wheel of time You diminish all things by Your imperceptible actions, and thus You are the Supreme Personality of Godhead... O Lord, You are the supreme creator of this universe and the ultimate controller of all moving and nonmoving living entities. You are Hrishikesha, the supreme controller of all sensory activity, and thus You never become contaminated or entangled in the course of Your supervision of the infinite sensory activities within the material creation. On the other hand, other living entities, even yogis and philosophers, are disturbed and frightened simply by remembering the material objects that they have supposedly renounced in their pursuit of enlightenment." (*Bhag*.11.6.15, 17)

Because Krishna is the source of everything, it is not possible for others to determine His origin, not even the demigods who have their source from Lord Krishna: "Neither the hosts of demigods nor the great sages know My origin, for, in every respect, I am the source of the demigods and sages." (*Bg*.10.2)

Arjuna also admits to this fact in the *Bhagavad-gita* after having understood Krishna's real characteristics: "O Krishna, I totally accept as truth all that You have told me. Neither the gods nor demons, O Lord, know Thy personality. Indeed, You alone know Yourself by Your own potencies, O origin of all, Lord of all beings, God of gods, O Supreme Person, Lord of the universe! (*Bg*.10.14-15) O great one, who stands above even Brahma, You are the original master. Why should they not offer their homage up to You, O limitless one? O refuge of the universe, You are the invincible source, the cause of all causes, transcendental to this material manifestation. (*Bg*.11.37) You are air, fire, water, and You are the moon! You are the supreme controller and the grandfather. Thus I offer my respectful obeisances unto You a thousand times, and again and yet again! Obeisances from the front, from behind and from all sides! O unbounded power, You are the master of limitless light! You are all-pervading, and thus You are everything! (*Bg*.11.39-40) You are the father of this complete cosmic manifestation, the worshipable chief, the spiritual master. No one is equal to You, nor can anyone be one with You. Within the three worlds, You are immeasurable." (*Bg*.11.43)

Even the immeasurable spiritual area called the Brahman is actually a tool that Krishna uses in which to create the cosmic manifestation. As He explains, "The total material substance, called Brahman, is the source of birth, and it is that Brahman that I impregnate, making possible the births of all living beings, O son of Bharata [Arjuna]. It should be understood that all species of life, O son of Kunti, are made possible by birth in this material nature, and that I am the seed-giving father. (*Bg*.14.3-4) Of all that is material and all that is spiritual in this world, know for certain that I am both its origin and dissolution. (*Bg*.7.6) I am the generating seed of all existences. There is no being--moving or unmoving--that can exist without Me. (*Bg*.10.39) Know that I am the original seed of all existences, the intelligence of the intelligent, and the prowess of all powerful men." (*Bg*.7.10)

In this way, Lord Krishna creates the material manifestation, and later absorbs it back into Himself. Then at His will, He again creates. "At the end of the millennium every material manifestation enters into My nature, and at the beginning of another millennium, by My potency I again create." (*Bg*.9.7)

"My dear Lord, the original *purusha-avatara*, Maha-Vishnu, acquires His creative potency from You. Thus with infallible energy He impregnates material nature, producing the *mahat-tattva*. Then the *mahat-tattva*, the amalgamated material energy, endowed with the potency of the Lord, produces from itself the primeval golden egg of the universe, which is covered by various layers of material elements." (*Bhag*.11.6.16)

Because Lord Krishna is the source of everything, there is obviously nothing that He personally needs from it, nor is He ever entangled in it. He is like the warden of a prison who can go in or out of it at any time he wants. Yet He is still overseeing it. "O son of Pritha, there is no work prescribed for Me within all the three planetary systems. Nor am I in want of anything, nor have I need to obtain anything--and yet I am engaged in work. (*Bg*.3.22) There is no work that affects Me; nor do I aspire for the fruits of action. One who understands this truth about Me also does not become entangled in the fruitive reactions of work." (*Bg*.4.14)

Akrura also admitted to Lord Krishna that, "You create, destroy and also maintain this universe with Your personal energies--the modes of passion, ignorance and goodness--yet You are never entangled by these modes or the activities they generate. Since You are the original source of all knowledge, what could ever cause You to be bound by illusion?" (*Bhag*.10.48.21)

The summary process of how Lord Krishna manifests and gives facility to the universe and the living entities within it is described in Vasudeva's prayer to Lord Krishna: "O transcendental Lord, from Yourself You created this entire variegated universe, and then You entered within it in Your personal form as the

Supersoul. In this way, O unborn supreme Soul, as the life force and consciousness of everyone, You maintain the creation. Whatever potencies the life air and other elements of universal creation exhibit are actually all personal energies of the Supreme Lord, for both life and matter are subordinate to Him and dependent on Him, and also different from one another. Thus, everything active in the material world is set into motion by the Supreme Lord. The glow of the moon, the brilliance of fire, the radiance of the sun, the twinkling of the stars, the flash of lightning, the permanence of mountains and the aroma and sustaining power of the earth--all these are actually You. My Lord, You are water, and also its taste and its capacities to quench thirst and sustain life. You exhibit Your potencies through the manifestations of the air as bodily warmth, vitality, mental power, physical strength, endeavor and movement. You are the directions and their accommodating capacity, the all-pervading ether and the elemental sound residing within it. You are the primeval, unmanifested form of sound; the first syllable, *om*: and audible speech, by which sound, as words, acquires particular references. You are the power of the senses to reveal their objects, the senses' presiding demigods, and the sanction these demigods give for sensory activity. You are the capacity of the intelligence for decision-making, and the living being's ability to remember things accurately. You are false ego in the mode of ignorance, which is the source of physical elements; false ego in the mode of passion, which is the source of the bodily senses; false ego in the mode of goodness, which is the source of the demigods; and the unmanifest, total material energy, which underlies everything. You are the indestructible entity among all the destructible things of this world, like the underlying substance that is seen to remain unchanged while the things made from it undergo transformation." (*Bhag.*10.85.5-12)

"Thus, these created entities, transformations of material nature, do not exist except when material nature manifests them within You, at which time You also manifest within them. But aside from such periods of creation, You stand alone as the transcendental reality." (*Bhag.*10.85.14)

Being the source of everything, Lord Krishna explains how He is also the source of genuine religion. "The Supreme Personality of Godhead said: 'O brahmana, I am the speaker of religion, its performer and sanctifier. I observe religious principles to teach them to the world, My child, so do not be disturbed.'" (*Bhag.*10.69.40)

Lord Krishna goes on to say that the understanding of how He is the origination of everything is the knowledge which can free a person from sins: "He who knows Me as the unborn, as the beginningless, as the Supreme Lord of all the worlds--he, undeluded among men, is freed from all sins." (*Bg.*10.3) This is the special nature of this spiritual knowledge of understanding who is Lord Krishna.

KRISHNA AS THE SOURCE OF ALL AVATARS OF GOD

Herein we can begin to see how numerous references establish Sri Krishna as the Absolute Truth, yet it is also established that He is not simply another *avatar* or incarnation of God, but He is the source of all other *avatars* of the Lord. This is verified in the *Bhagavatam* verse (1.3.28) where it explains: *ete chamsha-kalah pumsaha / krishnas tu bhagavan svayam / indrari-vyakulam lokam / mridayanti yuge yuge*, which means, "All of the (previously mentioned) *avatars* are either plenary portions or portions of plenary portions of the Lord, but Lord Sri Krishna is the original Personality of Godhead. All of them appear on planets whenever there is a disturbance created by the atheists. The Lord incarnates to protect the theists."

From this we can understand that Sri Krishna either descends directly, or it is one of His plenary portions who appears in order to perform the necessary activities. This is further explained in the following verses, which shows that even Maha-

Vishnu, the Creator of the cosmic manifestation, and Garbhodakashayi Vishnu, the expansion in each universe, are plenary portions of Lord Krishna: "The Supreme original Personality of Godhead, Lord Sri Krishna, expanding His plenary portion as Maha-Vishnu, the first incarnation, creates this manifold cosmos, but He is unborn. The creation, however, takes place in Him, and the material substance and manifestations are all Himself. He maintains them for some time and absorbs them into Himself again." (*Bhag.*2.6.39)

"The Personality of Godhead is pure, being free from all contaminations of material tinges. He is the Absolute Truth and the embodiment of full and perfect knowledge. He is all-pervading, without beginning or end, and without rival. O Narada, O great sage, the great thinkers can know Him when completely freed from all material hankerings and when sheltered under undisturbed conditions of the senses. Otherwise, by untenable arguments, all is distorted, and the Lord disappears from our sight." (*Bhag.* 2.6.40-41)

This next verse explains how from Lord Krishna in the spiritual world Maha-Vishnu expands into the material arena which rests in the great Brahman, who then manifests the material cosmic creation. "Karanarnavashayi Vishnu [Maha-Vishnu] is the first incarnation [*avatar*] of the Supreme Lord, and He is the master of eternal time, space, cause and effects, mind, the elements, the material ego, the modes of nature, the senses, the universal form of the Lord, Garbhodakashayi Vishnu, and the sum total of all living beings, both moving and nonmoving." (*Bhag.* 2.6.42) Here we can remember that Maha-Vishnu is the form of the Lord from whom all the universes are created, while Garbhodakashayi Vishnu is His expansion that enters each and every universe.

"I myself [Brahma], Lord Shiva, Lord Vishnu, great generators of living beings like Daksha and Prajapati, yourselves [Narada and the Kumaras], heavenly demigods like Indra and Chandra, the leaders of the Bhurloka planets, the leaders of the earthly planets, the leaders of the lower planets, the leaders of the Gandharva [angel-like beings] planets, the leaders of the Vidyadhara planets, the leaders of the Charanaloka planets, the leaders of the Yakshas, Rakshas and Uragas, the great sages, the great demons, the great atheists and the great spacemen, as well as the dead bodies, evil spirits, jinn, kushmandas, great aquatics, great beasts and great birds, etc.--in other words, anything and everything which is exceptionally possessed of power, opulence, mental and perceptual dexterity, strength, forgiveness, beauty, modesty, and breeding, whether in form or formless--may appear to be the specific truth and the form of the Lord, but actually they are not so. They are only a fragment of the transcendental potency of the Lord." (*Bhag.*2.6.43-45)

In Brahma's prayers to Lord Krishna, in a later portion of the *Bhagavatam*, He continues to explain, "Are You not the original Narayana, O supreme controller, since You are the Soul of every embodied being and the eternal witness of all created realms? Indeed, Lord Narayana [Maha-Vishnu] is your expansion, and He is called Narayana because He is the generating source of the primeval water of the universe. He is real, not a product of Your illusory Maya." (*Bhag.*10.14.14)

Once when Lord Krishna was beginning to prepare for leaving this world to return to His abode, all the demigods, sages, and celestial and subtle beings approached Him when He lived in Dvaraka. Then they offered prayers to the Lord which further reveals Lord Krishna's supremacy over all other incarnations and demigods. It is explained:

"The powerful Lord Indra, along with the Maruts, Adityas, Vasus, Ashvinis, Ribhus, Angiras, Rudras, Vishvadevas, Sadhyas, Gandharvas, Apsaras, Nagas, Siddhas, Charanas, Guhyakas, the great sages and forefathers, and the Vidyadharas and Kinnaras, arrived at the city of Dvaraka, hoping to see Lord Krishna. By His transcendental form, Krishna, the Supreme Lord, enchanted all human beings and spread His own fame throughout the worlds.

The Lord's glories destroy all contamination within the universe." (*Bhag.*11.6.2-4)

Many Hindus and followers of the Vedic tradition show great respect to these Vedic demigods, and rightly so, but such demigods can also come under the influence of Lord Krishna's illusory energy. In this next verse, we see how Lord Krishna takes it upon Himself to relieve Lord Indra of his pride and ignorance. Lord Indra is the king of heaven who is known for his own mystical or magical abilities, which tend to be a source of pride for him, which encourages him to do inappropriate things. In one such incident, Lord Krishna explained, "By My mystic power I will completely counteract this disturbance caused by Indra. Demigods like Indra are proud of their opulence, and out of foolishness they falsely consider themselves the Lord of the universe. I will now destroy such ignorance." (*Bhag.*10.25.16)

In summarizing the contents of the *Srimad-Bhagavatam* as Suta Gosvami begins to close his talk near the end of this *Purana*, he states: "I bow down to that unborn and infinite Supreme Soul, whose personal energies effect the creation, maintenance and destruction of the material universe. Even Brahma, Indra, Shankara [Shiva] and the other lords of the heavenly planets cannot fathom the glories of that infallible Personality of Godhead." (*Bhag.*12.12.67)

Thus, from different angles of thought, it is established from these and other references in the Vedic texts that Lord Krishna is the Supreme Being and source of all other *avatars* or incarnations of God and demigods.

WHY LORD KRISHNA DESCENDS INTO THIS WORLD

Why the Lord descends into this world is for multiple purposes, but primarily for two reasons. One of which is that, since He originally enunciated the ancient religious path of the *Vedas* for the benefit of the whole universe, whenever that becomes obstructed by the demoniac or wicked atheists He descends in one of His forms, which is in the transcendental mode of goodness. Thus, He again establishes the righteous Vedic path. He is the same Supreme Person, and in His *avatara* as Krishna appeared in the home of Vasudeva with His plenary portion, Balarama [His brother]. This was the second reason He appears in this world, which is to relieve the earth of the burden of the demoniac. As Krishna, He came to kill the hundreds of armies led by the kings who were but expansions of the enemies of the demigods, and to spread the fame of the Yadu dynasty. (*Bhag.*10.48.23-24)

Sri Krishna Himself explains this in the *Bhagavad-gita*: "Although I am unborn and My transcendental body never deteriorates, and although I am the Lord of all sentient beings, I still appear in every millennium in My original transcendental form. Whenever and wherever there is a decline in religious practices, O son of Bharata, and a predominant rise of irreligion--at that time I descend Myself. In order to deliver the pious and to annihilate the miscreants, as well as to reestablish the principles of religion, I advent Myself millennium after millennium. One who knows the transcendental nature of My appearance and activities does not, upon leaving the body, take his birth again in this material world, but attains My eternal abode, O Arjuna." (*Bg.*4.4-9)

Arjuna, after understanding the position of Lord Krishna, recognized His superior position and said, "Thus You descend as an incarnation to remove the burden of the world and to benefit Your friends, especially those who are Your exclusive devotees and are rapt in meditation upon You." (*Bhag.*1.7.25)

The sages at Kuruksetra, while addressing Lord Krishna, also summarized the reason for Lord Krishna's appearance in this world. They explained that at suitable times He assumes the mode of pure goodness to protect His devotees and punish the wicked. Thus, the Supreme Personality descends to maintain the eternal path of the *Vedas* by enjoying His pleasure pastimes. (*Bhag.*10.84.18)

Introduction 29

It is also described that when the Lord assumes a humanlike body, it is to show His mercy to His devotees. Then He engages in the sort of pastimes that will attract those who hear about them. Then they may become dedicated to Him. (*Bhag.*10.33.36) These pastimes of the Lord are so powerful that they can remove the sins of the three planetary systems and deliver those who are trapped in the continuous cycle of birth and death. (*Bhag.*10.86.34) Those who desire to serve the Lord should hear of these activities. Hearing such narrations of these pastimes destroy the reactions to fruitive work [karma]. (*Bhag.*10.90.49)

It is through Lord Krishna's pastimes that He calls all the conditioned souls to Him through love. Thus, by His wondrous activities He attracts all beings to return to their natural, spiritual position by reawakening their dormant love and service to Him. This is the purpose of human life, which provides the best facility and intellect for understanding our spiritual identity and connection with the Lord. As Sukadeva Gosvami explained to Maharaja Pariksit, "He, the Personality of Godhead, as the maintainer of all in the universe, appears in different incarnations after establishing the creation, and thus He reclaims all kinds of conditioned souls amongst the humans, nonhumans and demigods." (*Bhag.*2.10.42)

"To show causeless mercy to the devotees who would take birth in the future of this age of Kali-yuga, the Supreme Personality of Godhead, Krishna, acted in such a way that simply by remembering Him one will be freed from all the lamentation and unhappiness of material existence." (*Bhag.*9.24.61) However, Lord Krishna also explains that when He descends in His human form, the fools who are ignorant of His spiritual nature and supreme dominion over everything deride and criticize Him. (*Bg.*9.11)

Nonetheless, Lord Krishna Himself further explains the reasons for His appearance in this world to King Muchukunda: "My dear friend, I have taken thousands of births, lived thousands of lives and accepted thousands of names. In fact, My births, activities and names are limitless, and thus even I cannot count them. After many lifetimes someone might count the dust particles on the earth, but no one can ever finish counting My qualities, activities, names, and births. O King, the greatest sages enumerate My births and activities, which take place throughout the three phases of time, but never do they reach the end of them. Nonetheless, O friend, I will tell you about My current birth, name and activities. Kindly hear. Some time ago, Lord Brahma requested Me to protect religious principles and destroy the demons who were burdening the earth. Thus, I descended in the Yadu dynasty, in the home of Anakadundubhi. Indeed, because I am the son of Vasudeva, people call Me Vasudeva." (*Bhag*.10.51.36-40)

HOW LORD KRISHNA TOOK BIRTH IN THE MATERIAL WORLD

The Supreme Being in His form as Sri Krishna appeared on this planet 5,000 years ago and performed His pastimes for 125 years before returning to His spiritual abode. The *Vishnu Purana* (Book Four, Chapter Twenty-four) establishes that the age of Kali-yuga began in 3102 BCE, near the time when Lord Krishna left this world. There are many stories in the Vedic literature which narrate how Krishna engages in loving activities with His friends and relatives when He appears in this world, and how He performs amazing feats which thrill and astonish everyone, both while on this planet and in His spiritual abode. However, He brings His spiritual domain and His numerous pure devotees with Him when He descends into this world. Descriptions of the many activities and pastimes which go on in the spiritual world are found in such texts as *Srimad-Bhagavatam, Vishnu Purana, Mahabharata, Caitanya-caritamrta*, and Sanatana Goswami's *Brihat Bhagavatamritam*, and others, which explain the many levels and unlimited nature of the spiritual realm. Indeed, the body of the Lord is described as full of eternal bliss, truth, knowledge, the most dazzling splendour, and is the source of all that exists.

Introduction

It is described that when the Lord appeared on this planet in the nineteenth and twentieth *avatars*, He advented Himself as Lord Balarama and Lord Krishna in the family of Vrishni [the Yadu dynasty], and by so doing He removed the burden of the world. (*Bhag*.1.3.23)

The story of Lord Krishna's birth is a unique narrative, as told in the Tenth Canto of *Srimad-Bhagavatam*. About 5,000 years ago when the earth was overburdened by the military might of the demoniac who had taken the forms of rulers and kings, the spirit of mother earth took the shape of a cow and approached Lord Brahma to seek relief. Concerned with the situation on earth, Lord Brahma, Lord Shiva and other demigods went to the shore of the ocean of milk. Within that ocean is an island that is the residence of Lord Vishnu. After mentally offering prayers to Lord Vishnu, Brahma could understand the advice the Lord gave him. This was that He would soon appear on the surface of the earth in order to mitigate the burden of the demoniac kings. Therefore, the demigods and their wives should appear in the Yadu dynasty in order to serve as servants of Lord Krishna and increase the size of that dynasty.

Then one day Vasudeva, Krishna's father, and his wife, Devaki, were riding home from their wedding. Devaki's brother, the demoniac King Kamsa, was driving the chariot. Then a voice of warning came from the sky announcing that Kamsa would be killed by Devaki's eighth son. Kamsa was immediately ready to kill his sister, but Vasudeva instructed him and talked him out of the idea. Kamsa was still not satisfied, so Vasudeva said he would bring all of the children to Kamsa as they were born. Then Kamsa could kill them. As the children were born, at first Kamsa decided not to kill them. But later Kamsa learned from the sage Narada Muni that the demigods were taking birth and appearing in the Yadu and Vrishni dynasties and were conspiring to kill him. Kamsa then decided that all the children in these families should be killed, and that Vasudev and Devaki should be imprisoned in his jail in Mathura. Narada Muni had also told Kamsa that in his

Close up of the lotus eyes of baby Krishna, who displays His charming characteristics that attract so many

previous life he had been a demon named Kalanemi who was killed by Lord Vishnu. Thus, Kamsa became especially infuriated and a dedicated enemy of all the descendants of the Yadu dynasty.

Anantadeva (Balarama) first appeared in the womb of Devaki as her seventh pregnancy. It was Yogamaya, Krishna's internal potency, who made the arrangement to transfer Anantadeva from the womb of Devaki to that of Rohini, a wife of Nanda Maharaja in Gokul, from whom He appeared as Balarama. Then, with the prayers and meditations of Vasudeva, Lord Krishna appeared within his heart, and then within the heart of Devaki. So, Devaki's eighth pregnancy was Krishna Himself. Thereafter, she became increasingly effulgent, which drew the attention of Kamsa, who wanted to kill Krishna. Thus, he became absorbed in thoughts of Krishna. Devaki also drew the attention of the many demigods who came to offer prayers to her and the Lord in her womb.

When the Lord appeared, He first exhibited His four-armed Narayana form to show that He was the Supreme Lord. Vasudeva and Devaki were struck with wonder and offered many prayers. Yet, fearing Kamsa, Devaki prayed that Krishna withdraw His four-armed form and exhibit His two-armed form.

The Lord also told them of how He had appeared two other times as their son in His *avatar* forms of Prishnigarbha and Vamanadeva. This was the third time that He was appearing as their son to fulfill their desires. That night, during a rainstorm, Lord Krishna desired to leave the prison of Kamsa in Mathura and be taken to Gokul. By the arrangement of Yogamaya, Krishna's illusory energy, the shackles and prison doors were opened and Vasudeva was able to leave the prison and take Krishna to Gokul, thus saving the child from the danger of Kamsa. At this time, Yogamaya herself had taken birth from Mother Yashoda as a baby girl. This baby girl was actually Krishna's energy, Yogamaya. When Vasudeva arrived at Nanda Maharaja's house in Gokul, everyone was in deep sleep. Thus, he was able to place Lord Krishna in the hands of Yashoda, while taking her own newly born baby girl, Yogamaya, back with him. When he returned, he placed the baby girl on Devaki's bed, and prepared to accept his place in the prison again by putting the shackles back on. Later, when Yashoda awoke in Gokul, she could not remember whether she had given birth to a male or female child, and easily accepted Lord Krishna as her own.

When the baby girl, Yogamaya, began crying in the morning, it drew the attention of the doorkeepers of the prison, who then notified King Kamsa. Kamsa forcefully appeared in the prison to kill the child. Devaki pleaded with him to save the baby. Instead, he grabbed the little girl from her arms and tried to dash the baby against a rock. However, she slipped from his hands and rose above his head, floating in the air while exhibiting her true form as the eight-armed Durga, one of the forms of Yogamaya. Durga told Kamsa that the person for whom he was looking had already taken birth elsewhere. Thus, Kamsa became filled with wonder that Devaki's eighth child appeared to be a female, and the enemy he feared had taken birth elsewhere. Then he released Devaki and Vasudeva, being apologetic for all that he had done. Yet, after conferring with his ministers, they decided that they had best try to kill all the children that had been born in the past ten days in the attempt to try to find and kill Kamsa's enemy, Krishna. Thus started the atrocities of Kamsa and his ministers, which he would eventually pay for when Lord Krishna would kill him. Meanwhile, Lord Krishna started His pastimes with His devotees in Gokul and Vrindavana to display His unique characteristics, personality and beauty.

In this way, as Sri Uddhava explained to Vidura, "The Lord appeared in the mortal world by His external potency, *yogamaya*. He came in His eternal form, which is just suitable for His pastimes. These pastimes were wonderful for everyone, even for those proud of their own opulence, including the Lord Himself in His form as the Lord of Vaikuntha. Thus, His [Sri Krishna's] transcendental body is the ornament of all ornaments... The Personality of Godhead, the all-compassionate controller of both the material and spiritual creations, is unborn, but when there is friction between His peaceful devotees and persons who are in the material modes of nature, He takes His birth just like fire, accompanied by the *mahat-tattva*." (*Bhag.*3.2.12, 15)

JANMASTAMI--KRISHNA'S BIRTH FESTIVAL

The annual celebration day of Krishna's birth in this world is called Krishna Janmastami. It is one of the biggest of the Vedic festivals. It is held in the typical pattern of preparation, purification, realization, and then celebration. On the day of the festival, people will fast and spend the day focused on Krishna, meditating and chanting the Hare Krishna mantra and other prayers or songs devoted to Lord Krishna. Often times, there will also be plays and enactments of the birth and pastimes of the Lord. Thus, offering their obeisances and focusing their minds on Lord Krishna, the devotees hold themselves in such single-pointed concentration throughout the day. This, along with the fasting, indicates the overcoming of the false ego and the attachment to the body. After relieving ourselves of such hindrances, we engage in the worship of the Lord as the evening brings us closer to the occasion of His divine appearance. Therein, after a full day of purification, the Supreme appears and we realize our own connection with the Lord, who then manifests as the ultimate worshipable object of our purified consciousness. Then at the stroke of midnight Lord Krishna takes birth, which is commemorated by a midnight *arati* ceremony. Thus, this climax at night represents our overcoming the darkness of ignorance and reaching the state of purified spiritual knowledge and perception. Therein we overcome the influence of the mind and senses and enter the state of steady awareness wherein there is full spiritual awakening. If one can follow this process, then he or she can experience the real meaning of Krishna Janmastami.

MISUNDERSTANDING THE ACTIVITIES OF LORD KRISHNA

The activities and pastimes of Lord Krishna are full of meaning and purpose, all of which reveal the highest Truth. The level of perception depends on the person's depth of spiritual understanding. If a person has little depth in his or her spiritual realization and the life of Lord Krishna, then interpretations of such activities of the Lord can result in wrong or even absurd conclusions. This is the danger when those who are spiritually inexperienced wish to comment on something of which they have no real understanding, though they think they do.

For example, some people feel that if Lord Krishna encouraged Arjuna to fight in the war of Kuruksetra, as was instructed in the *Bhagavad-gita*, then this means that He was endorsing violence. However, we should point out that Lord Krishna never wanted war and exhibited much tolerance to the atrocities that the Kauravas displayed toward the Pandavas. But too much tolerance may also be seen as a sign of weakness and can make the abusers more egoistic and cruel, allowing them to think they can get away with whatever they want. When such a person is a ruler of a country, he must be removed. That is compassion for the rest of society. If such a ruler is allowed to continue, he will create more havoc that will affect everyone.

Lord Krishna wanted to protect *dharma*, the ways of truth, morality, balance, and Vedic culture, and asked the Kauravas, especially Duryodhana, to give up their evil ways. He even tried to negotiate for peace, but the Kauravas wanted no part of it. The Pandavas only wanted a small portion of land to live on, which was their rightful heritage. But the Kauravas said they would not give enough land to even push in a needle. So, they would not change. Thus, finally there was no alternative but war. However, even then Lord Krishna said He would only be Arjuna's chariot driver and not take up any weapon, even though He could have destroyed the whole world with a glance. So, He actually had no personal interest in fighting. The Lord acted in the appropriate manner to protect society and *dharma*. In this way, war may be utilized to protect *dharma* and the general welfare of society when necessary. To stand by and watch wickedness spread through the world without taking any action is a worse evil.

Even when Krishna killed His own uncle, Kamsa, He did so because Kamsa had completely given up all *dharma* and moral standards, and would not accept anyone's advice. He ruled in a cruel way and made so many plans and attempts to kill Krishna, thus terrorizing the whole society. So, finally there was a showdown when Kamsa invited Krishna and Balarama to a wrestling match that had been planned as another attempt to kill Them. Therein Krishna finally killed Kamsa. However, by this act of losing his body, Kamsa was delivered from his evil mentality and was transferred to a new situation after having been purified by the touch of the Lord. Thus, Kamsa lost his body, but his soul was lifted up and he achieved liberation.

Some people may also say that Lord Krishna consorted with women and the wives of other men, which shows devious standards. Yet, this idea again exhibits how ignorant such people are. First of all, He was only six or seven years old at the time He performed His *rasa* dance with the cowherd girls of Vrindavana, which holds much deep significance that few can fully understand. He is the Lord of everyone no matter what their position. He wanted to make everyone happy, and to awaken each soul to their relationship with the Supreme. To do this He wanted to break the limitations of pride and shame and whatever bonds keep us from an unbroken focus on God and our service to Him. Such bonds exist only within the mind, but we must become free from these unwanted conceptions. This was but one small purpose in bringing those select souls in the form of the girls of Vrindavana to the unlimited spiritual bliss of divine love with the Supreme Being. This is no common thing, most of which ordinary people cannot fathom or imagine. Therefore, one must look deep into Lord Krishna's activities. Otherwise, without proper insight, one may arrive at a wrong conclusion as to the purpose and meaning in the Lord's activities, or even what is the real identity of the Lord.

When Shiva went to see the Lord in His form as Vishnu, Shiva pointed out in his prayers how the Lord is perceived by different people in different ways, according to their level of understanding and consciousness. He said "Those who are known as the impersonalist Vedantists regard You as the Impersonal Brahman. Others, known as the Mimamsaka philosophers, regard You as religion. The Sankhya philosophers regard You as the transcendental person who is beyond *prakriti* [material nature] and *purusha* who is the controller of even the demigods. The followers of the codes of devotional service known as the *Pancharatras* regard You as being endowed with nine different potencies. And the Patanjala philosophers, the followers of Patanjali Muni, regard you as the supreme independent Personality of Godhead, who has no equal or superior." (*Bhag*.8.12.9) In this way, though one's consciousness and ideas of what the Absolute is prevents one from arriving at a true understanding, the Supreme Being remains unaffected, waiting for us to purify and spiritualize our consciousness to perceive the ultimate reality as He is.

THE BEAUTY OF KRISHNA

Lord Krishna's beauty is described in numerous prayers, poems, and portions of the Vedic literature. So we could provide many verses that describe this aspect of Krishna. An example of this is found when Lord Brahma relates Lord Krishna's form in the many verses of his *Brahma-samhita*. He also explains the beauty of Lord Krishna in his prayers that he directly offered to the Lord in the *Bhagavatam*. He says that Lord Krishna's body is dark blue like a new cloud. His garments are like brilliant lightning, and the beauty of Krishna's face is enhanced by His earrings and the peacock feather He wears on His head. He stands beautifully while wearing garlands made from the forest flowers, carrying a herding stick, a buffalo horn, and a flute. (*Bhag*.10.14.1)

His personal form is so attractive that it is considered the reservoir of all beauty. In fact, all beautiful things emanate from Him. His form is so attractive that it directs one's attention away from all other objects. Those same objects then seem devoid of attractiveness after seeing Lord Krishna. Thus, He attracts the minds of all people. His words also captivated the minds of all who remembered them. Even seeing His footprints, people were attracted. Thus, Krishna spreads His glories which are sung everywhere throughout the universe in the most sublime and essential Vedic verses. Lord Krishna says that by hearing and chanting about His glorious pastimes, the conditioned souls within this world could cross the ocean of ignorance. (*Bhag*.11.1.7)

The attractive nature of God is further described in the *Caitanya-caritamrita* (Madhya-lila, 17.139-140): "The transcendental qualities of Sri Krishna are completely blissful and relishable. Consequently Lord Krishna's qualities attract even the minds of self-realized persons from the bliss of self-realization. Those who are self-satisfied and unattracted by external material desires are also attracted to the loving service of Sri Krishna, whose qualities are transcendental and whose activities are wonderful. Hari, the Personality of Godhead, is called Krishna because He has such transcendentally attractive features."

Many of the Gosvamis of Vrindavana who had personally realized the attractive features of the Supreme wrote many books about the transcendental personality of God. One of the greatest of these saints was Rupa Gosvami (1489-1564 CE) who wrote a list of Krishna's characteristics in his book, *Bhakti rasamrita-sindhu*. This list describes 64 different qualities of God that are mentioned in the Vedic literature. This again confirms that the Lord is not merely an impersonal force, but a person who interacts in every way with the creation and the living entities that are within the creation that manifests from Him.

Close up of Sri Krishna as the Deity in the Detroit Krishna temple

The list includes the following qualities: 1) beautiful features of the entire body; 2) marked with all auspicious characteristics; 3) extremely pleasing; 4) effulgent; 5) strong; 6) ever youthful; 7) wonderful linguist; 8) truthful; 9) talks pleasingly; 10) fluent; 11) highly learned; 12) highly intelligent; 13) a genius; 14) artistic; 15) extremely clever; 16) expert; 17) grateful; 18) firmly determined; 19) an expert judge of time and circumstances; 20) sees and speaks on the authority of the scriptures--the *Veda*; 21) pure; 22) self-controlled; 23) steadfast; 24) forbearing; 25) forgiving; 26) grave; 27) self-satisfied; 28) possessing equilibrium; 29) magnanimous; 30) religious; 31) heroic; 32) compassionate; 33) respectful; 34) gentle; 35) liberal; 36) shy; 37) protector of surrendered souls; 38) happy; 39) well-wisher of devotees; 40) controlled by love; 41) all-auspicious; 42) most powerful; 43) all-famous; 44) popular; 45) partial to devotees; 46) very attractive to all women; 47) all-worshipable; 48) all-opulent; 49) all-honorable; and 50) the Supreme controller.

These fifty qualities, however, may also be found in varying degrees in some of the *jivas* or common living entities in this universe. But they are found in Lord Krishna to an unlimited degree. But besides these 50 qualities, there are five more which may also be manifested at times in the forms of Lord Brahma and Shiva. These are: 51) changeless; 52) all-cognizant; 53) ever-fresh; 54) *sat-cid-ananda-vigraha*--possessing a transcendental form of eternity, full of knowledge and absolute bliss; and 55) possessing all mystic perfection.

Beyond the above mentioned qualities, which may be seen in other forms of Divinity such as the demigods, Lord Krishna has the following exceptional qualities which are also manifested in the form of Narayana or Vishnu, which is His form as the Lord of the spiritual Vaikuntha planets. These, which cannot be applied to anyone else, are: 56) inconceivable potency; 57) uncountable universes are generated from His body; 58) the original source of all incarnations; 59) the giver of salvation to the enemies He kills; and 60) the attractor of liberated souls.

Besides the above-mentioned traits, Lord Krishna has four more qualities that are found only in Him, and not even in His forms of Vishnu, not to mention any of the demigods. These are: 61) the performer of wonderful pastimes (especially his childhood pastimes); 62) surrounded by devotees endowed with unsurpassed love of Godhead; 63) the attractor of all living entities in all universes through the expert playing of His flute; and 64) possessor of unexcelled beauty without rival. All of these qualities are those of someone who has a highly developed form and personality. Ultimately, these qualities are those of the form of the Supreme Being, Krishna, who can reciprocate in loving exchanges in a way that no other form of God or any of the demigods can manifest. You do not find such a loving reciprocation in the personality of Brahma or Shiva. This is why Sri Krishna is the God of love like none other.

Even the Bible verifies that God has a most beautiful form and is not formless, as is shown in the next few verses. As we read these, we can recognize their similarity to the Vedic description of God's form: "My beloved is white and ruddy, the chiefest among ten thousand. His head is as the most fine gold, his locks are bushy, and black as a raven. His eyes are as the eyes of doves by the rivers of waters, washed with milk, and fitly set. His cheeks are as a bed of spices, as sweet flowers; his lips like lilies, dropping sweet smelling myrrh. His hands are as gold rings set with the beryl; his belly is as bright ivory overlaid with sapphires. His legs are as pillars of marble, set upon sockets of fine gold; his countenance is as Lebanon, excellent as the cedars. His mouth is most sweet; yea, he is altogether lovely. This is my beloved, and this is my friend." (*Song of Solomon* 5.10-16)

Obviously, there is no more elevated truth or higher bliss than the personal form of the Supreme. As Sri Krishna says: "O conqueror of wealth [Arjuna], there is no truth superior to Me." (*Bg*.7.7) Many great transcendental scholars have accepted this fact, including Ramanujacharya, Madhvacharya, Vallabhacharya, Sri Chaitanya Mahaprabhu, Baladeva, as well as Lord Brahma, who, after performing many austerities for spiritual purification, became perfectly self-realized and, getting a glimpse of the Lord's spiritual nature, composed the *Brahma-samhita* many thousands of years ago and described what were his confidential realizations. One such verse is the following: "Krishna, who is known as Govinda, is the Supreme Personality of Godhead. He has an eternal blissful spiritual body. He is the origin and He is the prime cause of all causes." (*Brahma-samhita* 5.1)

HOW TO UNDERSTAND GOD

Sometimes people say that they want to see God, or that God is not perceivable. And this is confirmed in the Vedic scripture, but with additional points of instruction on how we can perceive the Supreme Being. The *Svetasvatara Upanishad* (4.20) explains, "His form of beauty is imperceptible to mundane senses. No one can see Him with material eyes. Only those who realize, through deep pure-hearted meditation, this Supreme Personality, who resides in everyone's heart, can attain liberation."

Krishna *lila* or His pastimes are eternally going on in the spiritual world, whereas they appear to be happening only at certain points in time within the material energy. However, one who has purified his or her consciousness can still witness these activities even while in the material body. This can especially happen at the holy places (*dhamas*) where the spiritual and material energies overlap, and where the spiritual world appears within this material domain. Such places include Vrindavana, Mathura, Jagannatha Puri, Dwaraka, etc. And when the Lord is pleased with your service, He may reveal Himself to you. In this way, many greatly elevated and pure devotees of Krishna have been able to have personal *darshan* of the Lord and witness His pastimes even while in the material body. Then they may leave instructions for the rest of us to follow so that we can do the same. This is verification that the process of devotion, bhakti-yoga, works.

The *Srimad-Bhagavatam* (10.14.29) continues with this point. "My Lord, if one is favored by even a slight trace of the mercy of Your lotus feet, one can understand the greatness of Your Personality. But those who speculate to understand the Supreme Personality of Godhead are unable to know You, even though they continue to study the *Vedas* for many years."

The *Katha Upanishad* (1.2.23) also relates, "The Supreme Soul can neither be attained by studying the *Veda*, nor by sharp intelligence, nor by hearing many discourses on the scriptures. However, the Lord reveals His original transcendental form to the soul who embraces Him within the heart as the only Lord and Master. That soul alone can attain Him--the Supreme Soul, the Personality of Godhead, the Lord of the heart."

Since Krishna is the Supreme Being and source of all enjoyment, it is in our best interest to engage in His service, for that will also connect us to Him and give us that great pleasure and bliss that we are always trying to find. That is the point of devotional service, called *bhakti-yoga*, which is the process of connecting (*yog*) with the Supreme through devotion (*bhakti*). In this way, our inherent loving propensity is directed toward the supreme lover and natural object of love, God. There is no better way of finding God than this. In other words, through devotion we do not try to see God, but we act in such a way that God sees us and reveals Himself to us. Then everything is accomplished. There can be no greater achievement in the human form of life than that. Everything else is temporary; it comes and goes. Only our spiritual achievements last eternally because they are connected with the immortal soul. Therefore, reawakening our relationship with the Supreme is the highest goal in human existence.

Since it is established in the Vedic texts that the Absolute is a person, then meditating on the personal form of God rather than the impersonal feature is the highest form of meditation. This is verified in *Bhagavad-gita* (12.2): "The Supreme Personality of Godhead said: 'He whose mind is fixed on My personal form, always engaged in worshipping Me with great and transcendental faith, is considered by Me to be the most perfect.'"

Herein, we can understand that realizing the Absolute Truth in the form of the Supreme Person is much easier and much more attractive than struggling to realize, meditate on, or merge into the great white light of the impersonal *brahmajyoti*, or some other nonpersonal aspect of God. By understanding the Supreme Personality, all other facets of the Absolute, such as the Brahman effulgence and Paramatma or Supersoul, are also understood. In fact, those who are absorbed in Brahman realization can easily become attracted to understanding the Supreme Personality as did such sages as Sukadeva Gosvami and the Kumaras, as noted in *Srimad-Bhagavatam*:

"Let me offer my respectful obeisances unto my spiritual master, the son of Vyasadeva, Sukadeva Gosvami. It is he who defeats all inauspicious things within this universe. Although in the beginning he was absorbed in the happiness of Brahman realization and was living in a secluded place, giving up all other types of consciousness, he became attracted by the most melodious pastimes of Lord Sri Krishna. He therefore mercifully spoke the supreme *Purana*, known as *Srimad-Bhagavatam*, which is the bright light of the Absolute Truth and which describes the activities of Lord Krishna." (*Bhag.*12.12.68)

Since Lord Krishna is the Supreme Personality, then naturally there are certain ways in which to understand Him. This is a science, which we can more deeply explain later. But for now we can offer a summary of the instructions that point the way. The main point of consideration is that if we are trying to understand Lord Krishna, then we need to know what pleases Him, which is something that we can find from His direct instructions.

The key is explained directly by Lord Sri Krishna Himself when he says: "Knowledge about Me as described in the scriptures is very confidential, and it has to be realized in conjunction with devotional service. The necessary paraphernalia for that process is being explained by Me. You may take it up carefully. All of Me, namely My actual eternal form and My transcendental existence, color, qualities, and activities--let all be awakened within you by factual realization, out of My causeless mercy." (*Bhag*.2.9.31-32)

To start on this process, one needs to hear from one who knows and is acquainted with the qualities of Lord Krishna and can explain them to others. This is established in this famous verse:

> *yasya deve para bhaktir*
> *yatha deve tatha gurau*
> *tasyaite kathita hy arthaha*
> *prakashante mahatmanaha*

"Unto those great souls who have implicit faith in both the Lord and the spiritual master, all the imports of Vedic knowledge are automatically revealed." (*Svetasvatara Upanishad* 6.23)

Lord Krishna also says, however, that, "I am never manifest to the foolish and unintelligent. For them I am covered by My internal potency, and therefore they do not know that I am unborn and infallible." (*Bg*.9.25)

Lord Brahma concurs with this point and verifies the need for the performance of devotional service, in which he says to Lord Krishna, "My dear Lord, devotional service unto You is the best path for self-realization. If someone gives up that path and engages in the cultivation of speculative knowledge, he will simply undergo a troublesome process and will not achieve his desired result. As a person who beats an empty husk of wheat cannot get grain, one who simply speculates cannot achieve self-realization. His only gain is trouble." (*Bhag*. 10.14.4)

As Lord Krishna establishes the foundation for attaining the means to understand Him, He also explains how to begin the process. "Only by practicing unalloyed devotional service with full faith in Me can one obtain Me, the Supreme Person. I am naturally dear to My devotees, who take Me as the only goal of their loving service. By engaging in such pure devotional service, even the dogeaters can purify themselves from the contamination of their low birth." (*Bhag*.11.14.21)

In his summary of the *Srimad-Bhagavatam*, Sri Suta Gosvami also explains the above point: "Remembrance of Lord Krishna's lotus feet destroys everything inauspicious and awards the greatest good fortune. It purifies the heart and bestows devotion for the Supreme Soul, along with knowledge enriched with realization and renunciation." (*Bhag*.12.12.55)

Lord Krishna continues His instructions to Arjuna: "My dear Arjuna, only by undivided devotional service can I be understood as I am, standing before you, and can thus be seen directly. Only in this way can you enter into the mysteries of My understanding. (*Bg*.11.54) For one who worships Me, giving up all his activities unto Me and being devoted to Me without deviation, engaged in devotional service and always meditating upon Me, who has fixed his mind upon Me, O son of Pritha, for him I am the swift deliverer from the ocean of birth and death. (*Bg*.12.6-7) All that you do, all that you eat, all that you offer and give away, as well as all austerities that you may perform, should be done as an offering unto Me. In this way, you will be freed from all reactions to good and evil deeds, and by this principle of renunciation you will be liberated and come to Me." (*Bg*.9.27-28)

Herein it is as if Lord Krishna is speaking directly to us, that if we follow through with this process, we will be successful even at the time of death, which is certainly the final test of life in whatever we may have done. This is the topmost process, through which steady progress will bring us to spiritual awakening. This is further related by Lord Krishna in His instructions to Brahma:

"The person who is searching after the Supreme Absolute Truth, the Personality of Godhead, must certainly search for it up to this, in all circumstances, in all space and time, and both directly and indirectly. O Brahma, just follow this conclusion by fixed concentration of mind, and no pride will disturb you, neither in the partial nor in the final devastation." (*Bhag*.2.9.36-37)

"By regularly hearing, chanting and meditating on the beautiful topics of Lord Mukunda [Krishna] with ever-increasing sincerity, a mortal being will attain the divine kingdom of the Lord, where the inviolable power of death holds no sway. For this purpose, many persons, including great kings, abandoned their mundane homes and took to the forest [for performing such spiritual pursuits]." (*Bhag.*10.90.50)

Here it becomes clear that for those who hear and chant the holy name and topics of Krishna, millions of grievous sinful reactions become immediately burned to ashes. Of course, the most important time for remembering the Lord and chanting His name is at the time of death. That is why it is said that those who chant "Krishna, Krishna" at the time the body expires become eligible for liberation, entering into the spiritual domain.

The *GopalaTapani Upanishad* (1.6) states, "One who meditates on this Supreme Person, glorifies Him, and worships Him, becomes liberated. He becomes liberated."

In conclusion, Lord Krishna simply explains that, "Thus I have explained to you the most confidential of all knowledge. Deliberate on this fully, and then do what you wish to do. Because you are My very dear friend, I am speaking to you the most confidential part of knowledge. Hear this from Me, for it is for your benefit. Always think of Me and become My devotee. Worship Me and offer your homage unto Me. Thus you will come to Me without fail. I promise you this because you are My very dear friend. Abandon all varieties of religion and just surrender unto Me. I shall deliver you from all sinful reactions. Do not fear." (*Bg.*18.63-66)

THE RESULT OF FAILING TO UNDERSTAND KRISHNA

Failing to have enough faith in Lord Krishna, or in getting to know Him, is not quite the same as you might find in some other faiths or religions wherein they say you will go to eternal hell if you are a non-believer, or are an infidel worthy of death, or whatever. But failing to investigate Him and realize what is our final destination is considered a waste of this particular life. Lord Krishna Himself explains:

"One may be well versed in all the transcendental literature of the *Vedas*, but if he fails to be acquainted with the Supreme, then it must be concluded that all of his education is like the burden of a beast or like one's keeping a cow without milking capacity." (*Bhag*.11.11.18)

"Those who worship the demigods will take birth among the demigods; those who worship ghosts and spirits will take birth among such beings; those who worship ancestors go to the ancestors; and those who worship Me [Krishna] will live with Me." (*Bg*.9.25)

In this way, we can begin to see the futility of following some materialistic path or a secondary spiritual method without the process for reaching an understanding of Lord Krishna. "Among all the eternal, conscious beings, there is One who supplies the needs of everyone else. The wise who worship Him in His abode attain everlasting peace. Others cannot." (*Katha Upanishad* 2.2.13)

Therefore, a person is allowed to proceed through life in the way he or she wants. Lord Krishna allows each person to develop in their own way, and to continue wandering throughout the universe and through various activities until they begin to inquire about the purpose of life, or become ready for a deep spiritual path. Materialistic activities are not the way to find everlasting peace, and most of us need to discover that for ourselves. However, a person cannot be helped until he or she is ready. So, until then, they may be offered the spiritual knowledge they need, but they must decide for themselves how much of it they wish to utilize. Just as when Sri Krishna spoke the whole *Bhagavad-gita* to Arjuna, at the end of it He asked Arjuna what he wished to do. He had to make up his own mind. He was not forced to do anything. In the same way, we can only offer this knowledge for the benefit of humanity, and they can decide what they wish to do, or how long they wish to continue their existence in the material worlds.

"They are truly ignorant who, while imprisoned within the ceaseless flow of this world's material qualities, fail to know You, the Supreme Soul of all that be, as their ultimate, sublime destination. Because of their ignorance, the entanglement of material work forces such souls to wander in the cycle of birth and death." (*Bhag*.10.85.15)

Therefore, regardless of what else we do, we should recognize how advantageous it is to add the process of engaging in devotional service to Lord Krishna in this lifetime. We may not even be able to become perfect at it, but it nonetheless accelerates our spiritual development. Otherwise, regardless of what else we have accomplished materially, our life remains incomplete. "Caught in the grip of ignorance, self-proclaimed experts consider themselves learned authorities. They wander about this world befooled, like the blind leading the blind." (*Katha Upanishad* 1.2.5)

It is only through this spiritual education that we can understand our real identity and transcendental nature beyond the body and all material activities. Without that, we remain ignorant of our true potential and the final shelter that is awaiting us in the spiritual domain.

DESCRIPTIONS OF LORD KRISHNA'S ETERNAL SPIRITUAL ABODE

The Vedic texts describe that there are innumerable spiritual planets in the spiritual sky beyond this material creation, each having one of the unlimited forms of the Lord with countless devotees engaging in His service. This is our real, eternal home. In the centre of all the spiritual planets of Vaikuntha (meaning the spiritual sky where there is no anxiety) is the planet known as Krishnaloka or Goloka Vrindavana. This is the personal abode of the original Supreme Personality of God, Sri Krishna. Krishna enjoys His transcendental bliss in multiple forms on that planet, and all the opulences of the other Vaikuntha planets are found there. This planet is shaped like a lotus flower and many kinds of pastimes are taking place on each leaf of that lotus, as described in *Brahma-samhita*, verses two and four: "The superexcellent station of Krishna, which is known as Gokula, has thousands of petals and a corolla like that of a lotus sprouted from a part of His infinitary aspect, the whorl of the leaves being the actual abode of Krishna. The whorl of that eternal realm, Gokula, is the hexagonal abode of Krishna. Its petals are the abodes of *gopis* [friends] who are part and parcel of Krishna to whom they are most lovingly devoted and are similar in essence. The petals shine beautifully like so many walls. The extended leaves of that lotus are the garden-like *dhama*, or spiritual abode of Sri Radhika, the most beloved of Krishna."

The only business that Sri Krishna has in the spiritual realm is transcendental enjoyment. The only business of Krishna's eternal servants or devotees is to offer enjoyment to Him. The more enjoyment the devotees offer to Krishna, the happier He becomes. The happier Krishna becomes, the more His devotees become enlivened and taste eternal, transcendental ecstasy. In this way, there is an ever-increasing competition of spiritual ecstasy between Krishna and His parts and parcels, the devotees. This is the only business in the spiritual world, as confirmed in *Brahma-samhita*, verse 6: "The Lord of Gokula is the Transcendental Supreme Godhead, the own Self of eternal ecstasies. He is superior to all superiors and is busily engaged in the enjoyments of the transcendental realm and has no association with His mundane [material] potency."

Though it is not possible to experience spiritual pastimes or to see the form of the Supreme with ordinary senses, by spiritualizing our senses by the practice of devotional yoga we can reach the platform of perceiving the Supreme at every moment. At that time we start becoming Krishna conscious and can begin to enter into the pastimes of Krishna, although we may still be

Sri Krishna and Srimati Radharani, His greatest devotee, in the ever-increasing joy of the spiritual world situated within this material body. If we become fully spiritualized in this manner, there is no doubt that when we give up this material body, we will return to the spiritual world. Until then, we can continue studying the Vedic texts to remember and be conversant about the beauty and loveliness of the spiritual world, as described as follows:

"Vrindavana-*dhama* is a place of ever-increasing joy. Flowers and fruits of all seasons grow there, and that transcendental land is full of the sweet sound of various birds. All directions resound with the humming of bumblebees, and it is served with cool breezes and the waters of the Yamuna River. Vrindavana is decorated with wish-fulfilling trees wound with creepers and beautiful flowers. Its divine beauty is ornamented with the pollen of red, blue and white lotuses. The ground is made of jewels whose dazzling glory is equal to a myriad of suns rising in the sky at one time. On that ground is a garden of desire trees, which always shower divine love. In that garden is a jewelled temple whose pinnacle is made of rubies. It is decorated with various jewels, so it remains brilliantly effulgent through all seasons of the year. The temple is beautified with bright-coloured canopies, glittering with various gems, and endowed with ruby-decorated coverings and jewelled gateways and arches. Its splendour is equal to millions of suns, and it is eternally free from the six waves of material miseries. In that temple there is a great golden throne inlaid with many jewels. In this way one should meditate on the divine realm of the Supreme Lord, Sri Vrindavana-*dhama*." (*Gautamiya Tantra* 4)

"I worship that transcendental seat, known as Svetadvipa where as loving consorts the Lakshmis [Goddesses of fortune], in their unalloyed spiritual essence, practice the amorous service of the Supreme Lord Krishna as their only lover; where every tree is a transcendental purpose-tree; where the soil is the purpose-gem, water is nectar, every word is a song, every gait is a dance, the flute is the favourite attendant, effulgence is full of transcendental bliss and the supreme spiritual entities are all enjoyable and tasty, where numberless milch-cows always emit transcendental oceans of milk; where there is eternal existence of transcendental time, who is ever present and without past or future and hence is not subject to the quality of passing away even for the duration of half a moment. That realm is known as Goloka only to a very few self-realized souls in this world." (*Brahma-samhita*, 5.56)

By studying and hearing about the beauty of the spiritual world, we will understand that everything we are looking for in life has its origin in that eternal realm. There, as it is described, one finds freedom from all pains and suffering, and the atmosphere is unlimitedly full of ever-expanding beauty, joy, happiness, knowledge, and eternal, loving relationships. In that realm, no one has the difficulties of maintaining a material body because everyone has spiritual forms. So, it is a world full of recreation only, without the struggle for maintaining our existence. There is never any hunger, and we can feast and never get full. Neither is there any lamentation over the past or fear of the future. It is said that time is conspicuous by its absence. Thus, the needs of the soul for complete freedom and unbounded love and happiness are found in the spiritual atmosphere. That is our real home.

CHAPTER ONE

What is Real Knowledge

WHAT LORD KRISHNA SAYS TO BE THE MOST IMPORTANT KNOWLEDGE

First of all, this world has innumerable varieties of activities and topics regarding knowledge or what is considered to be important knowledge in which we can become totally absorbed or even lose ourselves. There is so much to know, but how do we make sure we do not get lost into things which may not be as important as we think? Any particular field of activity or study has its own sort of language, principles, rules, or specialties. Yet, if we are going to look into the teachings that Lord Krishna has left for us to ponder, then we also must know what He claims to be the most important form of knowledge that we should take most seriously and never neglect. By that I mean that whatever else we accomplish or learn, there will be those things in particular that makes life whole, and without which life remains incomplete, imperfect, unfulfilled. Do you know what that is?

The importance of starting with this topic in understanding the teachings of Lord Krishna is that real knowledge consists of that which brings a person to understand who and what we really are, as spiritual beings, along with understanding our connection to God, and the means to act on that understanding and get free from continued material existence. So we are not talking about knowledge in which we acquire a life skill, or enhance our occupation or career, which is needed to survive but is a very basic level of life. What we are talking about is going beyond all that and reaching the real purpose of human existence, which is to realize our spiritual identity and attain freedom from any further rounds of continued birth and death in this material world. Without that, we have failed to perfect our existence, and have failed to acquire any real knowledge, which is actually the beginning of human life, above and beyond mere animalistic existence. So this is why we should first learn what Lord Krishna has to say about this.

Lord Krishna explains that the real process of knowledge and the advancement of the human race begins with and depends on the development of humility, pridelessness, nonviolence, tolerance, simplicity, finding and approaching a genuine and realized spiritual master, cleanliness, steadiness and self-control; renunciation of the objects of sense gratification, absence of false ego, the perception of the evil in the cycle of birth, death, old age and disease; nonattachment to children, wife, home and the rest, and even-mindedness amid pleasant and unpleasant events; constant and unalloyed devotion to Him; resorting to solitary places, detachment from the general mass of people; accepting the importance of spiritual self-realization, and the philosophical search for the Absolute Truth. All of these Lord Krishna declares to be knowledge, and what is contrary or opposite to these is ignorance.[1]

So, these are the principles that we need to focus on so that we can begin to advance properly. However, in our daily lives there are also other kinds of knowledge or information with which we will come in contact. By understanding their potential, we should be aware of the destination or result that following such knowledge will provide. As Lord Krishna explains, that knowledge through which the one uniting spiritual essence can be seen in all types of existence, undivided though appearing to be divided in different forms of life, is knowledge in the mode of goodness. But knowledge or an understanding which causes us to perceive different types of living beings in different bodies, or the contrasting variances between the living entities, even in the same species, is knowledge in the mode of passion. Such knowledge will lead to quarrels, non-cooperation, and disharmony on the planet. And that knowledge that will cause one to be attached to one kind of activity or outlook, which excludes knowledge of the Truth, and which is limited to the body, causing one to continue in the cycles of birth and death, is knowledge in the mode of darkness.[2] By understanding these descriptions, we can recognize which level of knowledge most of the people on this planet are absorbed in and utilize. The amount of quarreling in this world indicates that most everyone is absorbed in knowledge in the mode of passion. And the result? Quarrels, non-cooperation, and disharmony on the planet

Lord Krishna goes on to explain: that understanding by which one knows what should or should not be done, what should be feared or not, and what is liberating or binding to earthly existence, is understanding in the mode of goodness. That understanding is in the mode of passion when it cannot provide the means for perceiving between the religious way of life and the non-religious, or activity that should or should not be done. The understanding in the mode of ignorance, under the influence of illusion and darkness, makes one unable to perceive the difference between non-religious activities and those that are religious, and, thus, causes one to strive in the wrong direction.[3]

So here we are beginning to see how different levels of knowledge or understanding bring us to various perceptions of what is good or bad, or wanted and unwanted. That is how we form our motivations and activities that bring forth various results, some of which may be spiritually progressive and others that can be detrimental, not only to ourselves but all of society.

Real knowledge is that which is spiritual [everything else, for the most part, is generally a type of craftsmanship or technology, or managerial methodology]. Spiritual knowledge is based on and matures to the platform of discrimination between spirit and matter, and understanding what is real and false. It is cultivated through the process of scriptural evidence, developing austerity [singleness of purpose], direct experience or perception, logical inference, and by hearing or reading the historical narrations of the *Puranas*. In this way, the real goal of knowledge is to understand that the Absolute Truth alone is the actual reality, which was present before, during and after the destruction of the material creation.[4]

Through this process we can recognize that the ultimate goal of knowledge is reached when you are fully endowed with the conclusive understanding provided by the *Vedas*, and when you have realized by practice the definitive purpose of that information. Then you will be able to perceive the pure Self, your spiritual identity, and your mind will be satisfied. Then you will attain a stage of peace, undisturbed by any difficulty in life, and you will become dear to all living beings, even the demigods.[5]

So to clarify, as you advance in genuine knowledge, it brings about your perception of your spiritual identity and your relationship to the universe, as well as other living beings, and ultimately to God. This is the highest revelatory knowledge because, through realization, it allows you to see how to act in this life according to this spiritual relationship with all beings. As Lord Krishna says, "Those who have perfected their philosophical research and realized knowledge automatically recognize My lotus feet to be the supreme spiritual object and destination. Such realized transcendentalists are most dear to Me, and through their perfect knowledge maintain Me in happiness. A small fraction of spiritual knowledge which can produce such perfection of life cannot be duplicated through austerities, pilgrimage to holy places, chanting mantras, or giving in charity and other pious acts. Therefore, it is through real knowledge that you can understand your real Self. Then, by your advancement through clear realization of Vedic knowledge, you should worship Me in loving devotion."[6]

This is the conclusion of understanding who and what you are and the connection between the soul and ultimate reality, or God. Then deeper levels of realization and direct perception into the mysteries of life can begin to unfold. But before we reach this stage, there are other things we also need to understand.

HOW THIS VEDIC KNOWLEDGE IS DESCENDING DOWN THROUGH TIME

In the *Bhagavad-gita*, Lord Krishna explains the importance of this Vedic knowledge as an instruction for the benefit of all humanity, and how it is descending down through time to the present day: "I instructed this imperishable science of yoga to the sun-god, Vivasvan, and Vivasvan instructed it to Manu, the father of mankind, and Manu instructed it to Ikshvaku. This supreme science was thus received through the chain of disciplic succession, and the saintly kings understood it in that way. However, in time that succession was broken and the genuine knowledge became lost. Therefore, that ancient science regarding the relationship with the Supreme is again told to you by Me because you are My devotee and friend. For this reason you can understand the spiritual mystery of this science." [7]

Arjuna then asked how he was to understand that Krishna instructed this science to the sun-god, Vivasvan, since he was senior to Krishna. Krishna then explained that both He and Arjuna have passed through many, many lives, but only Krishna could remember all of them while Arjuna could not. Although Krishna is unborn and His spiritual body never deteriorates, He is the Lord of all sentient beings and appears in every millennium in His original transcendental body. [8]

In this way, we can understand the antiquity of this knowledge. First of all, it exists as an eternal sound vibration, *shabda-brahman*, outside the influence of the material energy. It then appears within this material creation by the arrangement of the Supreme Being. In the references above, Lord Krishna explains a little about this arrangement.

This is further corroborated in the *Mahabharata* (Shanti Parva 348.51-52) in which it is related that it was in the beginning of Treta-yuga that this science of our relation with the Supreme was delivered to Manu by Vivasvan. In order to spread this information for the benefit of mankind, he taught it to his son,

Maharaja Ikshvaku, who was the king of planet earth at that time and the forefather of the Raghu dynasty in which Lord Rama later appeared. In this way, we can see that the knowledge of *Bhagavad-gita* existed in human society since that time.

So to get an idea as to the timeframe of which we are speaking, we need to understand that the beginning of Treta-yuga, when Manu received this knowledge from Vivasvan, was about 2,326,000 years ago. This is calculated as follows: Treta-yuga lasts for 1,200,000 years. Dvapara-yuga, which follows, lasts 800,000 years. And the present yuga of Kali lasts for 432,000 years, of which 5,000 has already passed. So this brings us to 2,426,000 years ago. And Manu later gave this knowledge to his own son and disciple, Ikshvaku. Yet, before this, Lord Krishna spoke this knowledge to His disciple, the sun-god, Surya or Vivasvan, which places the length of time that the Vedic knowledge has been within this creation at a considerably earlier date. And now we find that Lord Krishna is again speaking the *Bhagavad-gita* to Arjuna just before the battle at Kuruksetra 5,000 years ago. It is calculated that Lord Krishna left this world near the year of 3102 BCE, at which time the age of Kali-yuga also began. So it was some years before then [some calculate that the battle of Kuruksetra was near 3143 BCE] when this knowledge was again spoken by Lord Krishna and has been a source of inspiration and guidance ever since.

Lord Krishna Himself explains clearly how and why the Vedic sound vibration was established in this world from the beginning of creation, and how it has since been carried forward for the benefit of humanity. The Supreme Lord said that it was by the influence of time that the spiritual sound of the Vedic knowledge became lost during the universal annihilation. Therefore, "when the next cycle of creation took place, I spoke the Vedic knowledge to Brahma because I Myself am the religious principles enunciated in the *Vedas*. Lord Brahma then spoke this Vedic knowledge to Manu, his eldest son, and the seven great sages headed by Bhrigu Muni then accepted the same knowledge from Manu. Then from the forefathers headed by Bhrigu Muni and other sons of Brahma appeared many children and descendants who assumed different forms as demigods, demons, human beings, Guhyakas, Siddhas, Gandharvas, Vidyadharas, Caranas, Kindevas, Kinnaras, Nagas, Kimpurushas, and so on. All of the many universal species and their leaders appeared with different natures and desires generated from the three modes of material nature. Because of their different natures and characteristics, there are a great many Vedic rituals, mantras, and rewards [to accommodate them all]. Therefore, due to the great variety of desires and natures among human beings, there are many different theistic philosophies of life, handed down through tradition, customs, and spiritual disciplic successions. However, there are also teachers who do not teach these systems and directly support atheistic views." [9] In this way, there are many levels of Vedic knowledge for the upliftment of the numerous varieties of living beings.

How the Vedic knowledge in the form of the *Srimad-Bhagavatam* appeared is further described. It is explained that the Absolute Truth revealed this incomparable torchlight of knowledge to Lord Brahma. Brahma then spoke it to Narada Muni who later spoke it to Krishna-Dvaipayana Vyasa [Srila Vyasadeva]. Srila Vyasa revealed this *Bhagavatam* to the greatest of sages, Shukadeva Gosvami, who also mercifully spoke it to Maharaja Pariksit.[10] Since then it has been handed down through the disciplic successions, such as the Brahma-Madhva-Gaudiya *sampradaya*, and has been delivered to the people of the world for their ultimate benefit, which we are explaining herein.

CHAPTER TWO

The Rarity of Human Birth

One important aspect of the value of genuine knowledge and the understanding of life is to know how rare it is to achieve a human birth. Among the millions of species of existence, and the number of beings in each, whether it is insects, plants, aquatics, reptiles, fowl, animals, bacteria, etc., humans do not occupy the most populous form of life.

As it is explained, while again and again rotating in the cycle of birth and death amongst the different species of life because of a person's own past activities, only by good fortune does the helpless living entity happen to become a human being. This human birth is very rarely obtained.[1]

Only after many births and deaths one can reach the rare form of human life. Although it is temporary, it nonetheless affords a person the exceptional opportunity to attain the highest perfection of any existence. Therefore, any human who is truly sober should quickly endeavor to attain the ultimate perfection of life, as long as he or she has not lost the body which is always subject to die. The fact of the matter is that gratification of the senses can be found in any species of life, while reaching the perfection of spiritual consciousness and awareness of Krishna is available to the living being only in the human form.[2]

As Sri Krishna explains, the human body can be compared to a perfectly constructed boat, with a spiritual master as the captain, and the instructions of the Supreme Being, Himself, as the favorable winds taking it on the proper course. With these advantages available only in the human form, a person who does not utilize his or her human existence to make spiritual progress to cross the ocean of material existence must be considered the killer of his own soul.[3]

The residents of both heaven and hell desire and pray for birth on planet earth because human life gives the facilities for attaining spiritual knowledge and love of God. Yet, life in heaven or in hell does not efficiently provide the same possibilities. Someone who is wise should never want promotion to heaven or hell. However, a human being should also not desire permanent life on earth. It is by such absorption in this sort of bodily consciousness that makes one foolishly negligent of one's best spiritual interest. Therefore, a wise person, knowing the temporary nature of life, should utilize the material body for spiritual perfection and not foolishly neglect this rare opportunity before death catches up with him.[4]

Those who find themselves in a human body, which is desired and prayed for even by the demigods, and utilize their human form to become spiritually progressed are extremely fortunate. However, if they should disregard this important opportunity, they are certainly working against their own best interest and attain a most unfortunate end. Therefore, what mortal man who has achieved this human life, which is the gateway to heaven or liberation from any further material existence, would willingly become attached to material property, which is worthless compared to the spiritual treasure waiting for him?[5]

So, as Lord Krishna concludes, for these reasons, once a person achieves this human form, those who are intelligent should free themselves from all material contamination of the modes of nature and engage in loving service to Him, the Supreme Being, and not waste this human life.[6]

"In this way, having attained this human form, which gives one the opportunity to realize Me, one can engage in My devotional service and achieve Me, the reservoir of all pleasure and happiness, the Supreme Soul of all existence, residing in the heart of every living being."[7]

Lord Krishna further explains to Uddhava that there are numerous kinds of created bodies--some with one leg (trees and plants), others with two, four, or more legs, and some with no legs (like aquatics), but of all these, the human form is actually dear to Me. Although I can never be perceived by ordinary sense perception, it is in this human form that living beings can use their intelligence and faculties of perception to search for Me.[8]

This is the great blessing that we have in the human form of life. Other forms do not have the intelligence by which they can come to fully understand the Supreme Being to the point of reawakening their love for God and returning back to the Supreme abode.

CHAPTER THREE

The Temporary Nature and Purpose of Material Existence

In gaining real knowledge about ourselves and the universe and our relation with God, as we travel the road to spiritual realization, Lord Krishna gives plenty of instruction regarding the temporary nature of this material existence. What is the point? The point is that if we are looking for anything truly substantial, effective, or deeply satisfying, the material world gives only a shadow of that for which we hanker. If the whole material manifestation is temporary, then naturally everything in it is also just as temporary, including whatever happiness that we are trying to find within it.

In this regard Sri Krishna describes that the nonpermanent appearance of happiness and distress and their disappearance in due course are like the natural changes of the winter and summer seasons. They are perceived according to the desires and acceptance or nonacceptance of such things to the senses. Therefore, one must learn to tolerate such changes without being disturbed.[1]

For example, sometimes for no apparent reason one's body is attacked by cruel people or violent animals. Yet at other times one may receive offerings of great respect or worship. One who remains neither angry nor satisfied in such situations is actually intelligent.[2]

Those who can perceive the Truth have concluded that of the nonexistent, or that which is based on the temporary illusory energy, there is no endurance, and of that which is based on Truth, there is no end.[3] Therefore, since it is the senses coming in contact with the temporary material nature which cause the interpretation within the mind of whether something is agreeable or disagreeable, the intelligent person does not partake in such sources of misery, which are due to their contact with the material senses. Such pleasures have a beginning and end, so the wise man does not delight in them.[4]

The Supreme Lord, in His form as Anantadeva, also explained to King Chitraketu that as one can remember the great trouble that is found within the field of fruitive activities [working for one's own selfish interest] in the endeavor for happiness, and how one often receives the reverse of one's hopes and desires, an intelligent man should cease from such desires. By such material endeavors one cannot achieve the ultimate goal of life. However, if one should engage in [the spiritual activities of] devotional service to the Lord without selfish intent, he or she can achieve the highest goal of life and attain freedom from the miserable conditions that accompany one who is living in this material world.[5]

Therefore, although the one who performs fruitive activities does so with the desire of perpetual happiness, it is often seen that such materialistic workers are unhappy or infrequently happy. This shows that they are not in control of their destiny, nor fully aware of their own best interest.[6] It is seen that even an intelligent person is not always happy, yet a great fool may appear happy. Thus, expecting to be happy merely through expertly performing materialistic activities is a false hope based on ego. Even if people do know how to achieve happiness and avoid unhappiness through materialistic enterprises, they still cannot avoid death, which is not at all pleasing, especially to one who has acquired his desired material objects. For one who is at death's doorstep, what happiness can such things provide? Of what use are those objects which are expected to provide happiness that are ultimately vanquished by time?[7]

Even if one on earth performs pious activities and rituals to satisfy the demigods [higher beings], he may go to heaven where he may enjoy the heavenly pleasures like a demigod, or be surrounded by angels or heavenly women. Nonetheless, he still uses up and exhausts the reactions of his pious activities and will again soon fall back down to the earthly realm.[8]

Krishna further explains that from the highest planet to the lowest in this material universe are all places of misery wherein repeated birth and death take place. However, when a person attains His abode in the spiritual realm, he or she never takes birth again.[9] "The whole cosmic creation is under Me. By My will it is manifested again and again, and by My will it is annihilated at the end." [10]

An intelligent person knows that any material activity is subject to constant change, and that even on the planet of Lord Brahma there is simply unhappiness because of this. Such a wise man can plainly see that as all things he has seen are temporary, so all things anywhere within this universe have a beginning and end.[11]

Sri Krishna goes on to tell Lord Brahma that, "Whatever appears to be of value, if it is without relation to Me, has no reality. Know it is My illusory energy, that reflection which appears to be in darkness." [12] With a similar view, Lord Vishnu told King Prithu that it is due to the interaction between the three modes of material nature [goodness, passion and ignorance] that cause the constant changes within this material universe.[13]

As we can see, because of blind desires people often act in a way that gives them something other than what they hoped for. Or they may act so selfishly to get what they want even if it hurts others or at their expense. Lord Balarama [Lord Krishna's brother] also spoke to Sri Krishna and told Him that proud men offend others for the sake of personal opulence, kingdom, land, wealth, women, honor, and power because of being blinded by conceit.[14]

Lord Krishna went on to explain that people in this world wander through higher and lower destinations. These are achieved because of their activities in pursuance of their desires while in ignorance of the actual long-term result. In this way, people act without knowing their real destination or purpose.[15]

THE AFFECTS OF MAYA, THE ILLUSORY ENERGY

In this regard, Lord Balarama spoke to Lord Krishna that His *maya* [illusory energy] makes men forget their real selves, and, taking the body as their real identity, they view others in the consideration of being friends, enemies, or neutral parties. Those who are bewildered in such a way perceive the one Supreme Soul, who resides with each embodied soul, as many. It is this temporary material body, composed of the material elements, which is imposed on the soul and causes one to experience the continual cycle of birth and death [in the form of reincarnation].[16]

Lord Krishna also related to Uddhava how the illusory energy affects the conditioned souls. He said that the material universe that living beings perceive through the mind, eyes, ears, and other senses is an illusory creation that one imagines to be real because of the influence of *maya*. All of the objects perceived by the material senses are temporary. One whose consciousness is bewildered by the illusory energy perceives many material objects with varying levels of value or meaning. Thus, one remains absorbed in such dualistic conceptions and remains engaged in various activities based on the idea of good and evil, or whether it is favorable or unfavorable to be done.[17]

Lord Krishna goes on to explain that a pure soul should see that since the materially conditioned souls who are dedicated to sense gratification have accepted the temporary objects of pleasure as truth, all of their endeavors will, at some point, be terminated. This is likened to a dream in which one sees many objects that he thinks is real. But such things are merely creations of the mind and are ultimately useless [and come to an end when the dream is finished]. Similarly, one who is asleep to his real spiritual identity will also perceive many objects of varying degrees of value, but they are all creations of My illusory energy with no permanence. One who is motivated by the senses to interact with such objects (for temporary happiness) uselessly engages his intelligence.[18] One should see one's real self-interest in life always and thus remain detached from objects for which the senses hanker, such as wife, children, home, land, wealth, opulence, and so on.[19]

Just as a dream is a creation of one's intelligence with no actual substance, similarly material emotions such as lamentation, happiness, or distress are all creations of My illusory energy. In other words, material existence has no essential reality.[20] It has no actual relation with the immortal soul.

Therefore, as an embodied soul loses external consciousness when his senses are overcome by the illusion of dreaming, so a person absorbed in the material duality must encounter illusion and death.[21]

FINDING REAL FULFILLMENT

The point is that we need to know where to look for the real fulfillment for which we are all seeking. We are spiritual in nature, and that means we are eternal, full of knowledge and full of bliss: *sat-chit-ananda*. So we are always looking for that. But how do we find it?

Lord Krishna tells us that by the cultivation of knowledge you should learn about Him and approach Him, the Supreme Being. By understanding the truth of the Lord's pure, transcendental existence, you should give up the false idea that the material world is an independent reality.[22]

Coming to this conclusion of all knowledge, you should next give up the false conception of material variety that you impose upon your own soul, and cease your material existence. The mind should be fixed on Me, since I am all-pervading.[23]

In this paragraph Lord Krishna explains the high standard view of the person who becomes spiritually realized. He says, you should see that the material world is a distinct illusion appearing in the mind, because material objects have an extremely flickering existence and are here today and gone tomorrow. It is like the red circle created by twirling a fiery stick in the air. It is a blur which is seen, but not actually there. All such types of perception are actually *maya*, illusion, and exist like images in a dream.[24] Having understood the temporary illusory nature of material existence, and if you can pull your consciousness away from illusion, you should remain without material desires. By experiencing the higher taste of the happiness of the soul, you should give up the fruitive desires associated with the performance of material activities [for the pleasure of the mind and senses]. Even if you interact with objects or people within this material world, you should remember that it is not the ultimate reality and that you have given it up. With such constant focus up till the time of death, you will not fall again into illusion.[25] In such an absorbed state of consciousness, just as a drunken man does not notice whether he has worn his shirt or coat, if you are self-realized and focused in your eternal spiritual identity, you will not notice whether the temporary body is sitting or standing, or if by My will your body is finished or if you have attained a new body. Though the material body will continue to move about according to your destiny, as long as your karma is still in effect, a self-realized soul who is awakened to the absolute reality and thus situated in the highest stage of yoga, will not surrender to the demands of the material body, knowing it to be like that visualized in a dream.[26]

In this way, the start, end, and maintenance [like the past, present and future] are the stages of material existence. Yet that which continues through all these phases and remains alone from one creation to another, even after all such phases are annihilated, is the one eternal. In conclusion, from the four types of evidence that include Vedic knowledge, direct experience, traditional wisdom, and logical induction, you can understand the temporary nature of the material world. It is by that which a person can become detached from the duality that exists within this world.[27]

By these forms of evidence, you should study and realize that this material manifestation has a beginning and end, and so is not the ultimate reality. Thus, you should live in this world without being attached.[28]

Knowing that the material body is subject to death, but through its proper use can still award the spiritual perfection of your life, being a wise person you should not foolishly neglect to take advantage of this opportunity before death claims you. In this way, giving up all material attachment and desire, you can understand Me, the Supreme Being and achieve perfect peace.[29]

CHAPTER FOUR

Our Real Identity as Spiritual Beings

An essential part of understanding spiritual knowledge, and an important aspect of the teachings of Lord Krishna, is that we realize our spiritual identity. Why it is suggested that we become detached from the world, or our body, or to see beyond the influence of the illusory energy makes no sense until we perceive that we are spiritual beings in a temporary material form. That is the key to spiritual advancement. Without understanding this main point, there is really little more we can truly comprehend or penetrate within the realm of spiritual knowledge and realization.

Out of all the spiritual teachings of the world religions, Lord Krishna has much to say about this, especially in what may be considered direct instructions from God. So now let us learn what Lord Krishna says about it. Remember, this is the heart or the essential spiritual teaching that He has given us, and does not include all of the other numerous verses found in the Vedic texts in which He explains this topic. And neither does it, nor can it, include the other innumerable verses that have filled the Vedic texts as given by other prominent personalities or incarnations of God that further elaborate on this same subject. There are so many portions of the Vedic literature that go into details about our spiritual identity and how to perceive it that it lends credence to the fact that there is no other scripture in the world that deals so extensively in allowing the individual to understand one's spiritual identity to the depth that the Vedic literature does.

So first of all, we need to realize that we cannot know what the purpose of life is, or what we should do with this existence, if we do not know who and what we are. For example, when Arjuna was hesitant to engage in battle with those who had mistreated his family and usurped his rightful claim to his kingdom, Lord Krishna told Arjuna in the *Bhagavad-gita* (*Bg*.2.11-13) that though he seemed to be speaking like a learned philosopher, the truth of the matter was that Arjuna did not understand that the wise lament neither for the living nor the dead. This was because there was never a time when Lord Krishna did not exist, nor Arjuna, nor any of the kings that were on the battlefield. And regardless of whatever might happen in the immediate future, there is never a time when any of them, or us, will cease to be. One can see that as the embodied soul passes through this life from boyhood to youth to old age, the soul similarly passes into another body at the time of death. Those who realize this and know their spiritual identity are not bewildered by such a change.

Lord Krishna goes on to explain that a person should know that which pervades the body through consciousness or awareness is indestructible. "No one is able to destroy the imperishable soul. It is the body only of the indestructible, immeasurable and eternal living entity that is subject to being destroyed. He who thinks that the living being can kill someone or is killed does not know this reality. One who is in spiritual knowledge understands that the Self neither kills nor can be killed. For the soul there is never birth nor death. Nor having once been does he ever cease to be. He is unborn, eternal, ever-existing, undying, and primeval. He does not die when the body is slain. Therefore, how can a person who knows that the soul is indestructible, unborn, eternal and immutable, kill anyone or cause anyone to kill?" [1]

"Just as a person puts on new garments when the old ones need replacing, similarly the soul accepts new bodies and gives up the old and useless ones." [2]

"The soul can never be cut into pieces by any weapon, burned, nor moistened by water or withered by the wind. The soul is unbreakable and insoluble, neither can it be burned nor dried. The soul is everlasting, all-pervading, unchangeable, immovable, and eternally the same. It is said that the soul is invisible, inconceivable, immutable, and unchangeable. In this way, there is no need to grieve for the body." [3]

"He who dwells in the body is eternal and can never be slain. Therefore, you need not grieve for any creature [since all beings are, in essence, spirit souls].[4] And when you have thus learned the truth, you will know that all living beings are but part of Me, and that they are in Me and are Mine." [5]

Since all living beings are but spirit souls, Krishna then explains that a person is even more advanced in spiritual knowledge when he views all beings with an equal mind. It does not matter whether they are honest well-wishers, or are friends, pious, or if they are envious or act like enemies, or sinners, or even if they are merely indifferent and impartial.[6]

Nonetheless, it is not easy to understand the nature of the soul from a materialistic point of view. Lord Krishna says, "Some look on the soul as amazing, some describe him as amazing, and some hear of him as amazing, while others even after hearing about him cannot understand him at all." [7]

It should be known that the living beings are without beginning, and whatever transformations they undergo, such as changes of body, are caused by the interactions of the material energy. It is nature that is the cause of all material activities, changes, and arrangements, while the living entity within the body is experiencing the various sufferings and enjoyments caused by such changes within this world.[8]

Krishna describes the predicament of the embodied living entities like so: The living entities in this material world of conditional life are in fact My eternal, fragmented parts. But due to the conditioned life [in which the living being forgets his real spiritual identity], they struggle very hard with the six senses, which include the mind.[9] There are two classes of beings, those who are fallible and those who are infallible. In the material world every entity is fallible, while in the spiritual world the living beings are all infallible [and not subject to the spiritual forgetfulness found in material existence].[10]

Lord Krishna goes on to explain: The reality to be perceived is that the material activities are performed by the body, which is created from the material energy, while the Self does nothing. When such a sensible person ceases to see different identities, caused by different material bodies, he attains the conception of Brahman, the Absolute. Thus he sees that beings, spirit souls, are expanded everywhere. With such a spiritual vision a person can see that the soul is transcendental and eternal, completely beyond the modes of nature. Even within the material body the soul is never entangled, just as the sky does not actually mix with anything, but is all-pervading due to its subtle nature. In this way, the soul is also in the body but is not mixed with it. As the sun illuminates the universe, so the soul within the body illuminates the entire body with consciousness. One who can knowingly see the difference between the body and the soul within it, and can understand the process of liberating the soul from this bondage, attains the supreme goal of life.[11]

THE LIVING BEING IN MATERIAL EXISTENCE

Lord Krishna in His expansion as Lord Anantadeva said to King Chitraketu, "When a living being thinks himself different from Me and forgets his spiritual identity of qualitative oneness with Me in eternity, knowledge and bliss, then his material, conditional life begins. In other words, instead of identifying his interest with Mine, he becomes interested in his own bodily concerns and expansions like his wife, children, and material possessions. In this way, by the influence of his actions, his material existence continues, life after life, and death after death.[12]

Lord Krishna explains to Uddhava that the subtle and gross material bodies are created by material nature, which are the Lord's expanded potencies. But material existence occurs when the living entity falsely accepts the qualities of the gross and subtle bodies [physical form, mind and intelligence] as being his true nature. Such an illusory state can be destroyed only by real knowledge [which is transcendental to the material environment].[13]

The living being in material nature follows the ways of material existence due to his association with the material energy, such as the modes of nature. Thus, [taking the unnecessary changes of life, such as birth and death, as the normal course of events] he meets with the good and evil reactions amongst various species of life.[14]

However, as the Lord says in His form as Kapiladeva, when the living being is unaffected by the fluctuating modes of material nature, and remains unchanged and free (detached) from proprietorship, he stays separate from the reactions of the modes and, even when in a material body, remains independent just as the sun stays aloof from its reflection on the water. When the living entity is under the spell of material nature and false ego, thinking he is the material body, he becomes absorbed in material activities. Then, by the influence of the false ego, he thinks he is the proprietor of so many things. Because of his association with the material modes of nature [and the materialistic level of consciousness], the conditioned soul transmigrates into different species of life in higher and lower situations. Until he is relieved from these material activities [and conceptions of life], he must accept this condition because of his faulty work and consciousness. Realistically, the living being is transcendental to material existence, but because of his desire to control material nature to suite his own wishes, his material existence continues, and he is affected by so many disadvantages, like in a dream. Therefore, it is the duty of every conditioned soul to engage his polluted consciousness in serious devotional service to the Lord with detachment for material results. Thus his mind and consciousness will be under full control [and will become purified].[15]

Lord Vishnu further explained to King Prithu that one who is advanced in intelligence and eager to perform welfare activities for others is considered best among human beings. An advanced human being is never malicious to others. Those with advanced intelligence are always conscious that the material body is different from the soul. If someone who is advanced because of executing the instruction of the previous spiritual masters is carried away by the influence of material energy, then all of his advancement is considered a waste of time. Those who are in full knowledge of the bodily conception of life, and who know that bodily desires are the results of being influenced by the illusion, do not become addicted to the body and its pleasures. A highly learned person who has no attachment to the body will not be affected by the products of material energy, such as house, home, wife, children, or wealth. The individual soul is one, pure, and non-material. It is the reservoir of all good qualities, and transcendental to the body and mind. When one is situated in My loving service without motive for material gains, he gradually becomes very satisfied within.[16]

This is the way the soul becomes naturally engaged in his real occupational service, and then becomes very peaceful. When the soul can engage in the service that is natural to him, rather than being forced to serve and feed the demands of the temporary material body, which can give only fleeting feelings of pleasure, then the soul easily becomes very happy.

It is only due to the contact with the soul that one's vital breath, intelligence, mind, and body are functional. It is only due to contact with the soul that our friends, wife, and children are dear to us. Therefore, what object can be more dear than one's own self [soul]?[17] In this way, we can recognize that it is actually the soul in everyone that is dear to us, and not merely the body, which will one day be lost.

As Lord Balarama [Lord Krishna's first expansion as His own brother] explained to Rukmini, the material body, which has a beginning and end, is composed of the physical elements, along with the senses and modes of nature. The body, which is imposed on the soul by material ignorance, causes one to experience the cycle of birth and death. In actuality, the soul is like the sun, which never comes in contact with, nor separates from, the sense of sight and what is seen. Similarly the soul never undergoes contact with or separation from the insubstantial, material objects. Such transformations as birth and death are undergone by the body but never the soul, just as changes are seen for the moon's phases, but never occur for the moon itself, though the new moon day may be called the "death" of the moon. So as a sleeping person sees himself undergoing changes within the illusion of a dream, one who is unintelligent undergoes material existence in the same way. Therefore, with transcendental knowledge you can dispel the grief and confusion that is weakening your mind.[18]

Just as fire, which burns and illuminates, is different from firewood which is what is burned to give illumination, similarly the soul, the seer within the body, is separate from the material body. Thus the spirit soul and the material body have different characteristics.[19]

Lord Krishna goes on to tell Uddhava that the living entity, called the *jiva*, is part and parcel of Him, but due to ignorance the conditioned souls have been suffering in material bondage since time immemorial. But by knowledge, they can be liberated from such existence. Both the individual spirit souls and the eternally liberated Supreme Lord [as the Supersoul in the heart] is within the material body. It is as if by chance two birds have made a nest together in the same tree--the body. Of these two birds, who are friends, one is eating the fruits of the tree, whereas the other who is in a superior position does not eat. The bird who does not eat is the Supreme Lord, who perfectly understands His own position and that of the *jiva*, the eating bird. The *jiva* soul, however, does not understand himself or the Lord. He is covered by ignorance and eternally conditioned, whereas the superior bird, the Supreme Lord, is eternally liberated. One who is enlightened in spiritual realization sees himself as transcendental to the body, although living within one, just as a person who has awakened from a dream no longer identifies with the body in the dream. Nonetheless, a foolish person will think that he is the body, just as a dreamer continues to identify with the dream as long as he is not awoken from it. An enlightened person who is free from the contamination of material or bodily desires does not consider himself to be the performer of those bodily activities. He knows it is only the senses that come in contact with any sense objects.[20]

How a person falls into material consciousness is more thoroughly explained. Lord Krishna says that a person without proper intelligence will first identify himself with the temporary body and mind [by becoming attached to his various ideas and speculations about who he is and what he wants to do]. Then when such a false understanding manifests within one's consciousness, material passion pervades the mind, which motivates one into activities that actually cause suffering. Once the mind, though naturally fixed in goodness, becomes polluted with passion, it absorbs itself in thinking and planning the means for material advancement. Thus, such a person becomes burdened with innumerable and unnecessary material desires. One who does not control the mind and senses comes under their influence for more material desires. Thus, he is bewildered by strong waves of passion for gaining the fruits of material activities, although seeing clearly that the results are often future unhappiness. Although a learned person may be bewildered in such a way, he should carefully bring the mind under control. By seeing how he has been influenced by material desires based on the modes of nature, he does not lose himself in attachments.[21]

Naturally, the mind has a tendency to enter into engagement with the material sense objects, and the sense objects enter into the mind [through attachment and longing]; but these are all merely designations that cover the spirit soul, which is actually My part and parcel.[22]

Understand that those states of existence that appear to have a separate existence from Me, the Supreme Lord, actually have no real existence. They merely create the illusion of separation from Me, the Absolute Truth, just as someone in a dream imagines different activities and rewards. In the same way, because of confusingly perceiving a separation from God, the materially conditioned living being performs fruitive activity thinking them to be the means for future rewards and arrangements [which will satisfy his mind and body]. While awake the living being enjoys the temporary characteristics of the body and mind. While dreaming he enjoys similar activities within the mind. When in deep dreamless sleep all such experiences merge into ignorance, and he is aware of nothing. The point of this is to understand that within all three states of consciousness the living being is above them, or separate in identity and remains the same. With such an understanding, he can become the controller of his senses [and does not become attached to the temporary material sense objects of this world].[23]

In this way, by understanding the unique position of the Absolute Truth through discriminating logic, one should expertly refute one's own mental misidentification with matter and cut asunder all doubts about one's own identity. One should thereafter avoid all lusty activities of the material senses by attaining the natural ecstasy from one's own soul or spiritual identity. The conclusion is that the material body, which is merely made of material elements like earth, air, fire, and water, is not the true self; nor are the senses or the mind, nor are the elements or the controllers of such elements, like the demigods. Neither is one's intelligence, material consciousness, nor one's ego. All of these simply exist within the realm of temporary matter.[24] The soul within the body is self-luminous and separate from the gross material body and subtle body. It remains fixed within the changing material existence, just as the ethereal sky. In this way, the soul has no end and is beyond any material comparison.[25]

SEEING THE SPIRITUAL UNITY BETWEEN US

If we can understand this information properly or deeply enough, we would not only understand our true spiritual identity, but also see the spiritual unity we share with all other beings. The essence of this perception has been related in the ancient Vedic texts, as we find in the *Svetasvatara Upanishad* (6.11) which states, "He is the one God hidden in all beings, all pervading, the self within all beings, watching over all worlds, dwelling in all beings, the witness, the perceiver." If one can truly understand this and become enlightened in this way, he will see that he is a part of the Supreme Reality and realize his union with all beings. Within that enlightenment one can reach Divine Love. This love is based on the spiritual oneness and harmony between all beings, which is sublime. It is a source of spiritual bliss. It is a love based not on bodily relations or mutual attraction, but it is based on being one in spirit, beyond the temporary nature of the body. This is the love for which everyone searches, from which springs forth peace, harmony, and unity, of which all other kinds of love are mere reflections. This state of being is reached only through spirituality. Therefore, a life without spirituality is a life incomplete. All have the need to fill their souls with spirituality, the presence of God, in order to feel fullness, peace, contentment, and unity.

As Lord Krishna says in the ancient Vedic text of *Bhagavad-gita* (6.30): "To him who sees Me in everything and everything in Me, I am never lost, and he is not lost to Me."

To begin seeing how things really are, and to recognize the Divinity in each of us, we have to start adjusting our consciousness. This takes place by being trained in spiritual knowledge and by the practice of yoga which purifies the mind. When the mind becomes purified and the false ego no longer influences our vision, we become sensible people. As the *Bhagavad-gita* (13.31-32) says, when a sensible man ceases to see different identities due to different material bodies, he attains the spiritual conception. Those with the vision of eternity see that the soul is transcendental, eternal, and beyond the modes of nature. Despite being within the material body, the soul is above material contact.

As the son is a part and parcel of the father, similarly, we are all individual parts of the Supreme Spiritual Father. In fact, the whole creation displays different energies that are expansions of the Supreme Energetic. Thus, there is diversity within the variegated material energy which expands from the Supreme Being. These expansions manifest in millions of species of life, as explained in the Vedic literature. Therefore, although we are in different material bodies, we are all expansions of the same spiritual energy. This is oneness and unity in diversity. On the spiritual platform, which is absolute, we are all the same. We are all spiritual beings, servants of the Supreme Being, undergoing life in the material creation. That is real unity. This perception is the perfection of the spiritually conscious person. He sees all living entities as reflections of the One, the Supreme Being. Thus, in a broad sense, there is one interest only amongst us all. Spiritually there is no clash.

We are all but small reflections of the Supreme Consciousness. When we put the greater whole above ourselves, and realize that we all contribute to the condition of this planet, then uniting with a common cause and with that Supreme Consciousness will be easy.

This planet does not allow us to be isolated, like individual islands. We all must work together and interface with others on some level. One lesson that this school of life on this planet forces us to learn is that when we come together willingly to communicate, with a positive purpose, or to pray together, and to unite for the good of the whole, then harmony and peace can exist. That peace forms and manifests when we focus on our spiritual nature, which brings between us our unity in the Supreme. Making this the center of our existence will easily bring peace, unity, and harmony in this world because it brings in the spiritual vibration that emanates from the Supreme. That vibration is one of spiritual love. It is all that is eternal. All else is temporary. Therefore, focusing on and using our energy on temporary emotions such as envy, jealousy, and anger, will only keep us far away from the Supreme, and from reaching any peace or unity between us.

We have to recognize how similar we are in order to expand our heart toward others we may have previously rejected. This is how love and understanding can dissolve the boundaries that keep us stifled as a society and individuals, and keep us from entering higher dimensions of consciousness. There is no other way to grow spiritually. A lack of love for each other reflects a lack of love for God.

When we think in spiritual consciousness, we do not recognize others by their differences. We see our similarities. This is easy when we think in terms of being sons and daughters of the same Supreme Father. We all belong to the One. Only in this way can there be universal love among all living entities. Only in this way can we begin to think that we are all related to each other. Once we establish our relationship with the Supreme, then we can establish our true relationship with everyone else. Our spiritual nature is eternal, and our spiritual relation with the Supreme is eternal. Therefore, our spiritual relationship with each other is also eternal. It is not subject to time and circumstances. This central point has to be established in order for there to be universal peace, brotherhood, equality, and unity in the world.

In essence, we are all consciousness in material forms. Consciousness cannot be destroyed. It is the essence of God in each of us. We are all spiritual beings, reflections of the Divine. We are not our beliefs, our cultures, or our minds and bodies. We are all divine souls on a wondrous journey through Truth and back to Truth. We have all manifested from God, the Supreme Truth, and we are all evolving back to God. As the *Manu-samhita* (12.125) relates, "Thus, he who by means of Self sees the self in all created things, after attaining equality with all, enters into Brahman [the spiritual atmosphere], the highest place." That is the ultimate goal.

CHAPTER FIVE

Reincarnation and the Immortality of the Soul

We have heard what Lord Krishna says regarding the soul's eternal nature in the previous chapter. In this chapter He goes more deeply into it and explains the process of reincarnation. Since the soul is eternal but, in most cases in the material world, waiting to discover the way of liberation, the living being undergoes the continuation of the cycles of birth and death. So how this takes place is extensively explained in the numerous branches of the Vedic literature, but here it is summed up by Lord Krishna.

First of all He explains in the *Bhagavad-gita* (2.13) that, "As the embodied soul continually passes in this body from boyhood to youth to old age, the soul similarly passes into another body at death. The self-realized soul is not bewildered by such a change... As a person puts on new garments, giving up the old ones, similarly the soul takes on new material bodies giving up the old and useless ones."[1]

So the continuation of life in new bodies after death is as natural as changing clothes. There is no need to mourn the body's demise when a person dies for he or she will continue on in another form, like a change of outfit.

Lord Krishna goes on to relate: "It is said that the soul is invisible, inconceivable, immutable, and unchangeable. Knowing this, you should not grieve for the body. If, however, you think the soul is perpetually born and always dies, still you have no reason to lament. For one who has taken birth, death is certain; and for one who is dead, birth is certain. Therefore you should not lament."[2]

In this way, we can understand that lamenting for the temporary body is a sign of misunderstanding the reality of the situation. In actuality, the soul is our real identity and we are merely taking up residence in a material body for a short length of time. As we progress through life we develop a type of consciousness, depending on our activities and habitual thought patterns and desires. This consciousness is tested at the time of death and perceived by what we are thinking of and our state of being when we are forced to give up this body. As Lord Krishna explains, "Whatever state of being one remembers when he quits his body, that state he will attain without fail." [3] Thus, our consciousness takes us into the next form of existence according to what we deserve and desire.

"The living entity in the material world carries his different conceptions of life from one body to another as the air carries aromas. Thus taking another gross body, the living being obtains a certain type of ear, tongue, nose, and sense of touch, which are grouped about the mind. He thus enjoys a particular set of sense objects [suitable to his consciousness]." [4] So the final level of consciousness that a person develops in this life will provide him the means of acquiring the correct kind of body in the next life, with a certain set of senses, such as ear, nose, tongue, and sense of touch, so that he can live, enjoy, experience, or suffer in a certain way, and in the proper species that will accommodate such desires and consciousness. As it is said, out of love, hate or fear an embodied soul focuses his or her mind on something, and when done in such a way at the time of death, the person will attain the form that is being concentrated upon without fail. This is all based on what he is most attracted to, or what you could say he is meditating on, at the time of death. Furthermore, a person forms a type of karma according to his good or bad activities. This governs what a person deserves in his next life in terms of good or bad circumstances. But not everyone can apprehend how this process takes place.

"The foolish cannot understand," Krishna explains, "how a living entity can quit his body, nor can they understand what sort of body he enjoys under the spell of the modes of nature. But one whose eyes are trained in knowledge can see all this. The endeavoring transcendentalist, who is situated in self-realization, can clearly see this. But those who are not situated in self-realization cannot see what is taking place, though they may try to."[5]

"As long as the living being forgets his spiritual identity and perceives separate states of existence within the modes of material nature, he will be forced to take birth in various forms of existence in numerous varieties of experience."[6]

"The unintelligent person in a material body, which has been created by his previous karma, as a result of his various activities, thinks that he is the one who performs or is responsible for everything he does. However, bewildered by his false ego, or his thinking that he is the body, the foolish person is caught by the reactions of all of his activities, and thus he is carried along by the interactions of the modes of nature [which push and pull him to act in various ways]. An enlightened person, however, who is fixed in detachment to the body [seeing himself as a spiritual being who is merely inside the body], will engage his body in all kinds of functions, whether sitting, standing, bathing, seeing, touching, eating, etc., and is never entangled by them. He remains as a witness to all that he does and does not get caught in such activities like the deluded person."[7]

"In this way, the conditioned soul has been accepting material bodies since time immemorial. These bodies are like great trees that sustain one's material existence. Just as a tree produces blossoms and then bares fruit, similarly the material body produces various activities which bare fruit in the form of reactions for which the living being is accountable."[8]

This accountability is called karma, and as Lord Krishna further explains, "The material body moves according to the control of a higher destiny. Therefore, the living entity must live in such a body, along with the mind and senses, as long as one's karma is in effect. But a self-realized soul who knows the absolute reality, and is situated in the perfect stage of yoga, never surrenders to the demands of the body, knowing it to be just like a form seen in a dream." [9]

In conclusion, Lord Krishna explains the whole process of reincarnation as follows: The materialistic mind is shaped by the reactions to fruitive work. Because of the desires held within, it travels from one body to another. Because of false identity, the spirit soul follows along with it. Bound by its karma, or reactions to fruitive work [which instills the strength in one's habitual thought patterns], the mind always dwells on the objects for which the senses hanker, both those of this world and those that he has heard about which he hopes to acquire in the next. As a result, the mind appears to come into being and then suffer annihilation with the loss of the body. Thus it loses its ability to perceive past and future (lives). When the living being is released from this body and enters the next, which is a product of his karma, he immediately becomes absorbed in the new circumstances of pleasure and pain, and completely forgets the previous body. The complete forgetfulness of the previous material existence is called death. Birth is merely a living being's total identification with the new body, as if accepting the experience of a dream as reality. Thus, a person thinks that he is only now coming into being, just as a dreamer forgets all of his previous dreams once he starts a new one. As the mind begins to accept the identity of a new body, it also begins to interpret the various levels of good or bad experiences that seem to affect it in this new life.[10]

Because of the swift nature of time, material bodies are always undergoing creation and annihilation. But the subtle nature of time makes this imperceptible. Such different transformations take place just like those seen in the current of a river with ever-new water entering the area while the old moves away. Or like the stages exhibited by the light from a candle, such a flame emanates innumerable rays, all of which exhibit constant cycles of creation, transition, and elimination. Yet a foolish person says this is the light of the lamp, or this is the water of the river. Similarly, the material body is in constant transformation, yet those deluded by time think that at each moment the body is their real identity. In the same way, a living being does not actually take birth with a body, nor does he die. He is immortal. Only by illusion does it appear that a person is born and dies. Impregnation, gestation, birth, infancy, childhood, youth, middle age, old age, and death are the nine ages of the body. It is due to ignorance from material association that one identifies oneself with both positive and negative circumstances, even though the Self is different from the body. However, if one is fortunate, he can give up such a conception.[11]

A person can understand the likelihood of dying as well as rebirth by observing the death of one's own father or grandfather, or the birth of one's son. Thus, a person can be free from these dualities of life by understanding this realistically, and recognizing that the witness to one's birth and death, or one's own Self, is separate from the body. Yet, an unintelligent person will become completely bewildered by material nature if he fails to differentiate himself from it. Thus, he sinks deeper into the cycle of material existence. Due to his fruitive activities, a conditioned soul may come in contact with the mode of goodness and take birth among the demigods or wise men. Through the mode of passion he becomes a human being, or even a demon. And through the mode of ignorance he appears within the ghostly or animal species. Ultimately, the material life and experience of sensual pleasure is actually false. It is similar to a tree appearing to be quivering when its reflection is viewed on agitated water, or as if the earth is moving when one turns his eyes around in circles. It is a false impression, like that seen in a dream. In truth, the impermanent material existence does not stop for one who is engrossed in thinking about it, although it lacks reality. Therefore, one should not try to enjoy the temporary happiness that comes from the objects of the senses. Such an illusion based on the dualistic nature of the material energy will keep one from realizing the soul. Thus, even if one is insulted, ridiculed, or neglected by evil men, or even repeatedly beaten, tied up, or spat or urinated on by ignorant people, one who wishes to attain the highest goal of life should tolerate such difficulties and by intelligence keep oneself safely on the spiritual path.[12]

However, we should note that even though Lord Krishna taught individual tolerance of so many things in this world, He never taught that we should neglect or be indifferent to protecting and defending the righteous principles of Vedic Dharma. Without Dharma, the basis of moral standards, the world would fall into darkness. So, maintaining Dharma is also a means of protecting the people of this world for their own spiritual upliftment and their freedom to continue this path. Therefore, Lord Krishna taught the whole *Bhagavad-gita* to assure Arjuna of his duty to arise, awake, and stand up and protect the principles of Vedic Dharma for the future well-being of the world, and to punish those who were too sinful or evil, and acted in too much opposition to the proper rules of conduct, even if it meant fighting or going to war.

CHAPTER SIX

The Ways of Spiritual Development and Freedom

In the previous chapters we have now learned about the rarity of human life, its purpose, our real spiritual identity, the process of reincarnation, and the need to remain on the spiritual path. These are obviously the most important types of spiritual understanding and the highest goal of human life. So what are the genuine ways of spiritual development?

Lord Krishna explains to Uddhava, "Because I desire that human beings achieve perfection, I have presented three paths of advancement--the path of knowledge [jnana-yoga, pronounced gyana], the path of work [karma-yoga] and the path of devotion [bhakti-yoga]. Besides these three there is absolutely no other means of elevation. Among these three paths, jnana-yoga, the path of philosophical speculation, is recommended for those who are disgusted with material life and are thus detached from ordinary, fruitive activities. Those who are not disgusted with material life, having many desires yet to fulfill, should seek perfection through the path of karma-yoga. If somehow by good fortune a person develops faith in hearing and chanting My glories, such a person, being neither very disgusted with nor attached to material life, should achieve perfection through the path of loving devotion to Me [bhakti-yoga]. As long as one is not satiated by fruitive activity and has not awakened his taste for devotional service by *shravanam kirtanam vishnoh* [the hearing and chanting about the glories of Lord Vishnu, Krishna], one has to act according to the regulative principles of the Vedic injunctions. One who is situated in his prescribed duty, free from sinful activities and cleansed of material contamination, in this very life obtains transcendental knowledge or, by fortune, devotional service unto Me. Even the residents of heaven and hell desire human birth on the earth planet because human life facilitates the achievement of transcendental knowledge and love of Godhead, whereas neither heavenly nor hellish bodies efficiently provide such opportunities." [1]

JNANA-YOGA

The process of jnana-yoga is to attain spiritual realization, and ultimately liberation from material existence. The process is through cultivation of knowledge to discern what is the real difference between matter and spirit. Then the real self, and the Supreme Self, by logical analysis will become revealed.

Lord Krishna explains this process as follows: First of all, by neither praising nor criticizing the material nature or activities of others, you should see the world as a combination of both the material energy and the conditioned souls based on one Absolute Truth. Those who indulge in either praising or blaming the qualities and behavior of others will also become entangled in the illusory dualities and become distracted from his own real interest. It is through the involvement of such dualities that force a person to perceive his encounter with illusion and death. That which can be expressed with words or focused upon with the mind, which are both material, is not the ultimate truth. So what is actually good or bad within this material world?[2] One who understands this remains free from material duality and wanders freely in this world. Thereby, through perception and logical deduction, along with scriptural injunctions and realization, one should know this temporary world is not the ultimate reality. In this way, one should remain detached from the world to attain real freedom.[3]

Even though this material existence is ultimately meaningless, in terms of having no relation to the soul itself, as long as one remains foolishly attracted to the material body and senses, his material existence continues. The living being is above the material existence, but because of his attraction to the objects of sense perception, his material existence continues, just as one experiences so many disadvantages in a dream.[4] The soul does not actually experience such things as sadness, elation, fear, anger, greed, confusion, desires, or birth and death. It is only the false ego that causes one to feel such things.[5] The false ego is also material, and thus has no real existence, although it is perceived through the expression of the mind, speech, life air, and functions of the body. However, with the sword of spiritual knowledge, sharpened by the help of a genuine spiritual teacher, a sober person can cut off this false identity and connection, and live in the world free from material attachments.[6] Real *jnana*, or spiritual knowledge, leads one to perceive the difference between matter and spirit. It is also cultivated with scriptural explanations, the hearing of the Puranic narrations, austerity, as well as direct perception and logic. It leads to understanding the Absolute Truth which alone is all there was before the universal creation and will be all that there is after its destruction. It is also the ultimate reality, the time factor and ultimate cause of everything in between.[7]

In this way, jnana-yoga is to use cultivated knowledge, along with direct perception, logical analysis, and the directions from the spiritual authorities, to discern the difference between what is genuinely spiritual from what is temporary and material. Through this means one separates his real spiritual identity from the false bodily platform of life. Then one works within that framework of perception to attain full spiritual realization and qualification for liberation from this worldly existence.

As Lord Krishna continues to explain: By using discriminating logic to understand what is the Absolute Truth, one must remove his false misidentification with the material energy and curtail all doubts about the actual position of the soul. One should also avoid all sensual activities based on the material senses by being satisfied with the natural bliss that comes from the soul. Through this process it will become clear that one can see that the body, the senses, the life air, the demigods, the elements such as fire, water, earth, air, and ether, and even our own mind, intelligence, material consciousness, ego, are all material energy, and have nothing to do with the identity of the real Self.[8]

Once a person becomes such a wise man, whose consciousness is fixed in the identity of the Self, he no longer notices his bodily activities. He merely goes through the motions and knows that whether he is eating, standing, sitting, walking, lying, evacuating, etc., it is the body only that is acting according to its nature. Even if he sees an impure object or activity, he does not identify with it or become disturbed by it. He logically understands that such things are part of the illusory energy and distinct from what is real, the same way a man who has awakened from a dream looks back on the events in his dream, which is already fading from memory. The darkness or ignorance of material activities imposed on the living being expands into many varieties, which the materially conditioned soul accepts as reality [and important for his happiness]. But that same ignorance ceases by proper knowledge, and the soul remains the eternal identity. It is just as when the sun rises and destroys the darkness that was covering the eyes and lights everything in the area, it does not create but only reveals the objects that were there all along. Similarly, realization of Me, the Lord, destroys the darkness covering a person's consciousness [and reveals Me, the eternal reality that was there all the time].[9]

Ultimately, when one truly understands his or her spiritual identity, the real occupation of the living being then becomes clear, and that is to engage in the devotional service to the Supreme Soul. As Lord Krishna further explains in the process of jnana-yoga: until one has completely eliminated all material passion from his mind by the practice of devotional service to Him, one must still be very careful not to associate with the modes of material nature, which are products of the Lord's illusory energy.[10]

Finally, when one's vision and perception of reality become clear, one sees how the material elements are divided into twenty-eight separate parts. When one no longer sees these separated parts, which all spring from a single cause, but instead sees the cause itself, namely the Supreme Person, at that time one's direct perception and experience is called Self-realization, or *vijnana*.[11] This is the goal and the perfected outcome of jnana-yoga.

Lord Krishna in His form as Lord Kapiladeva summarizes the purpose of jnana-yoga, or philosophical investigation, as follows: "Philosophical research culminates in understanding the Supreme Personality of Godhead. After achieving this understanding, when one becomes free from the material modes of nature, he attains the stage of devotional service. Either by devotional service directly or by philosophical research, one has to find the same destination, which is the Supreme Personality of Godhead."[12]

HOW TO PERFORM KARMA-YOGA

The next path Krishna describes is karma-yoga. This path is for those people who are not disgusted with material life, but still have many desires yet to fulfill. The basic idea is that one's actions produce reactions, or karma. Good or pious activities will produce positive or uplifting results, taking one to a better next life. Selfish, sinful or impious activities produce regressive, negative or degrading results, taking one to a worse or hellish future existence. So with karma-yoga, you are taught to act in such a way that your many activities will not become entangling, nor produce results that create unfortunate or unwanted situations to endure in your future, either in this or your next life. Karma-yoga teaches the means by which your good and pious acts will create a positive or heavenly future life, or even allow you to attain liberation from any further existence in the material realm.

Lord Krishna explains more about the effects of karma on us as follows: It is by the force of karma that a living being takes birth, and by karma alone that brings his destruction. His happiness, distress, fear, and feeling of security all come from the effects of karma. Even if there is a Supreme Being who controls and awards others the results of their fruitive activities, it is still based on the types of activities that are performed by the person. There can be no awards of fruitive activities unless such acts are performed. In this way, living beings in this world are forced to experience the consequences of their previous work. Every individual is under the control of his or her own conditioned nature and must follow that nature. In fact, this entire universe is based on the conditioned nature of the living beings. It is karma that causes the conditioned living beings to accept and let go of various high and low material bodies.[13]

Krishna in the form of Lord Balarama also says that no one but oneself is responsible for one's joy or sorrow, because a man experiences the result of his own deeds.[14]

However, even though we may know how karma affects us, determining exactly what will bring good karma or bad karma can be a complex topic. It is not so easy to understand. Nonetheless, if you can grasp it, you can learn to act in such a way that you will be relieved from any further cycles of birth and death, which is the real goal of karma-yoga, as Lord Krishna relates herein: "Even the intelligent are bewildered in determining what is action and what is inaction. Now I shall explain to you what action is, knowing which you shall be liberated from all sins. The intricacies of action are very hard to understand. Therefore one should know properly what action is, what forbidden action is, and what inaction is. One who sees inaction [akarma or non-karmic activities] in action, and action [karma forming acts] in inaction, is intelligent among men, and he is in the transcendental position, although engaged in all sorts of activities. One is understood to be in full knowledge whose every act is devoid of desire for sense gratification. He is said by sages to be a worker whose fruitive action is burned up by the fire of perfect knowledge. Abandoning all attachment to the results of his activities, ever satisfied and independent, he performs no fruitive action, although engaged in all kinds of undertakings. Such a man of understanding acts with mind and intelligence perfectly controlled, gives up all sense of ownership over his possessions, and acts only for the bare necessities of life. Thus working, he is not affected by sinful [karmic] reactions. He who is satisfied with gain which comes of its own accord, who is free from duality and does not envy, who is steady both in success and failure, is never entangled, although performing actions. The work of a person who is unattached to the modes of material nature and who is fully situated in transcendental knowledge merges entirely into transcendence. A person who is fully absorbed in Krishna [transcendental] consciousness is sure to attain the spiritual kingdom because of his full contribution to spiritual activities, in which the consummation is absolute and that which is offered is of the same spiritual nature."[15]

So this is the summarization of how karma-yoga can free you from reactions that cause you to remain in the continuous cycles of birth and death. The path of karma-yoga is, nonetheless, a detailed process, which Lord Krishna further describes as follows:

"I have already explained that there are two classes of men who realize the Self. Some are inclined to understand Him by empirical, philosophical speculation, and others are inclined to know Him by devotional work. Not by merely abstaining from work can one be free from reaction [karma], nor by renunciation alone can one attain perfection. All men are forced to act helplessly according to the impulses born of the modes of material nature; therefore no one can refrain from doing something, not even for a moment. One who [artificially] restrains his senses and organs of action, when the mind still focuses on sense objects, deludes himself and is a pretender. While he who controls the senses by the mind and engages his active organs in works of devotion, without attachment, is far superior. So perform your prescribed duty, for action is better than inaction. A man cannot even maintain his physical body without work." [16]

So here Lord Krishna further describes how spiritual activities, though they may seem hardly any different than ordinary materialistic actions, keep one from being bound up by karmic reactions. Not mere pious activities but only genuine spiritual activities, or devotional service to the Lord, actually nullify and frees you from karma. Lord Krishna explains it this way:

"Work done as a sacrifice for Vishnu has to be performed, otherwise work binds one to this material world [through karma]. Therefore, perform your prescribed duties for His satisfaction, and in that way you will always remain unattached and free from bondage. I, the Lord of all creatures, sent forth generations of men and demigods at the beginning of creation, along with sacrifices to please Vishnu, and blessed them, saying, 'Be thou happy by this yajna [sacrificial ritual] because its performance will bestow upon you all desirable things.' Then the demigods, being pleased by such sacrifices, will also please you; thus nourishing one another, there will reign general prosperity for all. The demigods, being in charge of various necessities of life, and being satisfied by the performance of these yajnas [sacrifices, or those actions done in spiritual consciousness], supply all necessities to mankind. But he who enjoys these gifts, without offering them to the demigods in return, is certainly a thief [and thus builds karma]. The devotees of the Lord are released from all kinds of sins because they eat food that is first offered for sacrifice. But those who prepare food for personal sense enjoyment verily eat only sin. All living bodies subsist on food grains, which are produced from rains, which are produced by the performance of yajna [sacrifices] which are based on prescribed duties. Regulated activities are prescribed in the *Vedas*, and the *Vedas* are directly manifested from the Supreme Lord. Consequently the all-pervading Transcendence is eternally situated in acts of sacrifice." [17]

This means that the way to be free of karmic bondage through the process of devotional service is also the way we can reach the spiritual strata wherein we can personally experience the Divine. In the meantime we have to eat, but if we prepare food to be first offered to God, that spiritualizes the food and when we eat it also purifies us from merely eating for our own sensual pleasure and, thus, incurring more karma.

Lord Krishna goes on to explain that a man who does not follow the prescribed means for happiness in the Vedic system leads a life of sin, for a person delighting only in the senses lives in vain.[18] This means that a person who lives by his own interests without the regulations found in the Vedic literature, accumulates karmic reactions that hold him in this world. Thus he misses the opportunity for spiritual progress. Furthermore, if someone simply takes pleasure in the Self, and is illumined and satisfied in the Self, he has no duty [because the purpose behind the Vedic regulations has already been attained]. Such a realized person has no further purpose to fulfill in the discharge of the prescribed duties, nor does he have a reason for not doing them. In this way, by acting as a matter of duty, without being attached to the results, one can attain the Supreme.[19]

So herein we can understand that the prescribed pious activities are for our own spiritual benefit, and are meant to give us freedom from accumulating any more karma, which holds us in material existence. But even if someone is already spiritually realized, he has nothing more to attain from such pious rituals and activities. However, there is no reason for not doing them either. Such a person shows others by example how to attain the Supreme in this way. For as Lord Krishna says, "Just for the sake of educating the people in general, you should perform your work. For whatever action is performed by a great man, common men follow in his footsteps. And whatever standards he sets by exemplary acts, all the world pursues."[20]

The difference is that as those who are spiritually ignorant perform their duties with attachment to results, similarly the learned may also act, but without attachment, for the sake of leading people on the right path. Nonetheless, let not the wise disrupt the minds of the ignorant who are attached to fruitive action. They should not be encouraged to refrain from work, but to engage in work in the spirit of devotion.[21]

Thus, it is the intent of one's work that most determines whether such activities bind one with karma or frees one from it. When work is done as an offering or in the mood of devotion to the Supreme, then that activity is a way of purifying ourselves of karma, and advancing in spiritual understanding. That is the goal of karma-yoga.

Therefore, Krishna further explains that one who is in knowledge of the Absolute Truth does not engage himself in activities based solely for sense gratification, knowing the difference between work in devotion and work for fruitive results. The ignorant fully engage themselves in material activities and are attached to the results, but the wise should not disturb them even though their activities are inferior because of their lack of spiritual understanding. Therefore, you should surrender all your works unto Me, with mind intent on Me, and without desire for material gain and free from egoism. One who executes his duties according to My injunctions, following this teaching faithfully without envy, becomes free from the bondage of fruitive activities [karma]. However, those who disregard these teachings and do not practice them due to envy, are considered bereft of all knowledge, befooled and doomed to ignorance and material bondage [the karma that will keep one bound to the cycle of birth and death]. Even a man of knowledge acts according to his own nature, for everyone follows his nature. What can repression accomplish?[22]

Therefore, it is better to act according to one's nature and dovetail those activities into acts of devotion, pursuing the pleasure of the Supreme Being and working toward the benefit of others, rather than merely for one's own personal satisfaction of the mind and senses. This is actually the cause of bad karma, performing various activities out of lust for the selfish pleasure of the mind and senses. Lord Krishna further explains that we should therefore curb this great symbol of sin [lust] by regulating the senses, and slay this destroyer of knowledge and self-realization.[23]

Why is lust the destroyer of knowledge? Because, as has been explained, it keeps one motivated on the bodily platform of life in which one works to satisfy the mind and senses due to the conception that that is what it takes to be happy. Thus, one is forced to engage in all kinds of unnecessary activities that actually bind one in the web of karma, which forces one to continually undergo the cycles of repeated birth and death, and thus forego the opportunity to become Self-realized. As Krishna continues to explain, the senses are superior to dull matter; and mind is higher than the senses; intelligence is still higher than the mind; and the soul is even higher than intelligence. Thus, knowing oneself to be transcendental to the material senses, mind and intelligence, one should control the lower self [mind and senses] by the higher self [the soul and spiritual intelligence] and thus by spiritual strength conquer this insatiable enemy known as lust.[24] Once lust has been subdued, then the biggest cause of bad karma will be eliminated.

The process of performing karma-yoga and devotional or pious activities centers around the need for spiritual consciousness. It is not enough to merely abstain from sinful acts, but there must be positive deeds and proper understanding that promote one's consciousness and freedom from karma. Lord Krishna elaborates on this as follows: "There is no work that effects Me; nor do I aspire for the fruits of action. One who understands this truth about Me also does not become entangled in the fruitive reactions to work. All the liberated souls in ancient times acted with this understanding and so attained liberation. Therefore, as the ancients, you should perform your duty in divine consciousness."[25]

However, without this divine consciousness or intent in one's activities, even austerities or sacrificial rituals, etc., may not give one spiritual merit, or lead to freedom from karma. Lord Krishna explains: "Those who undergo severe austerities and penances not recommended in the scriptures, performing them out of pride, egotism, lust or attachment, who are impelled by passion and who torture their bodily organs as well as the Supersoul dwelling within are to be known as *asuras*, or demons." [26] In this way, we can see that those who undergo severe austerities, like say a boxer who needs to train and get his weight down to size, and do so with the intention of showing what he can do for fame, status, money, etc., are not performing activities that will stop the implications of karma. Being based on bodily performance and improvement for mundane purposes, such activities actually create karma and, thus, help further bind one to this world.

However, no matter how strict one follows the path of karma-yoga, trying to avoid sinful or reactionary activities and perform uplifting and beneficial endeavors, it can be difficult to do everything right. In fact, karma-yoga is meant to include bhakti-yoga or devotional acts dedicated to God since that is the surest way to perform the strongest purificatory actions. In summary, Lord Krishna says, "One who works in devotion, who is a pure soul, and who controls his mind and senses, is dear to everyone, and everyone is dear to him. Though always working, such a man is never entangled." [27]

Furthermore, even if one accidentally falls into karmic activities, or is still working out the adverse karmic reactions from past lives, or even this life, Krishna says that devotion to Him burns the sins committed by His devotees, just as a blazing fire turns wood into ashes.[28] So this is the protection one can receive by the servitude mentality of devotion to the Supreme. Devotion to the Supreme is, essentially, the process of bhakti, or bhakti-yoga. And since the processes that have been described in this chapter also include or culminate in devotional activities to the Supreme Being, this process will be thoroughly covered in a separate chapter.

CHAPTER SEVEN

How to Practice Mystic Yoga

Another process of spiritual development is the system of yoga. It is often systematized into raja-yoga or astanga-yoga. This is the eightfold system of yoga that has been quite popular in the Western countries. However, Lord Krishna does have some specific instructions regarding the mystic yoga system, which is what we will be reviewing here.

WORSHIPING THE BRAHMAN: LORD KRISHNA'S IMPERSONAL ASPECT

When it comes to yoga and meditation, many people think that the mystic yoga system is for meditating on the impersonal aspect of God. And, for the most part, the system of raja-yoga, astanga-yoga, and other such yoga systems, explain the means to do this. However, this may be more difficult to do correctly than most people think. Meditation means to concentrate your attention on something specific, or a particular object of worship. Meditating on nothing, or the void, or something that is *nirguna*, without qualities, is not so easy. Lord Krishna says, "But those who fully worship the unmanifested, that which lies beyond the perception of the senses, the all-pervading, inconceivable, fixed, and immovable--the impersonal conception of the Absolute Truth--by controlling the various senses and being equally disposed to everyone, such persons, engaged in the welfare of all, at last achieve Me. For those whose minds are attached to the unmanifested, impersonal feature of the Supreme, advancement is very troublesome. To make progress in that discipline is always difficult for those who are embodied. But for those who worship Me, giving up all activities unto Me and being devoted to Me without deviation, engaged in devotional service and always meditating on Me, who has fixed his mind upon Me, for him I am the swift deliverer from the ocean of birth and death." [1]

Herein Lord Krishna explains the difficulty in making spiritual advancement on the impersonalistic path, but if one is sincere, that person will continue and one day go beyond the Brahman to the point of understanding the Supreme Being, in which spiritual progress is much more effective.

In other words, many teachers suggest that the Brahman or *nirguna* level of realization is the ultimate level of understanding, and that giving God a form for us to meditate on is only for those who are too attached to the *mayic* world of forms. Or it is for people who want an easier system to use for the mind's thinking capacity because, as they say, it is easier for the mind to think of an object of some sort. However, as it is explained in the *Srimad-Bhagavatam* (3.32.26), the Supreme Personality alone is complete transcendental knowledge, but appears differently according to the different processes of understanding Him. Thus, He may appear as the impersonal Brahman, or the localized Paramatma or Supersoul in the heart of all living beings, or as the Supreme Personality of Godhead, Bhagavan, the topmost of all incarnations of the Lord.

As Krishna further says, He is the basis of the impersonal Brahman, which is the constitutional position of ultimate happiness, and which is immortal, imperishable and eternal.[2] So the Brahman or spiritual platform is the basis of immortality, but the foundation of the Brahman is actually Lord Krishna. It exists because of Him and emanates from Him. It is said elsewhere that the Brahman is the bodily rays of the Lord, which is made up of innumerable spiritual sparks, the *jiva* souls that are floating in the impersonal great white light of the Brahman known as the *brahmayoti*.

The need to understand the Truth that lies beyond the Brahman and how to perceive it is also summarized in the *Katha Upanishad* (2.3.8-11): "Beyond the *brahmajyoti* (the *nirguna* or formless Brahman of the monist) there is the Great Purusha, viz. Purushottama God who is all-pervading (as the *brahmajyoti*) and without any empirical attributes, but having *sat-chit-ananda*--the transcendental embodiment. He who realizes this Purushottama-tattva is finally liberated. Attaining a spiritual body he renders eternal service to the Purushottama. The transcendental Personality of Godhead is beyond the purview of occult vision. Nobody can behold Him with the physical eye. But He can be apprehended through a pure transparent mind imbibed with intuitive wisdom borne out of unalloyed devotional practices in the very core of one's own unstinted heart--those who have really got such vision have gained final beatitude. When the five organs of knowledge, together with the mind, are composed and withdrawn from sense perception and enjoyment, and the intellect does not rush on to its outward objects but is concentrated upon culturing devotion to God, then this state is called the highest state, or *paragati*, to realize the soul within. This state of controlling the senses by withdrawing them from the outer-world and directing them in a proper channel of culturing unalloyed devotion to God is indeed known as real yoga. When the yogi becomes quite free from all vagaries of mind and when yoga leads to this royal path of devotion, it destroys the very nescience [causes of darkness]."

As mentioned, the Lord is understood in three features, namely the impersonal Brahman, the localized Supersoul or Paramatma, and then as Bhagavan, the Supreme Personality. A person may start with one aspect, such as the Brahman. But enlightened sages have said that unless a person has realized all three features, one's realization of God is incomplete. Thus the process and purpose of meditation and yoga must be correctly understood. So if Krishna is the Absolute Truth, and, therefore, the ultimate authority on yoga, then let us see what He has to say about it.

LORD KRISHNA'S INSTRUCTIONS ON YOGA

Lord Krishna certainly provides instructions for this process. Lord Krishna begins by explaining that the process of yoga requires the stilling of the mind. One must get beyond the mind in order to reach the spiritual perception. If a person can control the mind, then he or she can reach the level of perceiving the higher self. But if the mind is uncontrolled, then it becomes the enemy of one who hopes to make such progress.

As Lord Krishna relates, "One who is unattached to the fruits of his work and who works as he is obligated is in the renounced order of life, and he is the true mystic: not he who lights no fire or performs no work. What is called renunciation is the same as yoga, or linking oneself with the Supreme, for no one can become a yogi unless he renounces the desire for sense gratification. For one who is a neophyte in the eightfold yoga system, work is said to be the means; and for one who has already attained to yoga, cessation of all material activities is said to be the means. A person is said to have attained yoga when, having renounced all material desires, he neither acts for sense gratification nor engages in fruitive activities. A man must elevate himself by his own mind, not degrade himself. The mind is the friend of the conditioned soul, and his enemy as well. For him who has conquered the mind [by stifling the habitual thought patterns], the mind is the best of friends; but for one who has failed to do so, his mind will be the greatest enemy. For one who has conquered the mind, the Supersoul is already reached, for he has attained tranquility. To such a man happiness and distress, heat and cold, honor and dishonor are all the same. A person said to be established in self-realization and is called a yogi when he is fully satisfied by virtue of acquired knowledge and realization. Such a person is situated in transcendence and is self-controlled, He sees everything--whether it be pebbles, stones or gold--as the same. A person is said to be still further advanced when he regards all--the honest well-wisher, friends and enemies, the envious, the pious, the sinner and those who are indifferent and impartial--with an equal mind."[3]

Krishna begins to describe the preliminaries of the inner yoga process by relating that one should shut out all external sense objects, keep the eyes and vision concentrated between the two eyebrows, and suspend the inward and outward breaths within the nostrils. By thus controlling the mind, senses and intelligence, the transcendentalist becomes free from desire, fear and anger. One who is always in this state is certainly liberated.[4]

Herein it is described how one needs to suspend the breathing, which is obviously more difficult than many people realize. The breath itself is said to be the last obstacle of deep meditation. Just as it is the gap between thoughts that is the place in which one is freed from the mind, and is the doorway to entering spiritual perception, the same can be said about the gap between breaths. So ultimately the breathing is supposed to be suspended to enter the deepest state of meditation. That is not easy, so we have to work with that as best we can.

Furthermore, in preparation for practicing this form of yoga, Krishna explains that one should always try to live alone in a secluded place, control the mind, and concentrate on the Supreme Self. The person should also remain free from desires and possessiveness. He should then lay kusha grass on the ground, cover it with deerskin [which helps keep away snakes, since yogis would often be in the forest at the time of this teaching] and a soft cloth. The yogi should then firmly sit on it and practice yoga by controlling the senses and mind and fixing it on one point. Then hold one's body, neck and head straight in a line and gaze at the tip of the nose [with eyes open but unfocused and half-closed]. Thus, with the mind free from agitation and fear, and any desires for sex, one should meditate on Me [Lord Krishna] within the heart and make Me the ultimate goal of life. By such practice of controlling the body, mind and senses, and by the cessation of material existence, the mystic yogi attains the kingdom of God. However, there is no possibility of becoming a yogi if one eats too much or too little, or sleeps too much or too little. He must be temperate in eating, sleeping, working, or recreation to alleviate all material pains through the practice of yoga. Only through such practice, when one disciplines his mental activities, remaining devoid of all desires of the senses, and becomes situated in Transcendence, is he said to have attained yoga. The yogi must remain steady in meditation on the Self just as a lamp remains steady in a windless place.[5]

This is the stage of perfection called trance, or *samadhi*. At this point one has the ability to see the Self by the pure mind, and to relish and rejoice in the Self. It is in that state wherein one enjoys himself through transcendental senses and experiences boundless spiritual happiness. When one is established in such a way, one never departs from this truth, nor does he think there is any greater gain. Once situated in this way, one is never shaken, even in the midst of great difficulty. This is certainly actual freedom from all miseries born from material contact. Therefore, one should practice this form of yoga with undeviating determination and faith. One should abandon every material desire based on the false ego [the conception that one is the material body] and control all the senses by the mind. Gradually, step by step, and with full conviction, by means of intelligence, one should become situated in trance by fixing the mind on the Self alone.[6]

So, as Sri Krishna continues to explain, in the practice of yoga, from wherever the mind wanders, due to its unsteady nature, one must bring it back under the control of the Self. In this way, for the yogi whose mind is fixed on Me attains the highest happiness. By his identity with Brahman [the spiritual strata], he is liberated, and his mind is peaceful, free from passions, and he is freed from sin. Steady in the Self, and free from all material contamination, such a yogi achieves the highest happiness, in touch with the Supreme Consciousness. Thereafter, a true yogi perceives Me in all beings, and sees every being in Me. Indeed, the self-realized person sees Me everywhere. For such a person who sees Me everywhere and everything in Me, I am never lost, nor is he ever lost to Me. The person who knows that I and the Supersoul within all creatures are one worships Me and remains always in Me in all respects. He who sees the true equality of all beings, both in their happiness and distress, is a perfect yogi.[7]

After practicing yoga throughout one's life, the goal is then to become liberated from any further material existence. It is not enough that yoga can make one more thoughtful, increase one's awareness, or make one's body more healthy. There are so many other ways by which a person can do that. But the real goal of yoga is to return to the spiritual realm. How that is done is also described by Lord Krishna. He explains that at the time of death one who fixes his life airs between his eyebrows and in full devotion engages in remembering Him, the Supreme Lord, will certainly attain the Supreme Being. The destination of one who is learned in the *Vedas*, and who chants *omkara* (*Om*) and who are great sages in the renounced order, enter into the Brahman [the spiritual sky]. The process for accomplishing this requires the yogi to be situated in complete detachment from all activities of the senses. Closing off the doors of the senses and fixing the mind on the heart, and raising the life air to the top of the head, one establishes himself in yoga. Then, being situated as such and vibrating the sacred syllable *Om*, the supreme combination of letters, if one thinks of the Supreme Lord as he quits his body, he will certainly reach the spiritual planets.[8]

When one has perfected himself in yoga, one can die at will. In this process, called *sva-cchanda-mrityu*, the yogi blocks the anus with the heel of his foot [which prevents the life airs from going downward]. He then lifts the life airs up through the *chakras*, which also carry the soul from the heart to the chest, neck, and finally to the top of the head. Situated within the *brahma-randhra*, the yogi then gives up his body and guides the spirit soul to the selected destination.[9] When the soul is at the top of the head, the skulls cracks, releasing the soul and the yogi's life airs out of the body, thus allowing it to travel to whatever target the yogi has focused his attention. This is the process for the mystic yogi to reach the spiritual realm.

IT IS NOT EASY FOR ONE TO REACH SPIRITUAL PERFECTION IN THIS FORM OF YOGA

However, even after hearing all about this system of yoga, Arjuna, who was being taught these things by Lord Krishna at the time, said that this system appears impractical and unendurable since the mind is so restless and unsteady. It is turbulent, obstinate and very strong. To subdue it is more difficult than controlling the wind.[10] Therefore, we must ask if Arjuna, who was a far more capable person 5,000 years ago than we are today, could perceive the difficulty of this system, then it behooves us to understand that it is also most difficult to use this system today and expect to reach perfection with it. The ultimate perfection with this form of yoga is that you become so focused on the Supreme within and around you that you attain liberation from any more cycles of birth and death in this material creation. However, now we are in Kali-yuga, an age of quarrel, difficulties, constant distractions, temptations and discomfort. So it is even harder to control the mind to such a degree as is expected through this system.

Nonetheless, Lord Krishna continued to advise Arjuna that even though it is very difficult to curb the restless mind, it is possible by constant practice and detachment. "Self-realization is difficult work for one whose mind is unbridled. But My opinion is that he whose mind is controlled, and who strives by the proper process [of continued practice], is assured of success."[11]

However, Arjuna was not so convinced and still questioned Lord Krishna. He asked what was the destination of someone who starts the process of self-realization but does not persevere, but gives up due to worldly-mindedness and does not attain success. Does such a person perish like a riven cloud, with no position anywhere?[12]

Here Arjuna is not merely asking about the astanga or eightfold path of yoga. He is asking about any kind of genuine process of self-realization. What happens when a sincere person still cannot continue to reach the goal? Lord Krishna answers him that such a transcendentalist does not meet with destruction either in this world or in the spiritual world. One who does good is never overcome by evil. Even an unsuccessful yogi [due to his pious credits], after many, many years of enjoyment on the heavenly planets of the pious, is born in a family of righteous people, or a wealthy family of aristocracy. Or he takes birth in a family of transcendentalists who are already on the spiritual path and great in wisdom. Yet, such a birth is most rare in this world. On taking such a birth, he again revives his divine consciousness of his previous life. Then he takes up the process again and continues to make further progress in order to achieve complete success. It is by virtue of the spiritual consciousness from his previous existence that he automatically becomes attracted to the yogic principles-- even without seeking them. Such an inquisitive transcendentalist, striving for yoga, stands always above the rituals prescribed in the scriptures. But when the yogi engages himself with sincere endeavor, and being washed of all contamination, then, after many, many births and deaths, he ultimately attains the supreme goal. A yogi is greater than the ascetic performing austerities, greater than the empiricist philosopher, and greater than one engaged in karmic activities for fruitive results. So in all circumstances be a yogi.[13]

    So herein Lord Krishna describes the positive opportunity that awaits anyone who makes any sincere endeavor on the path of spiritual advancement, even if they do not fully succeed in one lifetime. And then in the next verse He concludes what is the real goal of yoga, and again points out the ease and need for the process of loving devotion to Him when He says, "And of all yogis, he who always abides in Me with great faith, worshiping Me in transcendental loving service [*bhakti*], is most intimately united with Me in yoga and is the highest of all." [14]

    In a similar circumstance, after Lord Krishna explained the science of yoga to Uddhava, Uddhava had the same doubts as Arjuna, but made further suggestions for a person to reach spiritual perfection. He said that he feared that the method of yoga that had been described by Him is very difficult for one who cannot completely control his mind. So Uddhava requested Lord Krishna to explain a simpler way of attaining spiritual perfection. Uddhava explained that those yogis who try to steady the mind experience frustration because of their inability to perfect the state of trance.

Thus they weary in their attempts to control the mind. Therefore, swanlike men happily take shelter of Your lotus feet, the source of all transcendental ecstasy. But those who take pride in their accomplishments in yoga and karma fail to take shelter of You and are thus defeated by Your illusory energy.[15]

Lord Krishna similarly relates that sometimes the spiritual progress of a yogi or transcendentalist is halted by attachment to family members, disciples or others. But on the strength of their accumulated advancement, they will resume their yoga practice in the next life. They will never be trapped in the network of fruitive or karmic work.[16] Thereafter, Lord Krishna begins to explain the process of devotional service, bhakti-yoga, as the direct means of attaining the ultimate goal of yoga.

THE ESSENTIAL POINTS OF THIS YOGA SYSTEM

In spite of all these instructions, Lord Krishna also explains some of the pros and cons that many people may face in the mystic yoga system that He has described. He says that the yogi who is endeavoring for advancement, but who is not yet mature in his practice, may at times be overcome by various disturbances. Some of the obstructions or obstacles may be counteracted by certain yogic meditations or *asanas*, sitting postures. These are to be practiced together with controlled breathing. Other difficulties may be overcome by engaging in specific austerities, or using certain mantras or herbs. However, Krishna goes on to explain that these inauspicious difficulties can be removed gradually simply by constant remembrance of Him, and by the congregational hearing and singing of His holy names, or by following in the footsteps of the great masters of yoga. By various methods, some yogis free the body from disease and old age, and keep it perpetually young and healthy. Thus they engage in yoga for the purpose of achieving material mystic perfections.[17]

However, Krishna goes on to relate that this mystic bodily superiority or development is not valued very highly by others who are advanced in genuine spiritual knowledge. They consider that the endeavor for such perfection is useless since the soul is permanent but the body is destroyed in time. "So although the physical body may be improved by various processes of yoga, an intelligent person who has dedicated his life to Me, does not place much faith in the prospect of perfecting his physical body through yoga. In fact, he may even give it up." [18]

In this way, we may engage in yoga to help keep the body fit, in the same way we need to maintain our cars to keep them in shape and running properly. We do it so that they will give us good service for as long as possible, but not with the idea that we will reach a high degree of spiritual perfection with it, or hold onto our youth and thus increase our ability to gratify our senses. Lord Krishna advises that there are better ways to spiritually develop ourselves.

As explained elsewhere in a story to Uddhava by Lord Krishna, charity, prescribed duties, observance of both major and minor regulative principles, hearing from scriptures, the performance of pious work and purifying vows, are all meant for subduing and controlling the mind. Indeed, simply concentrating the mind on the Supreme is the highest yoga. But if one's mind is fixed [on Me] and pacified, then of what use is there for one to perform rituals, charity, or other pious work? And if one's mind remains uncontrolled in illusion, then of what use or benefit have these engagements been for him? [19]

Lord Krishna, when instructing King Muchukunda, also related that the minds of nondevotees, though they may engage in such practices as *pranayama*, are not fully cleansed of material desires. Thus material desires are again seen to arise in their minds [in spite of their practice].[20]

So after all the instructions on how a yogi could reach the spiritual domain, or what problems a yogi may face, Lord Krishna summarizes the process for how anyone can easily reach the supreme destination through the proper meditation, which is to simply think of Him. He says, "For one who remembers Me without deviation, I am easy to obtain because of his constant engagement in devotional service. After attaining Me, the great souls, who are yogis in devotion, never return to this temporary world, which is full of miseries, because they have attained the highest perfection." [21] This is the ultimate result or goal of practicing yoga and meditation.

Lord Krishna tells Uddhava the difference between ordinary yoga and *bhakti*, devotional meditation: "The unalloyed devotional service rendered to Me by My devotees brings Me under their control. I cannot be thus controlled by those engaged in mystic yoga, Sankhya philosophy, pious work, Vedic study, austerity, or renunciation." [22]

"Thus, one should meditate on My peaceful, transcendental form with four arms holding a conch-shell, the Sudarshana disc, club, and lotus flower. In this way, one should worship Me with fixed attention." [23]

In His form as Lord Kapiladeva, the Supreme points out that the yoga system which relates directly to the Supreme and the individual soul, which is meant for the ultimate benefit of everyone, and which causes detachment from all forms of material happiness and distress, is the highest yoga system.[24] [Complete] perfection in self-realization cannot be attained by any yogi unless he engages in devotional service to the Supreme Personality, for that is the most auspicious path.[25]

So, basically, meditation works like this: If out of affection, love, hate or fear a person focuses his concentration with intelligence upon a particular bodily form, he will certainly attain the form upon which he meditates.[26] Therefore, as Krishna further relates, "The mind that meditates on the objects of the senses certainly becomes entangled in such objects, but if one constantly remembers Me, then the mind is absorbed in Me. Therefore, one should reject all material processes of elevation, which are like the mental creations in a dream, and should completely absorb one's mind in Me. By such constant thinking of Me, a person becomes purified." [27]

DEVOTIONAL MEDITATION FREES ONE FROM THE ILLUSION

Even at the time when Lord Brahma, the secondary creator of the universe, was trying to figure out his position and purpose in this world, Lord Krishna instructed him. He told Brahma that he should situate himself in penance and meditation, and follow the rules of knowledge to receive His favor. Through this process Brahma would be able to understand everything within his heart. By being absorbed in the meditation of devotional service, in the course of Brahma's creative activities, he would see the Supreme Being in him as well as throughout the universe. He would also be able to see himself, all the living entities, and the entire universe within the Supreme Lord. He would further see the Lord and His energy spread all over the universe and within every living entity, just as fire is situated in wood. Only in this state of transcendental vision would Brahma be free from all kinds of illusion. When one is free from the conception of separated gross and subtle bodies, and when the senses are free from the influences of the modes of material nature, then you can realize your pure spiritual form in the Lord's association. At that time you can be situated in pure spiritual consciousness.[28]

THE HIGHEST LEVELS OF SPIRITUAL ENLIGHTENMENT

Since we have been discussing the path and goal of the yogic process for spiritual development, before we go much further, we should understand exactly what Sri Krishna says is the ultimate goal of yoga, or any spiritual process, and the highest form of spiritual understanding. This is especially in regard to what the yogi should realize. There are, of course, various paths which have been presented and even approved by Sri Krishna that we can use for our spiritual advancement, depending on what we need to learn and the way we need to learn it. But when it comes down to the most essential spiritual realization, what does Lord Krishna say about it?

We find the answers to this in the *Bhagavad-gita* (7.2-7) in which He relates: "I shall now declare unto you in full this knowledge both phenomenal and noumenal, by knowing which there shall remain nothing further to be known. Out of many thousands among men, one may endeavor for perfection, and of those who have achieved perfection, hardly one knows Me in truth. Earth, water, fire, air, ether, mind, intelligence, and false ego-- altogether these eight comprise My separated material energies. Besides this inferior nature, O mighty-armed Arjuna, there is a superior energy of Mine, which are all living entities who are struggling with material nature and are sustaining the universe. Of all that is material and all that is spiritual in this world, know for certain that I am both its origin and dissolution. O conqueror of wealth [Arjuna], there is no Truth superior to Me. Everything rests upon Me, as pearls are strung on a thread."

Thus, the essential realization for the spiritual *sadhaka* or initiate is to arrive at the realization of what is the Absolute Truth and know what or who He is. Herein Lord Krishna says that He is the basis of everything. This is the ultimate knowledge that He further explains to Arjuna, "because you are never envious of Me, I shall impart to you this most secret wisdom, knowing which you shall be relieved of the miseries of material existence. This knowledge is the king of education, the most secret of all secrets. It is the purest knowledge, and because it gives direct perception of the Self by realization, it is the perfection of religion. It is everlasting, and it is joyfully performed.[29] And when you have thus learned the truth, you will know that all living beings are but part of Me--and that they are in Me, and are Mine." [30]

Thus, the highest form of understanding is to know the superior nature of Lord Krishna, and that on the spiritual platform we are all of the same quality, but not of the same quantity or power. It is God who is the source of everything, as the powerhouse is the source of electricity. Even though electricity is the same everywhere and supplies power to the small light bulbs in our houses as well as to the big machines in factories, nonetheless, it is the powerhouse from which comes all the electrical force. So that powerhouse or source is obviously in a superior position, without which there would be no electricity at all. It is the same for God. God is the source of all energies, both spiritual, material, and the marginal, which are the innumerable living entities, the Lord's parts and parcels. After one understands the intricacies of this, then, as Lord Krishna further explains: "A true yogi observes Me in all beings, and also sees every being in Me. Indeed, the self-realized man sees Me everywhere. For one who sees Me everywhere and sees everything in Me, I am never lost, nor is he ever lost to Me. The yogi who knows that I and the Supersoul within all creatures are one worships Me and remains always in Me in all circumstances."[31]

Herein is the highest stage of yoga--to be fully aware of the Lord's superior position and to see His influence and recognize His energies everywhere. Thus, one becomes absorbed in spiritual consciousness. That is the end result of real yoga. Then one remains in constant awareness of the true spiritual reality. Such constant awareness is called *samadhi*. This awareness becomes a natural part of one's consciousness without the need to necessarily go into a trance through the process of meditation, *pranayama*, or yoga. In fact, all yoga is meant to lift one up to this stage of realization, without which the path of yoga remains incomplete. As Lord Krishna summarizes elsewhere, "Persons who try to reach the ultimate goal of life must expertly observe the Supreme Absolute Person and the living entity, who are one in quality in their relationship as part and whole. This is the ultimate understanding of life. There is no better truth than this."[32]

THE MYSTIC PERFECTIONS ATTAINED THROUGH YOGA

There are particular mystic powers that the yogi can attain from the regulated practice of yoga when he or she has conquered the senses, steadied the mind and perfected the breathing exercises, and fixed the mind on the Supreme. In the *Srimad-Bhagavatam*

Chapter Seven

(Eleventh Canto, Fifteenth Chapter) Lord Krishna explains that the masters of yoga have established that there are 18 types of mystic perfection, or *siddhis*. Of these are eight primary, being dependent on the Supreme, and ten are secondary, born from the mode of goodness. Among the eight primary mystic perfections, there are three that can transform the body. These are *anima*, *mahima*, and *laghima*. These powers are, respectively, becoming smaller than the smallest, like an atom; becoming greater than the greatest; and lighter than the lightest, like a feather or even an element that can ride the rays of the sun. Through what is called *prapti* one can acquire whatever one wants, and reach great distances away. Through *prakamya-siddhi* one can experience any enjoyable object, either in this or the next world. With *ishita-siddhi* one can manipulate nature, or the subpowers of *maya*. With the *vashita-siddhi* one can go unimpeded by the modes of nature, or even bring others under his control. The *kamavasayita-siddhi* gives one the power to obtain anything from anywhere, up to the highest limit. These are natural powers that can be awakened or developed by an individual with the proper practice of yoga.

The ten secondary mystic powers arise from the modes of nature. In other words, by attaining a high level of the mode of goodness, these powers may manifest automatically. They are not necessarily signs of deep spiritual development. These include the power to free oneself from bodily disturbances such as hunger and thirst, hearing and seeing things far away, being able to move at the speed of mind, assuming different forms as one desires, entering the bodies of others, dying when one desires, witnessing the pastimes of the demigods and Apsaras or the celestial girls, executing one's determination, and accomplishing one's wishes without impediment. The power to know past, present and future; tolerance of heat and cold; knowing the minds of others; checking the power of fire, sun, water, poison, etc.; and remaining undefeated by others--these are the five perfections of the mystic powers of yoga and meditation. These are listed according to their names, characteristics, and how they are developed.[33] What follows is the descriptions by Lord Krishna of how these various powers are attainable by the yogi through meditation on His various forms and energies.

THE WAY TO MEDITATE

While Uddhava was talking with Sri Krishna, as described in the *Srimad-Bhagavatam* (11.14.31-46), Uddhava asked Him by what process should one meditate upon Him when they desire liberation through the yoga process. Also, he wanted to know what specific nature should the meditation be, and upon which form should a person meditate? So Krishna explained what a person should do. The instructions that follow are similar to Lord Krishna's instructions to Arjuna, as we have read from *Bhagavad-gita*, and also similar to the instructions given by the incarnation of Lord Krishna known as Lord Kapiladeva, who taught His mother Devahati, as found in the *Srimad-Bhagavatam* (Third Canto, Chapter Twenty-eight). But Kapila's instructions contained some additional points. So I have combined the instructions together to get as comprehensive a view as possible regarding the way to meditate. Furthermore, it may surprise some people how detailed the personal form of the Supreme Being is described within this process of meditation. Hearing and listening to the descriptions of the Lord's form is itself a type of meditation. So here are the full instructions:

As Lord Kapiladeva said to His mother, by practicing this system of meditation, one can become joyful and progressively advance towards the path of the Absolute Truth. One should perform one's own duties responsibly. One should be satisfied with whatever he achieves by the Lord's grace and worship the spiritual master. One should cease performing conventional religious practices and should only be attracted to the traditions that lead to ultimate liberation. One should also eat frugally and remain in a secluded place to raise the consciousness to the highest perfection of life. A person should also practice truthfulness and nonviolence, and avoid stealing. He should be satisfied with owning only as much as one needs for maintaining oneself. The *sadhaka*, practitioner, should abstain from sex life, perform voluntary austerity, be clean, and study the Vedic literature, and worship the Supreme Lord. One must also observe silence [speak only when necessary if something relevant has to be said, or simply avoiding gossip and trivial topics], acquire steadiness in the practice of *asanas*, sitting postures, and learn to control the breath. One must also withdraw the senses from sense objects and concentrate the mind on the heart.

As Lord Krishna explained to Uddhava, one who wants to meditate properly should sit on a seat that is not too high or too low. Keep the body straight and erect yet comfortable. Place the hands on one's lap and focus the eyes on the tip of the nose. Then purify the pathways of breathing. Once the senses are controlled, one may practice *pranayama* [breathing exercisers] step by step.

Lord Kapila explains that the yogi should clear the air passages by inhaling deeply, hold the breath in and then exhale. Or, one can reverse the process by first exhaling, hold the breath outside, and then inhale. This is done so the mind can become steady and free from external disturbances. By practicing such *pranayama*, one can concentrate the mind and become free from the desire for sinful activities and material association. By meditating on the Supreme Lord one can become free from the influence of the material energy.

As Lord Krishna continues, once this is completed, one should move the life air upward, from the lowest *muladhara-chakra* to the heart, where the sacred syllable *Om* (*omkara*) is situated like the sound of a bell. One should thus continue raising the sacred sound upward, and then join the *omkara* with the fifteen vibrations produced with *anusvara*, the nasal passage. Being focused on the *omkara*, one should practice the *pranayama* system ten times at each sunrise, noon and sunset. Thus, after one month one should gain control of the life air.

Keep the eyes half closed and fix the gaze on the tip of the nose. Being alert, one should meditate on the lotus flower situated within the heart. This lotus has eight petals and is situated on a straight lotus stalk. Then one should meditate on the sun, moon and fire, placing them one after the other within the whorl of that lotus flower. Placing My transcendental form within the fire, one should meditate upon it as the auspicious goal of all meditation. That form is perfectly proportioned, gentle and cheerful. It possesses four beautiful long arms, a charming, beautiful neck, a handsome forehead, a pure smile, and glowing, shark-shaped earrings extending from the two ears. That spiritual form is the color of a dark rain cloud and is dressed in golden-yellow silk. The chest of that form is the abode of Shrivatsa and the goddess of fortune. That form is also decorated with a conchshell, disc, club, lotus flower, and a garland of forest flowers. The two brilliant lotus feet are decorated with ankle bells and bracelets, and that form exhibits the Kaustubha gem [on His chest] along with an effulgent crown. The upper hips are beautified by a golden belt, and the arms are decorated with valuable bracelets. All of the limbs of that beautiful form capture the heart, and the face is beautified by merciful glancing. Pulling the senses back from the sense objects, one should be grave and self-controlled and should use the intelligence to strongly fix the mind upon all of the limbs of My transcendental body. Thus one should meditate upon that most delicate transcendental form of Mine.

Lord Kapila further describes that the Lord in the heart is superbly adorned with a pearl necklace, a crown and pairs of armlets, bracelets and anklets. He stands on the lotus of His devotee's heart. He is most charming to look at, and His serene aspect gladdens the eyes and souls of the devotees who behold Him. He is worshipable by all the inhabitants of every planet. He is ever youthful and always eager to bestow His blessings upon His devotees. One should meditate on the eternal form of the Lord until the mind becomes fixed.

In fixing the mind on this eternal form of the Lord, the yogi should not take a collective view of all His limbs, but should fix the mind on each individual limb of the Lord. The yogi should first start with the Lord's lotus feet, which are adorned with the marks of a thunderbolt, a goad, banner, and lotus. The splendor of their beautiful ruby nails resembles the moon and dispels any thick gloom in one's heart. The Lord's feet act like thunderbolts hurled to shatter the mountain of sin stored in the mind of the meditating devotees. One should therefore meditate on the Lord's feet for a long time. Next the yogi should fix his mind on the Lord's thighs, the storehouse of all energy. They are whitish blue, like the luster of the linseed flower, and appear most graceful. The yogi should then contemplate His rounded hips, which are encircled by a girdle that rests on the exquisite yellow silk cloth that extends down to the ankles. The yogi should then meditate on His moonlike navel in the center of His abdomen. From His navel, which is the foundation of the universe, sprang the lotus stem that contained all the different planetary systems. The lotus is the residence of Brahma, the first created being. Then the yogi should concentrate His mind on the Lord's nipples, which resemble a pair of most exquisite emeralds, whitish in hue because of the rays of the milk-white pearl necklaces adorning His chest.

The yogi should then meditate on the chest of the Supreme Personality, the abode of goddess Maha-Lakshmi, the goddess of fortune. The Lord's chest is the source of all transcendental pleasure for the mind and full satisfaction for the eyes. The yogi should then focus his mind on the neck of the Supreme Personality, who is adored by the entire universe. The neck of the Lord serves to enhance the beauty of the Kaustubha gem, which hangs on His chest. The yogi should then go on to meditate on the Lord's four arms, which are the source of power for the demigods who assist in controlling various aspects of the universal affairs. Next are the ornaments of the Lord, and the Lord's disc, the Sudarshan chakra, which contains a thousand spokes and a dazzling luster, as well as His conch shell that He holds in His hand. Then there is the Lord's club, Kaumadaki, which smashes the demoniac. One should also then concentrate on the Lord's nice garland that adorns the Lord's neck, and is surrounded by honey-seeking bumblebees that create a buzzing sound. The pearl necklace on the Lord's neck represents the pure living beings who engage in His service.

The yogi should then meditate on the lotus-like countenance of the Lord, who appears in this world out of compassion for His anxious devotees. The yogi meditates upon the beautiful face of the Lord, which is adorned with curly hair and decorated with lotus-like eyes and dancing eyebrows. There is also the glances cast by the Lord's eyes that soothe the most fearful agonies of His devotees, and the smiles full of grace. The Lord's benevolent smile dries away the tears of grief for all those who bow to Him. Next is the Lord's arched eyebrows that are so charming they captivate the sex-god, Cupid, for the good of the [celibate] sages. The yogi can also meditate on the Lord's captivating laughter, which reveals His small teeth that resemble jasmine buds rendered rosy by the splendor of His lips. Once devoting his mind to this, the yogi should desire to see nothing else. Through this course of meditation, the yogi develops pure love for the Supreme and he feels excessive joy, and his mind withdraws from all material activity.

As Lord Krishna continues explaining to Uddhava, one should then pull the consciousness back from all the limbs of that transcendental body. At that time, one should meditate only on the wonderfully smiling face of the Lord. Being established in meditation on the Lord's face, one should then withdraw the consciousness and fix it in the sky. Then giving up such meditation, one should become completely established in Me and give up the process of meditation altogether.

One who has fixed his mind on Me in this way should see Me within his own soul and see the individual soul within Me, the Supreme Personality. Thus, he sees the individual souls united with the Supreme Soul, just as one sees the sun's rays completely united with the sun. When the yogi thus controls his mind by intensely concentrated meditation, his illusory identification with material objects, knowledge, and activities is very quickly extinguished.

Lord Kapila concludes by describing that thus situated in the highest transcendental stage, the mind of the yogi ceases from all material reaction and becomes transcendental to all material conceptions of happiness and distress. At that time the yogi realizes the truth of his relationship with the Supreme. He discovers that pleasure and pain as well as their interactions are actually due to the false ego, or identification with the temporary body, a view that is a product of ignorance. Because he has achieved his real identity and is completely aware and focused on it, the perfectly realized soul has no conception of how the material body is moving or acting. He becomes a *jivanmukta*, a liberated soul while still in the body. The body of such a liberated yogi is taken charge of by the Supreme Person, and it functions until its destined activities are finished. The liberated devotee, being awakened to his spiritual constitutional position and thus situated in *samadhi* which is the highest stage of yoga, no longer accepts the by-products of the material body as his own. Thus he considers his bodily activities to be like those in a dream. Thus, the yogi can be in the self-realized position after conquering the insurmountable spell of *maya*, illusion.

In Lord Krishna's instructions to Uddhava, He summarizes the goal of yoga in another way. He tells the story of a brahmana, in which the brahmana teaches that after perfecting the yogic sitting postures and the breathing processes, one should then make the mind steady by regulated practice of yoga and detachment from worldly concerns. Then fix the mind on the single goal of yoga. The mind can easily be controlled by focusing it on the Supreme Personality. Once the mind is stable, it becomes free from polluted desires for material activities. That is when the mode of goodness increases, which empowers one to completely give up the modes of passion and ignorance. One can gradually even transcend the mode of material goodness [and enter pure goodness, the spiritual strata]. The fire of material existence is extinguished when the mind is free from the influence of the modes of nature. Then one can achieve the spiritual platform of directly relating with the object of meditation, the Supreme Lord. When one's consciousness is so fixed on the Absolute Truth, the Supreme Lord, one no longer perceives any duality or difference between external and internal reality.[34]

LEAVING THE BODY THROUGH YOGA: THE ULTIMATE PERFECTION

In the *Srimad-Bhagavatam* (2.2.15-38) Sukadeva Gosvami instructs King Pariksit on the means by which one attains the final and ultimate goal of yoga, and how to leave the body to reach the spiritual domain. He says that when a yogi desires to leave this planet, inhabited by human beings, he should not be concerned about the proper time and place, but should sit somewhere comfortably and begin regulating the life air and control the senses by the mind. The yogi should then merge his mind within himself by his intelligence, and then merge his spiritual identity into the Supersoul. Once this is done [if one can get this far], one should feel fully satisfied so that he ceases from all other activities and awareness.

In that transcendental state there is no influence of time, which affects even the demigods in the celestial realms. Nor is there any influence from the modes of material nature, namely goodness, passion and ignorance. One should then prepare to give up the body by first blocking the anus with the heel of one's foot. Then one needs to begin raising the life air from the base of the spine up through the different *chakras*, up from the navel to the chest, the heart, and on up to the root of the palate, and up between his eyebrows. Then, blocking the seven openings in the head, from which the life air could leave, he should maintain his focus on going back to the spiritual realm. If he is completely free from all material desires, he should then lift the life air up to the cerebral hole at the top of the head, the crown *chakra*, and give up all material and bodily connections, focused on going back to the Supreme. However, if a yogi still has desires for material enjoyment, even to reach the higher and more refined planets like Brahmaloka, or to attain other perfections, then he takes with him the materially conditioned mind and senses. [This means that another birth in a material body will follow. Such material desires can only be accommodated with another material body.]

A true transcendentalist is concerned only with a spiritual body. Thus, as a result of their devotional service, austerities and spiritual practices, they are unrestricted to move beyond the material worlds, but never can the fruitive workers or gross materialists attain such success.

On the way out of this material creation, the mystic yogi passes over the star system known as the Milky Way by illuminating the Sushumna. The Milky Way leads toward the highest planet, Brahmaloka. The yogi reaches the planet of the fire deity, Vaishvanara. There he becomes cleansed of all material contaminations and can thus go still higher to the circle of Shishumara. This Sishumara is the universal pivot and is called the navel of Garbhodakashayi Vishnu. The yogi then goes to the planet of Maharloka, which is inhabited by pure saints, like Bhrigu, who enjoy a duration of life extending to 4,300,000,000 solar years. This planet is worshipable even by other purified saints.

On Maharloka, the yogi can see all the planets of the universe burning to ashes at the end of Brahma's life once they have been touched by the flame that emanates from the mouth of Anantadeva. Thereafter, the yogi leaves for and reaches Satyaloka (Brahmaloka), the topmost planet in the universe, by airplanes or vehicles that are used by the great purified souls. On Satyaloka, life is considered to be some 15,480,000,000,000 solar years. On this planet there is neither old age or death, nor pain or sadness. However, there may be a feeling of compassion when witnessing the many conditioned souls who have no knowledge of the spiritual process of devotional service to God, and who thus undergo numerous miseries while in contact with the material energy. On Satyaloka, the yogi is able to be released from the layers of material sheaths that encompass his Self, and thus his form goes from earthly to watery, fiery, airy, and to the ethereal stage. In this way, he is relieved of the material subtle sense objects such as smelling, tasting, seeing, touching, hearing, and other organs for material activities. The yogi, thus relieved of both gross and subtle forms of covering, enters the final stage of false ego, or bodily identification of any kind. Therein he neutralizes the material modes of goodness and passion and reaches ego in goodness. Thereafter, all egoism merges into the *mahat-tattva*, the unmanifest material ingredients, and he reaches pure Self-realization. Then he attains freedom from all material influences and may leave the cosmic creation altogether. Only in that state can such a person attain the perfection of association with the Supreme Personality of Godhead in complete bliss and satisfaction in his natural and spiritual state of being, free from all material limitations and identifications. Whoever is able to reach this stage of existence and devotional sentiment is never again attracted to the material manifestation and never returns to it. Thus, the yogi returns to the Vaikuntha world in which there are innumerable spiritual planets, hundreds of times larger than any material universe.

Sukadeva Gosvami concludes by stating that this knowledge was originally described by Lord Krishna to Lord Brahma. That great personality Brahma studied the *Vedas* three times with great attention and concentration. After such a scrutinizing examination he concluded that attraction for the Supreme Lord Sri Krishna is the highest perfection of religion. It is therefore essential that every human being hear about, glorify, and remember that Supreme Lord always and everywhere. Those who hear the nectarean message of Lord Krishna, the beloved of the devotees, thus become purified of the polluted aim of life of material desires and aims, and thus go back to the spiritual realm, back to the lotus feet of Lord Krishna.

This has been a description of the process and the perfectional stage of mystic yoga and meditation, but the easier process of bhakti-yoga, which Lord Krishna especially recommends, and is the preferable process for this age or yuga, is more fully described later in Chapter Ten.

CHAPTER EIGHT

Recognizing the Energy of God Everywhere

In the previous chapter we learn that one who is becoming or has advanced to the stage of being Self-realized can recognize and see God everywhere. Such a person knows that everything is but a display of the Lord's energy. Such a Self-realized person can perceive God and His parts and parcels wherever he or she is, and thus remain in such consciousness, which is a type of constant awareness or *samadhi*.

However, even if we are not completely Self-realized, there are numerous ways we can begin to recognize different aspects of God's energy, and, thus, remain conscious of Him more easily. In the *Bhagavad-gita* (7.8-12) Lord Krishna begins to explain to Arjuna how to do this and relates that He is the taste in water, the light of the sun and moon, the *om* syllable in the Vedic mantras, as well as the quality of sound in the either and the ability in man. Thus, without the Lord's energy, such prowess in man to do something would not be possible. Krishna goes on to say that He is also the original fragrance of the earth, the heat in fire, the life-force in all that lives, and the penance of all ascetics. He is the original seed of all existences, the intelligence of the intelligent, and the prowess of all-powerful men. He is the strength of the strong, but without passion and desires. He is also sex life that is not contrary to religious principles [by which there can be the production of powerful children]. In fact, all states of being are manifested by His energy, no matter that they may be in goodness, passion or ignorance. He is everything, and does not come under the control of the material modes, but remains in control over everything.

Lord Krishna also relates that He is the source of all power and beauty: "The splendor of the sun, which dissipates the darkness of the whole world, comes from Me. And the splendor of the moon and of fire also come from Me. I enter into each planet, and by My energy they stay in orbit. I become the moon and thereby supply the juice of life to all vegetables. I am the fire of digestion in every living body, and I am the air of life, outgoing and incoming, by which I digest the four kinds of foodstuff."[1]

So this is how we can begin seeing the power of God in our everyday life, whether it be in seeing amazing feats of nature, or in simply perceiving God's energy in the ability that people display. In this way, we can see that everything comes from God.

Lord Krishna further explains it this way: "Physical nature is known to be endlessly mutable. The universe is the cosmic form of the Supreme Lord, and I am that Lord represented as the Supersoul, dwelling in the heart of every embodied being."[2]

Furthermore, as the wind always rests in space, though blowing everywhere, in the same way all beings rest in Me.[3] I am the father, the mother, support, and the grandsire of the universe. I am the object of knowledge, the purifier and the syllable *om*. I am also the *Rig*, *Sama* and the *Yajur* [*Vedas*]. I am the goal, the master, the witness, the abode, the shelter, and the most dear friend. I am the creation and the annihilation, the basis of everything, the resting place and the eternal seed. I control the heat, the rain and the drought. I am immortality and I am also death personified. Both being and non-being are in Me.[4]

Lord Krishna goes on and tells Arjuna that He will tell him of His splendorous manifestations, but only those that are the most prominent for His opulences are limitless. Krishna explains that He is the Self in the hearts of all creatures, as well as the beginning, middle, and end of all beings. He is Vishnu of the Adityas, of lights He is the radiant sun, and of stars He is the moon. He is the *Samaveda* of the *Vedas*, and Indra of the demigods. Of all the senses He is the mind, and in living beings He is the living force. Of all the Rudras He is Lord Shiva, and of the Yakshas and Rakshasas He is the lord of wealth, Kuvera. Of the Vasus He is fire [Agni] and of mountains He is Meru. Of priests He is Brihaspati, the lord of devotion. Of generals He is Skanda, the lord of war; and of large bodies of water, He is the ocean. Of vibrations He is the transcendental *om*. Of sacrifices He is the chanting of the Lord's holy names [*japa*]; and of immovable things He is the Himalayas. Amongst sages and demigods He is Narada Muni, and among perfected beings He is the sage Kapila. Among men He is the monarch, and of weapons He is the thunderbolt. Among the celestial snakes He is Ananta; of the aquatic deities He is Varuna; and among the dispensers of law He is Yamaraja, the lord of death. Among the Daitya demons he is the devoted Prahlada; of subduers He is time; among the beasts He is the lion, and among birds He is Garuda, the feathered carrier of Lord Vishnu. Of purifiers He is the wind; among the wielders of weapons He is His incarnation Lord Rama; of fish He is the shark; and of all flowing rivers He is the Ganges. He is the beginning, middle and end of all creations. Of all sciences He is the spiritual knowledge of the Self; and among logicians He is found as the conclusive truth. Of letters He is the letter A, and of creators He is Brahma. Krishna is all-devouring death and the generator of all things yet to be. Among women He is recognized as fame, fortune, speech, memory, intelligence, faithfulness, and patience. Of hymns He is the *Brihat-sama* sung to Lord Indra, and of poetry He is the sacred Gayatri verse sung daily by brahmanas. Of months He is November and December, and of seasons He is the flower-bearing spring. In the cheating processes among men He is recognized as gambling. He is also the splendor, victory, adventure, and the strength of the strong. Of the descendants of Vrishni He is recognized as Vasudeva, and of the Pandavas He is Arjuna. Of the sages He is Vyasadeva, and among great thinkers He is Ushana. Among punishments He is the rod of chastisement, and of those who seek victory He is morality. Of all secret things He is silence, and of the wise He is wisdom. Finally,

He summarizes that He is the generating seed of all existences. There is no being--moving or nonmoving--that can exist without Him.[5]

An almost verbatim description is given by Lord Krishna to Uddhava in the *Srimad-Bhagavatam* (11.16.11-41), in which case He also adds a few extra points. He goes on to say that among great things He is the total material creation. Among subtle things He is the spirit soul, and of things that are difficult to control He is the mind. Among the eight progressive states of yoga He is *samadhi*, the final stage of success, in which the soul is completely free from any illusion. Among those desiring victory, He is prudent political counsel, and He is the science of the soul among processes of expert discrimination by which one discerns the exact differences between matter and spirit. Among religious principles He is renunciation. Of all types of security He is the consciousness of the eternal soul within. Among the ages He is Satya-yuga, the age of truth. Among those who have divided the *Vedas* He is Krishna Dvaipayana Vedavyasa [Vyasadeva]. Among the Kimpurushas He is Hanuman, and among Vidyadharas He is Sudarshana. Among jewels He is the ruby, and is the lotus among beautiful things. He is the kusha among different types of grass, and of ingredients obtained from the cow the oblations of ghee poured into the fire. He is the quality of forgiveness of the tolerant, and the good attributes of those in the mode of goodness. He is also the devotional activities of His devotees. He is also the sweet taste of water. Lord Krishna says that even with time He might count the atoms within the universe, still He cannot count all of His ever-increasing opulences or potencies that He manifests within the innumerable universes. Whatever power, beauty, fame, opulence, humility, renunciation, mental pleasure, fortune, strength, tolerance, or spiritual knowledge there may be is simply an expansion of Lord Krishna's potencies.

Then Lord Krishna tells Arjuna, "O mighty conquerors of enemies, there is no end to My divine manifestations. What I have spoken to you is but a mere indication of My infinite opulences.

Know that all beautiful, glorious, and mighty creations spring from but a spark of My splendor. But what need is there, Arjuna, for all this detailed knowledge? With a single fragment of Myself I pervade and support this entire universe." [6]

More insight into this understanding is given in Chapter Eleven of the *Bhagavad-gita* in which Lord Krishna shows Arjuna His universal form. It is explained that understanding the real spiritual nature of Krishna makes one eligible for being free of sins and attaining immortality. As Lord Krishna relates, "He who knows Me as the unborn, as the beginningless, as the Supreme Lord of all the worlds--he, undeluded among men, is freed from all sins. Intelligence, knowledge, freedom from doubt and delusion, forgiveness, truthfulness, self-control and calmness, pleasure and pain, birth, death, fear, fearlessness, nonviolence, equanimity, satisfaction, austerity, charity, fame and infamy are created by Me alone. The seven great sages and before them the four other great sages [Sanaka, Sananda, Sanatana and Sanat-kumara] and the Manus [progenitors of mankind] are born out of My mind, and all creatures in these planets descend from them. He who knows in truth this glory and power of Mine engages in unalloyed devotional service; of this there is no doubt. I am the source of all spiritual and material worlds. Everything emanates from Me. The wise who know this perfectly engage in My devotional service and worship Me with all their hearts." [7]

In this way, a mystic, a yogi, or a devotee should reach the stage of never seeing anything as being separate from the Supreme Lord, knowing the original cause of all that be. Whatever is beautiful or wonderful, we should realize its source. Then whatever we see or appreciate in this way becomes a cause for furthering our spiritual upliftment. No matter whether it is the elements from which everything is made, the planets, the living beings, the rivers and oceans, it is all an expansion of the Supreme Lord's energy and potencies. Thus, by seeing everything as an expansion of the Supreme Being, such a spiritual person should be respectful to everything and everyone. So a perfected yogi or Vedic *sadhaka* sees everything in relation to the Supreme and sees everything that exists to be eternally situated in the Lord. It is said that for a yogi and spiritual follower who engages his or her senses in the material energy, and who is neither elated nor repelled by anything in this world because of seeing it all as the energy of God, is the greatest among devotees or mystics.[8] Just as woven cloth is made of the expansion of the lengthwise and crosswise threads, similarly this entire universe is expanded on the length and breadth of the potencies of the Supreme Lord and is situated in Him.[9] "The Supreme Personality of Godhead, who is greater than all, is attainable by unalloyed devotion. Although He is present in His abode, He is all-pervading, and everything is situated within Him."[10]

As Lord Krishna summarizes, "Within this world, whatever is perceived by the mind, speech, eyes, or other senses is Me alone and nothing besides Me. All of you please understand this by a straightforward analysis of the facts."[11]

CHAPTER NINE

Lord Krishna as the Supersoul

In the chapter about yoga we understood that one should meditate on the heart and focus our awareness on the Paramatma or Supersoul within. Yet, the Supersoul acts and is perceived in many different ways, both within all embodied beings and outside. The Supersoul is the plenary expansion of Lord Krishna who accompanies each and every soul through all aspects of life. Further explanation of the Supersoul is provided by Lord Krishna as He describes this aspect of Himself: "I am seated in everyone's heart, and from Me come remembrance, knowledge and forgetfulness. By all the *Vedas* am I to be known; indeed I am the compiler of the Vedanta, and I am the knower of the *Vedas*." [1]

"In this body there is another, a transcendental enjoyer who is the Lord, the Supreme Proprietor, who exists as the overseer and permitter [of everyone's activities], and who is known as the Supersoul.[2] That Supersoul is perceived by some through meditation, by some through the cultivation of knowledge, and by others through working without fruitive desire." [3]

By understanding the Supersoul in everyone, and His position, one actually makes tangible progress in their spiritual understanding, as explained: "One who sees the Supersoul accompanying the individual soul in all bodies and who understands that neither the soul nor the Supersoul is ever destroyed, actually sees. One who sees the Supersoul in every living being and equal everywhere does not degrade himself by his mind. Thus he approaches the transcendental destination." [4] Or as Lord Krishna relates to Uddhava in the *Srimad-Bhagavatam* (11.12.17) that as the Supreme Lord, He gives life to everyone and is situated in the heart along with the life air and primal sound vibration... He is the Supersoul of all living beings, and thus naturally their controller but also their well-wisher. As their creator, maintainer and annihilator, since all entities come from Him and are eternally His, He is not different from them in spiritual quality.[5]

Furthermore, one who is kind to all living beings, who is peaceful and fixed in spiritual knowledge, sees Me within all things. Such a person never falls into the cycle of birth and death again.[6]

Lord Krishna further explains that for the Supersoul, everywhere are His hands and legs, His eyes and faces, and He hears everything. In this way the Supersoul exists. The Supersoul is the original source of all senses, yet He is without senses [meaning material senses]. He is unattached, although He is the maintainer of all living beings. He transcends the modes of nature, and at the same time He is the master of all modes of material nature. The Supreme Truth exists both internally and externally, in the moving and nonmoving. He is beyond the power of the material senses to see or to know. Although far away, He is also near to all. Although the Supersoul appears to be divided [in the heart of every living being], He is never divided. He is situated as one. Although He is the maintainer of every living entity, it is to be understood that He devours [as time] and develops all [as the creator]. He is the source of light in all luminous objects. He is beyond the darkness of matter and is unmanifested [materially]. He is knowledge, He is the object of knowledge, and He is the goal of knowledge. He is situated in everyone's heart."[7]

So how does one begin to see the Supersoul in the heart? Descriptions exist in the Vedic texts, such as the *Srimad-Bhagavatam* (Second Canto, Second Chapter, verses 8-13). Therein it is described by Sukadeva Gosvami that others see the Supreme Personality who resides in the heart region, measuring only eight inches, and having four hands, each of which hold a lotus, a disc, a conchshell, and a club. His smile expresses His happiness and His eyes are like lotus petals. His garments are yellowish like the saffron of a kadamba flower. He is bedecked with valuable jewels and gold ornaments, and wears a glowing headdress and earrings. His lotus feet stand over the whorls of the lotus-like hearts of the great mystics. The Kaustubha gem, carved with a beautiful calf, rests on His chest. His torso is garlanded with flowers while other jewels rest on His shoulders. Valuable jewels are set in the rings on His fingers, and His waist is decorated with an ornamental wreath. His leglets, bangles, oiled and curling hair with a bluish tint, along with His smiling face are all very pleasing. This is the transcendental form upon which we must concentrate through meditation, as long as the mind can be focused on Him. This process of meditation should begin from the Lord's lotus feet, and then up to the calves, thighs, and then progress higher up to His smiling face. The more focused the mind can remain upon the different limbs of the Lord, the more one becomes purified.

In conclusion, the Lord in His form as Narasimhadeva instructed Prahlada to not be concerned whether he was in the material world or not. But he should always hear the instructions and messages given by the Lord and always remain absorbed in thought of Him, for He is the Supersoul that exists within everyone's heart. Therefore, one should give up fruitive activities and engage in ways of worshiping the Lord.[8]

How to do this is explained in the next chapter.

CHAPTER TEN

Realizing Lord Krishna as Bhagavan, the Supreme Being

In the previous chapters we have leaned that God has many energies and many forms, including the impersonal Brahman, the Paramatma or Supersoul, as well as Bhagavan, the Supreme Person. Many systems of yoga seem to focus on the impersonal Brahman or the Supersoul within. So how does one realize the personal aspect? Thankfully there are numerous instructions that have been given by Lord Krishna for our benefit in this regard. And who better to hear it from than Him? So what follows is the essential directions in this matter as given directly by Lord Sri Krishna so we can get started on this path.

THE PROCESS OF DEVOTIONAL SERVICE--BHAKTI-YOGA

Devotional service to Lord Krishna is also called bhakti-yoga, or the process of union with the Supreme Being through the development of spiritual love for Him. This is actually quite a confidential level of understanding and awareness. It is not meant for everyone, unless they are genuinely curious or interested, or sincerely searching for knowledge of the Absolute Truth. In that case, they have found what they are looking for. As Lord Krishna Himself explains, "This knowledge is the king of education, the most secret of all secrets. It is the purest knowledge, and because it gives direct perception of the self by realization, it is the perfection of religion. It is everlasting, and it is joyfully performed."[1]

Furthermore, the effectiveness of the path should not be taken lightly or thought of as only a sentimental view, as Lord Krishna relates: "Being freed from attachment, fear and anger, being fully absorbed in Me and taking refuge in Me, many, many persons in the past became purified by knowledge of Me--and thus they all attained transcendental love for Me. All of them--as they surrender to Me--I reward accordingly. Everyone follows My path in all respects.[2] A person who is fully absorbed in Krishna consciousness is sure to attain the spiritual kingdom because of his full contribution to spiritual activities, in which the consummation is absolute and that which is offered is of the same spiritual nature."[3]

So if bhakti-yoga is so effective, then how does it work? What is the potency in its methodology? Lord Krishna also begins to supply the answers to these questions. "The renunciation of work and work done in devotion are both good for liberation. But, of the two, work in devotional service is better than renunciation of works... Unless one is engaged in the devotional service of the Lord, mere renunciation of activities cannot make one happy. The sages, purified by works of devotion, achieve the Supreme without delay. One who works in devotion, who is a pure soul, and who controls his mind and senses, is dear to everyone, and everyone is dear to him. Though always working, such a man is never entangled."[4]

"One who performs his duty without attachment, surrendering the results unto the Supreme God, is not affected by sinful action, as the lotus leaf is untouched by water. The yogis, abandoning attachment, act with body, mind, intelligence, and even with the senses, only for the purpose of purification. The steadily devoted soul attains unadulterated peace because he offers the result of all activities to Me; whereas a person who is not in union with the Divine, who is greedy for the fruits of his labor, becomes entangled."[5]

Herein Lord Krishna reveals the difference between ordinary activities, even religious acts, and those actions performed as offerings for the pleasure of the Supreme. Devotional service itself is not only the means to remain free from material entanglement or karma, which forces one to continue in the rounds of birth and death in this material creation, but such devotional activities purify and free one from material existence. This is the power of such service to the Lord, no matter how simple it may be. It is the intention and love in the act that makes the difference. This is the secret of devotional activities which can make such a connection between the Infinite Lord and the infinitesimal *jiva* soul.

Another example of this is regarding offerings of food to Lord Krishna, which are sometimes called sacrifices. He says, "If one offers Me with love and devotion a leaf, a flower, fruit or water, I will accept it." [6] This means that Lord Krishna accepts only simple vegetarian foods, however nicely arranged they may be. Thus, there is no meat, fish, eggs, or insects that are offered to Krishna. And His sincerest devotees only eat what is offerable to Him. Therefore, devotees of the Lord eat only vegetables, fruits, juices, grains, milk, and water, and the thousands of preparations that are made of these combinations, as foods fit for human consumption. This also helps bring you to a *sattvic* consciousness, in the mode of goodness. Foods in *rajas* and *tamas*, or the modes of passion and ignorance, or are products of violence from animal slaughter, create a darker and less peaceful consciousness. So if you are trying to make spiritual progress, you should learn the difference and avoid the foods that are unsuitable. Then, after simple vegetarian foods are prepared with devotion for the Lord, they are offered to Him in the form of His Deity, or with prayers and mantras, and afterwards you may honor whatever is left as remnants of the offering and eat it as *prasada*, which means the mercy of the Lord.

Again, such offerings must be presented in love. Otherwise, if there is no love in the offering, it is not required that Lord

Krishna accept anything, regardless of how fancy or elaborate it may be. However, there are numerous items and activities that can be offered to God. As Lord Krishna further describes, "O son of Kunti, all that you do, all that you eat, all that you offer and give away, as well as all austerities that you may perform, should be done as an offering to Me. In this way you will be freed from all reactions to good and evil deeds, and by this principle of renunciation you will be liberated and come to Me."[7]

This is the system by which our lives can be easily dovetailed to become a series of devotional services offered to Lord Krishna. Thus, with this consciousness, everything that we do within the system of regulated service can be a type of meditation on the Supreme, which thus further purifies our consciousness and turns our ordinary or mundane life into an enjoyable and spiritual adventure. We have to understand that the purpose of life is not merely to solve all of our temporary problems, or facilitate the demands of our mind and senses. We are not these bodies, and thus we need to reach the level wherein we can actually perceive our spiritual identity and the relationship we have with the Supreme. Otherwise, for what purpose have we been born in this world? For what reason do we even exist? Any animal can find some amount of happiness through the satisfaction of its tongue, stomach, or genitals. Are we no better than that? Some people may not think so. But for those of us who are more aware, who have a higher consciousness than the animals, then reawakening our loving relationship with God and seeing the spiritual relation we have with each other is a most satisfying and meaningful process.

Lord Krishna further elaborates on the means to reawaken our relationship with Him. "Engage your mind in always thinking of Me, offer obeisances and worship Me. Being completely absorbed in Me, surely you will come to Me.[8] Though engaged in all kinds of activities, My devotee, under My protection, reaches the eternal and imperishable abode by My grace. In all activities just depend on Me and work always under My protection. In such devotional service, be fully conscious of Me. If you become conscious of Me, you will pass over all the obstacles of conditioned life by My grace. If, however, you do not work in such consciousness but act through false ego, not hearing Me, you will be lost." [9]

In this way, though it may appear that one devoted to Lord Krishna engages in numerous activities, still such actions are the means to make spiritual progress if they are done simply with the proper intention. Then we come under the protection of Lord Krishna Himself.

However, we should know that there are different levels of service, and naturally not everyone will be able to reach a high level of devotion in one lifetime. And Lord Krishna also knows and understands this, for which He relates the following instructions: "For one who worships Me, giving up all activities unto Me and being devoted to Me without deviation, engaged in devotional service and always meditating on Me, who has fixed his mind upon Me, for him I am the swift deliverer from the ocean of birth and death. Just fix you mind upon Me, the Supreme Personality of Godhead, and engage all your intelligence in Me. Thus you will live in Me always, without a doubt. However, if you cannot fix your mind upon Me without deviation, then follow the regulated principles of bhakti-yoga. In this way you will develop a desire to attain to Me. If you cannot practice the regulations of bhakti-yoga, then just try to work for Me, because by working for Me you will come to the perfect stage. If, however, you are unable to work in this consciousness, then try to act giving up all results of your work and try to be self-situated. If you cannot take to this practice, then engage yourself in the cultivation of knowledge. Better than knowledge, however, is meditation, and better than meditation is renunciation of the fruits of action, for by such renunciation one can attain peace of mind." [10]

So herein we have the step-by-step process through which we can attain a progressively higher level of consciousness and devotion toward Lord Krishna. If we are not immediately on the higher stage of devotion (and who is?), then we can follow the regulative principles of bhakti-yoga, or work with the idea that what I'm doing is an offering for the Lord. Then we can give up the sense of ownership of our activities, which can pave the way for peace of mind. Or we can cultivate knowledge about our spiritual selves and Lord Krishna. Reading books, such as this one or *Bhagavad-gita*, is itself a way of increasing our understanding and is also a meditation on Lord Krishna and His instructions. Through this process our doubts will disappear and we will progress in our understanding, knowledge and awareness to the point where we will have a natural attraction for Lord Krishna. Continuing with this process will bring our attraction to a loving attitude, which can expand to a deeper love, which gives way to a reciprocation between ourselves and the Lord. Then our relationship with God and our thoughts of Him will become fixed. Therein the joy and happiness which is always available, and for which we are always looking, become so apparent in our lives that we will never want to leave such a situation, nor lose such a consciousness of the Supreme. Then not only is Krishna dear to us, but we are also dear to Krishna.

    Lord Krishna directly describes who is dear to Him. He says, "one who is not envious but is a kind friend to all living beings, who does not think himself a proprietor, who is free from false ego and equal both in happiness and distress, who is always situated and engaged in devotional service with determination, and whose mind and intelligence are in agreement with Me--he is very dear to Me. He for whom no one is put into difficulty and who is not disturbed by anxiety, who is steady in happiness and distress, is very dear to Me. A devotee who is not dependent on the ordinary course of activities, who is pure, expert, without cares, free from all pains, and who does not strive for some [materialistic] result, is very dear to Me. One who neither grasps pleasure or grief, who neither laments nor desires, and who renounces both auspicious and inauspicious things, is very dear to Me. One who is equal to friends and enemies, who is equipoised in honor and dishonor, heat and cold, happiness and distress, fame and infamy, who is always free from contamination, always silent [not talking about useless topics] and satisfied with anything, who doesn't care for any residence, who is fixed in knowledge and engaged in devotional service, is very dear to Me. He who follows this imperishable path of devotional service and who completely engages himself with faith, making Me the supreme goal, is very, very dear to Me." [11]

The Lord also related to Kardama Muni that for those who serve Him in devotion through worship, especially persons who have given up everything for Him, there is never any question of frustration.[12] Even when teaching Prahlada, the Lord in His form as Narasimha said that there are many who are wise and highly elevated who try to please Him in many ways and moods, for He is the only person who can fulfill all the desires of everyone.[13]

Lord Krishna also relates to Uddhava that His devotees may or may not know what or who He is, or how He exists, but if they worship Him with unalloyed love, then He considers them to be the best of devotees.[14] This means that it is the love that is the most important. Knowledge and insight of what or who Lord Krishna is takes a secondary position over the love that is offered to the Supreme. Even if you cannot explain or describe much about Krishna, if you have love for God, then Krishna still accepts you as the best of any devotees. Out of so many hundreds of people who are attracted to spiritual life, few will be interested to understand Lord Krishna. And out of so many who are actually liberated from material existence, few will actually know the Supreme Person. And those that do know about Krishna, few will actually have fixed and unalloyed love for Him. Thus, those that do have such love are the best, whether they are in full knowledge of spiritual topics or not.

THE FOUNDATIONAL PRINCIPLES

To begin building our character in preparation to follow the higher principles of spiritual realization, Lord Krishna recommends the following points that should be applied as best we can to our outlook and actions. These are basic moralistic rules that help prepare us for higher levels of understanding and spiritual insight. These begin with the twelve primary disciplinary principles: 1) nonviolence, 2) truthfulness, 3) not coveting or stealing the property of others, 4) being detached, 5) having humility, 6) freedom from possessiveness, 7) trust in the principles of religion that have been outlined in the Vedic texts and in Lord Krishna's instructions, 8) also remain celibate or free from carnal activities, 9) remain silent from unnecessary or hurtful talks, 10) be steady minded, 11) be forgiving, and 12) be fearless in your spiritual pursuits.

The twelve elements of regulated prescribed duties are to maintain: 1) internal cleanliness, 2) external cleanliness, 3) chant the holy names of the Lord, 4) austerity or voluntary inconveniences for a higher cause, 5) sacrifice [of one's activities to please the Lord], 6) faith, 7) hospitality, 8) worship of Lord Krishna, 9) visit the holy places, 10) act and desire only what is good for the ultimate interest, 11) be satisfied or content, and 12) do service to the spiritual master. These twenty-four elements bestow all desired traits upon all who cultivate them.[15]

Lord Krishna then goes on to explain some of these as follows: 1) Absorbing the intelligence in Him is mental equilibrium, 2) self control is the discipline of the senses, 3) patiently enduring unhappiness or discomfort is tolerance, 4) conquering the urges of the tongue and genitals is steadfastness, 5) giving up all aggression toward others is real charity, 6) real austerity is the renunciation of lust, 7) real heroism is to conquer one's tendency to enjoy material life, 8) reality is seeing the Supreme Personality everywhere, 9) truthfulness means to speak the truth, and in a non-hurtful or pleasing way, 10) cleanliness is detachment in the performance of fruitive activities, 11) renunciation means the sannyasa [renunciant] order of life, or what is equal to it, 12) religious remuneration is devotion to the acharya with the purpose of acquiring spiritual instruction, 13) the greatest strength, both physical and mental, is the system of breath control, *pranayama*, 14) the true desirable wealth for human beings is religiousness, and 15) sacrifice is to the Supreme Personality of Godhead, or the means to absorb one's consciousness in the Supreme and that which is connected to Him.[16]

Continuing, He also says: 16) actual opulence is the Lord's own nature in which He exhibits the six unlimited opulences, namely strength, beauty, fortune, fame, renunciation, and knowledge, 17) the ultimate gain in life is achieving devotional service to the Lord, 18) real education is negating the false perception of duality within the soul, 19) real modesty is to be disgusted with improper activities, 20) beauty is to possess good qualities, 21) real happiness is to transcend the stages of material happiness and unhappiness, 22) real misery is to be implicated in searching for sex enjoyment, 23) a wise man knows the process of freedom from bondage to the body, 24) a fool is one who thinks he is this body and mind, 25) the real path of life is that which leads to Lord Krishna, 26) the wrong path is to work for gratifying the senses, 27) heaven is the predominance of the mode of goodness, 28) hell is the predominance of the mode of darkness or ignorance, 29) the Lord is everyone's true friend, acting as the spiritual master, 30) one's home is the human body, 31) being rich is being full of good qualities, 32) one who is dissatisfied with life is actually poor, 33) a wretched person is one who is controlled by the senses, 34) one who is not attached to sense gratification is the real controller, 35) one who is attached to gratifying his senses is a slave. A more elaborate description of these good and bad qualities is not necessary. To constantly see good and bad qualities is itself a bad quality. The best quality is to transcend the material forms of good and bad.[17]

THE ESSENTIAL WAYS FOR DEVELOPING LOVE FOR KRISHNA

Though the above principles are to be understood and followed as best we can, Lord Krishna nonetheless more concisely explains that the easiest ways for engaging in the spiritual activities of devotional service is simply by hearing about Him, seeing His Deity form, meditating upon Him, and chanting His names and glories. This is the way love for Him easily develops, and not necessarily by physical proximity.[18] And there are so many ways to do this. First hearing about Him is easy by reading the sacred texts, such as the *Bhagavad-gita*, *Srimad-Bhagavatam*, and others that describe Him and His pastimes, and that provide explanations by spiritual authorities. This can be done any time if one has such books. There are now so many temples in which one can go and get *darshan* or view Lord Krishna in His various forms, whether it be His form of Radha and Krishna, or Lakshmi and Vishnu, or Jagannatha, and so on. So the temples and one's going to the temple and participate in its programs, or helping fund or manage such temples, is a part of devotional service and one of the ways to make spiritual advancement and further the development of one's love for Him. Meditating upon Lord Krishna is easy by hearing about Him, serving Him by offering your activities to Him, or by chanting His holy names, either through *japa* meditation, which is chanting His names on beads a certain number of times each day, or by engaging in singing songs about Him, *bhajans* or *kirtans*. So this can be very easy for most people, and much simpler than trying to follow lots of rules and regulations.

As Lord Krishna further explains, as when He spoke to the kings who had been imprisoned by Jarasandha, we should live our lives and keep our minds fixed on Him, even when begetting generations of progeny, or encountering happiness and distress, or birth and death. But be detached from the body and that which is connected with it. As we remain self-satisfied through such detachment, we must keep our religious vows while keeping our minds fixed on the Lord. In this way, we can ultimately attain Him, the Supreme Absolute Truth.[19]

Lord Krishna provides the primary principles for beginning the process of developing love for Him. He describes this to Uddhava: "Because you love Me, I previously explained the process of devotional service. Now I will again explain the supreme process for achieving loving service unto Me." So these are the essential steps for beginning the regulated process by which a person can attain the spiritual love for Lord Krishna. He explains that it is: 1) through firm faith in the blissful narrations of His pastimes, 2) continued chanting of His glories, 3) attachment and participation in ceremonial worship of Him, such as at temples, 4) praising Him through beautiful hymns, 5) showing great respect for the process of devotional service, 6) offering Him or His Deity obeisances with one's body, 7) performing first-class worship of His devotees, 8) awareness of Him as the Supersoul in all living beings, 9) offering ordinary activities in devotional service to Him, 10) engaging your words to describe Him, 11) offering your mind to Him, as in thinking of Him in numerous ways that are appropriate for you, 12) rejecting material desires, 13) using your wealth to engage in His devotional service, 14) renouncing or being detached form material forms of sense gratification and happiness, 15) performing all of your pious activities, such as charity, religious principles, chanting, vows, and voluntary austerities with the purpose of achieving Him. These are the principles that, through constant practice, assist one to the level of achieving love of God. After attaining this there is no other purpose or goal to be accomplished for His devotee.[20]

To summarize in the words of Lord Kapiladeva, the pure devotee should engage in devotional service by giving respect to the spiritual master and the *acharyas*. You should also be compassionate to the poor and make friendship with persons who are your equals. All of your activities should be kept in line with the devotional regulations and with control of the senses. You should also try to hear about spiritual topics, and use your time in chanting the holy name of the Lord. You should keep your behavior straightforward and simple. You should also avoid the company of persons who are not spiritually advanced or inclined, although you should keep yourself friendly and non-envious toward everyone. When you are fully qualified with these spiritual attributes and your consciousness is purified, you will immediately become attracted whenever you hear the Lord's name and transcendental qualities. As air carries an aroma from its source and is caught by your sense of smell, similarly if you engage in the devotional service of the Lord in a continuous manner, you can also catch the Supreme Soul, who is present everywhere.[21]

This is the point of following the principles that purify our lives and consciousness. It enables us to reach the Supreme Being in realization and in establishing a union with the Lord in a loving connection. Lord Kapiladeva continues to explain that the manifestation of unadulterated devotional service is exhibited when one's mind is at once attracted to hear the spiritual name, qualities and activities of the Supreme Being who resides in everyone's heart. Just as the water of the Ganges naturally flows toward the ocean, the devotional ecstasy of service to the Lord, when uninterrupted by material conditions, easily flows towards Him.[22]

THE WAY TO WORSHIP THE DEITY FORM OF THE LORD

Lord Krishna also explains to Uddhava the process of how to worship the Lord at the temple, or if you have Deities of the Lord in your home. He says that through these activities you can give up false pride and prestige, which is always a hindrance on the path of spiritual advancement. You may purify yourself by seeing, touching, worshiping, serving, and offering prayers of glorification and obeisances to His Deity form and to His pure devotees. You should hear with love and faith the narrations of His glories,

The beautiful Deities of Sri Sri Radha-Kunjabihari of the Detroit Krishna temple. Kunjabihari means Lord Krishna who sports in the pleasure groves in the spiritual atmosphere of Vrindavana.

participate in praising them, and thus meditate on Him. Whatever you acquire can be offered to Him, and even offer yourself as an eternal servant and thus give yourself completely to Him. Krishna says that you should always discuss His birth and activities and enjoy life by participating in the festivals, such as Janmastami, His appearance day celebration, which facilitates in glorifying His pastimes. You should also participate in the ceremonies at His temples by singing, dancing, playing musical instruments, and certainly talking with others, especially Vaishnavas, about Lord Krishna. You should also observe the other regular festivals by attending the ceremonies, make offerings, as well as go on pilgrimages to the holy places if you can. Religious vows such as the Ekadasi day should be observed, wherein one fasts for the day or at least eats no grains or beans. You should also take initiation according to the instructions in the *Vedas*, *Pancharatra*, and similar texts. You should also assist in lovingly constructing temples wherein you and others can install the Deity of Lord Krishna, which is His home, and then help with His worship with establishing flower and fruit gardens and areas that celebrate His pastimes, and in cleaning the temple. Having cleaned the temple by dusting and then using water and pure antiseptic, you should sprinkle scented water and decorate the temple with *mandalas*, thus acting just like Lord Krishna's own servant. However, a devotee should never act with pride and advertise his devotional services. You should be careful and not do such things as use lamps that have been offered to the Lord's Deity for other purposes simply because there is a need for light somewhere. Also, you should never offer anything that has been already offered or used by others. You should offer whatever you most want in this world, or whatever is most dear to you. Such an offering with love qualifies you for eternal life.[23]

Lord Krishna goes on to explain that if you have executed such devotional performances and pious works for His satisfaction, and worship Him in His Deity form with fixed attention, you will obtain unflinching devotional service to Him. By the excellent quality of this service, a worshiper like yourself will obtain realized knowledge of Him.[24]

IN THE END YOU GO BACK TO KRISHNA

As Lord Krishna in His *avatara* as Lord Kapiladeva says, His devotee becomes self-realized by His unlimited causeless mercy. Thus, when freed from all doubts, you will steadily progress toward your destined abode, which is directly under the protection of the Lord's spiritual energy of unadulterated bliss. This is the real perfectional goal of life for any living being. In this way, when you give up your material body, you go back to that transcendental abode and never come back to this world.[25]

Therefore, as Lord Kapiladeva continues, He does not find a greater person than one who has no outside interest than His and who therefore engages and dedicates all of his activities and life unto Him.[26] Thus, even if one is a family man who lives a decent and devotional life with the idea of giving his family the best of spiritual environments, he is still a first-class devotee. Or if a person is a businessman, if he is dedicated to the purpose of doing business with the idea of supporting or expanding the means of serving God, then he is also a prime candidate for making the most of this life in terms of spiritual advancement. He may be engaged in so much business, but if his intent or meditation is to find the means or raise the funds for worshiping the Supreme Person in various ways, then he or she becomes the manifest energy of Seshanaga or Sankarshana who is the support of Lord Vishnu. So such a person exhibits his or her devotional ability as the support of the service of God. The time and results of one's engagement in activity of business becomes purified by using the results, such as the funds that are earned, in the service of God. Ordinarily this would be considered karma-yoga, to offer the results for a spiritual purpose. But when one directly uses it as an offering for the service of Lord Krishna, then it becomes a part of one's devotional service, bhakti-yoga. This endeavor, and one's thought and meditations on it, qualifies one for detachment and spiritual advancement, which is the goal of yoga, and the ultimate attainment of love of God. And this is what paves the way for liberation from the material world and entrance into the Lord's abode, the ultimate aim of life.

This process is much easier than we may think. It only takes a little daily practice. As the Personality of Godhead in His form as Lord Kapiladeva said: "My dear mother, the path of self-realization which I have already instructed to you is very easy. You can execute this system without difficulty, and by following it you shall very soon be liberated, even within your present body. Those who are actually transcendentalists certainly follow my instructions, as I have given them to you. You may rest assured that if you traverse this path of self-realization perfectly, surely you shall be freed from fearful material contamination and shall ultimately reach Me. Persons who are not conversant with devotional service certainly cannot get out of the cycle of birth and death." [27] Thus, the most sure way of spiritual development and reaching the ultimate goal of life is described herein.

WHY LORD KRISHNA ADVISES US TO ENGAGE IN THE PROCESS OF BHAKTI-YOGA

Bhakti-yoga is the devotional service performed for Lord Krishna, or one of His incarnations, such as Lord Vishnu, Lord Ramachandra, etc. Lord Krishna explains that, "Work done as a sacrifice for Vishnu has to be performed, otherwise work binds one to this material world. Therefore, O son of Kunti [Arjuna], perform your prescribed duties for His satisfaction, and in that way you will always remain unattached and free from bondage." [28]

"Those who know Me as the Supreme Lord, as the governing principle of the material manifestation, who know Me as the one underlying all the demigods and as the one sustaining all sacrifices, can, with steadfast mind, understand and know Me even at the time of death.[29] And whoever, at the time of death, quits his body remembering Me alone, at once attains My nature. Of this there is no doubt. Whatever state of being one remembers when he quits his body, that state he will attain without fail. Therefore, Arjuna, you should always think of Me in the form of Krishna and at the same time carry out your prescribed duty. With your activities dedicated to Me and your mind and intelligence fixed on Me, you will attain Me without doubt." [30]

In this way, we can begin to understand that devotional service ultimately brings us to the level of being able to see Lord Krishna directly. It is by this method that numerous other saintly sages and yogis have come to be able to directly see the Lord. The point to remember is that the more spiritual we become, the more we can perceive that which is spiritual. The more purified our consciousness is, or the higher the vibrational level upon which our consciousness functions, the more we can see and enter into that higher level of existence or reality. It awakens our transcendental senses that exist within us. So the process of continued service to Krishna and His devotees will bring about the purification which will allow us to enter into Krishna's domain, even within this very lifetime, if we are fortunate enough.

As Lord Krishna relates, "The form which you are seeing with your transcendental eyes cannot be understood simply by studying the *Vedas*, nor by undergoing serious penances, nor by charity, nor by worship. It is not by these means that one can see Me as I am. My dear Arjuna, only by undivided devotional service can I be understood as I am, standing before you, and can thus be seen directly. Only in this way can you enter into the mysteries of My understanding. One who is engaged in My pure devotional service, free from the contaminations of previous activities and from mental speculation, who is friendly to every living entity, certainly comes to Me." [31]

"One can understand the Supreme Personality of Godhead as He is only by devotional service. And when one is in full consciousness of the Supreme Lord by such devotion, he can enter into the kingdom of God."[32]

Lord Krishna also explains that the residents of both heaven and hell want to take a human birth on earth since such a human life provides the best facility to achieve transcendental knowledge and love of God. Neither heavenly nor hellish bodies provide the efficient means for such opportunity.[33] This is the fortunate nature of life on this earth planet and in these humans bodies, which we often take so much for granted.

Furthermore, Lord Krishna describes that the highest level of happiness that can be attained is when we have a taste for serving Him. He says that if you fix your consciousness on Him, giving up your material desires, you will share a happiness with Him that cannot be experienced in any way by those who remain engaged in sense gratification. If you do not desire anything of this world, and have achieved peace through controlling the senses, and if your consciousness is equipoised in all situations, and when your mind is satisfied in Him, you will find happiness wherever you go.[34] If or when you are without any desire for personal gratification, and when the mind is attached to Him, peaceful and without false ego, merciful to all living beings, and when your consciousness is not affected by the prospects for gratifying the senses, then you can find a happiness that cannot be known or achieved in any other way, especially by those who lack such qualities.[35]

THOSE WHO RENDER DEVOTIONAL SERVICE TO LORD KRISHNA

As we can see, many people in this world are not interested in serving God. But those who do are distinguished by certain characteristics as described by Lord Krishna Himself. He says, "O best among the Bharatas [Arjuna], four kinds of pious men render devotional service unto Me--the distressed, the desirer of wealth, the inquisitive, and he who is searching for knowledge of the Absolute. Of these, the wise who are in full knowledge in union with Me through pure devotional service are the best. For I am very dear to them, and they are dear to Me. All these devotees are undoubtedly magnanimous souls, but he who is situated in knowledge of Me I consider verily to dwell in Me. Being engaged in My transcendental service, he attains Me. After many births and deaths, he who is actually in knowledge surrenders unto Me, knowing Me to be the cause of all causes and all that is. Such a great soul is very rare."[36]

Krishna goes on to explain that persons who have acted piously in previous lives and in this life, whose sinful actions are completely eradicated and who are freed from the duality of delusion, engage themselves in His service with determination. Those intelligent persons who are endeavoring for liberation from old age and death take refuge in Him through devotional service. They are actually Brahman because they entirely know everything about transcendental and fruitive activities.[37]

As Krishna says to Arjuna, "Those who are not deluded, the great souls, are under the protection of the divine nature. They are fully engaged in devotional service because they know Me as the Supreme Personality of Godhead, original and inexhaustible. Always chanting My glories, endeavoring with great determination, bowing down before Me, these great souls perpetually worship Me with devotion. Others, who are engaged in the cultivation of knowledge, worship the Supreme Lord as the one without a second, diverse in many, and in the universal form."[38]

"Those who worship Me with devotion, meditating on My transcendental form--to them I carry what they lack and preserve what they have."[39]

"And whoever knows Me as the Supreme Personality of Godhead, without doubting, is to be understood as the knower of everything, and he therefore engages himself in full devotional service, O son of Bharata. This is the most confidential part of the Vedic scriptures, O sinless one, and it is disclosed now by Me.

Whoever understands this will become wise, and his endeavors will know perfection." [40]

THOSE WHO DO NOT TAKE UP DEVOTIONAL SERVICE

What Sri Krishna says about those people who do not engage in His service is also disclosed herein. He says, "Ignorant and faithless persons who doubt the revealed scriptures do not attain God consciousness. For the doubting soul there is happiness neither in this world nor in the next.[41] Those whose minds are distorted by material desires surrender unto demigods and follow the particular rules and regulations of worship according to their own natures.[42] Whatever a man may sacrifice to other gods, O son of Kunti, is really meant for Me alone, but it is offered without true understanding... Those who do not recognize My true transcendental nature fall down." [43]

Furthermore, "Those miscreants who are grossly foolish, lowest among mankind, whose knowledge is stolen by illusion, and who partake of the atheistic nature of demons, do not surrender unto Me.[44] Those who are not faithful on the path of devotional service cannot attain Me, but return to birth and death in this material world." [45]

Lord Krishna also explains to Uddhava that if a person engages in meticulous study of the Vedic literature and even becomes expert in it, yet makes no progress in understanding the Supreme Personality, then one's study is like that of a person who works so hard to take care of a cow that gives no milk. In this way, there is no substantial result from one's study, except for the work alone. Such a man who works to take care of a cow that gives no milk, or an unchaste wife, useless children, or a body that is totally dependent on others, or has wealth that serves no rightful purpose, is certainly most miserable. In the same way, one who studies Vedic knowledge that does not contain the Lord's glories is also miserable. Therefore, an intelligent person should never accept literature that does not contain the descriptions of the Supreme Being's activities, which purify the universe. It is He that creates, maintains and annihilates the complete material manifestation. And among all of His incarnations, His forms of Krishna and Balarama are the most beloved. Any so-called knowledge that does not contain information on the activities of Lord Krishna is simply barren of the highest truth and not acceptable to those who are actually intelligent.[46]

BHAKTI-YOGA GIVES ONE THE SAME RESULTS AS MYSTIC YOGA AND MORE

With the explanations that follow we can understand that a separate endeavor for engaging in the mystic yoga tradition is not needed. Whatever spiritual goals you may wish to attain can be acquired simply by engaging in devotional service to the Supreme. Sri Krishna explains this: "One who can control his senses by practicing the regulated principles of freedom can obtain the complete mercy of the Lord and thus become free from all attachment and aversion.[47] And of all yogis, he who always abides in Me with great faith, worshiping Me in transcendental loving service, is most intimately united with Me in yoga and is the highest of all.[48] He who meditates on the Supreme Personality of Godhead, his mind constantly engaged in remembering Me, undeviated from the path, he, O Partha [Arjuna], is sure to reach Me... One who at the time of death, fixes his life air between his eyebrows and in full devotion engages himself in remembering the Supreme Lord, will certainly attain to the Supreme Personality...[49] After attaining Me, the great souls, who are yogis in devotion, never return to this temporary world, which is full of miseries, because they have attained the highest perfection."[50]

This is the powerful effect of the process of thinking and dedicating your activities to Lord Krishna. However, the same result can also be acquired by proper association with those who are spiritually advanced. In this regard, the Supreme Lord personally told Uddhava that it is by associating with His pure devotees that you can destroy your desires for the objects that can gratify the senses. It is this purifying association that can bring the Lord under the control of such a devotee. You may perform the astanga-yoga system, engage in philosophical analysis of the elements of material nature, or practice nonviolence and other ordinary principles of piety, like dig wells, give in charity, plant trees, or other public welfare activities. You may even chant the *Vedas*, perform penances, take up the renounced order of life, worship the demigods, chant confidential mantras, or visit the holy places. But all such activities cannot bring Him under your control.[51] Even though you may engage with great endeavor in the mystic yoga system, or philosophical speculation, or charity, vows, penances, rituals, or even studying the *Vedas* and teaching the Vedic mantras to others, still you cannot achieve Him by these means alone.[52]

However, by example we can see that as the residents of Vrindavana, headed by the *gopis* [cowherd girls devoted to Krishna], were always completely attached to Him with the deepest love, they could not find any other comfort or happiness in their separation from Him when Krishna's uncle Akrura took Him and Balarama to Mathura. All of the nights in which the *gopis* spent with Krishna in Vrindavana went by like a moment. And now, bereft of His association, the *gopis* felt those same nights drag on forever, as if each night were a day of Brahma. Just as the great sages in yoga trance merge into self-realization, just like the river merging into the ocean, and are thus oblivious to any material names and forms, in the same way the *gopis* of Vrindavana were so completely attached and absorbed in thought of Him that they did not think of their own bodies, or of anything of this world, not even of their future. Their complete consciousness was simply absorbed in Krishna. Though they were not completely aware of His actual position, by their thoughts and association with Him, they all attained Him, the Supreme Absolute Truth.

Therefore, as Lord Krishna says, "Abandon the Vedic mantras as well as the procedures in the supplementary Vedic literature and all their injunctions. Simply take shelter of Me alone, for I am the Supreme Personality of Godhead situated within the heart of all conditioned souls. Take shelter of Me wholeheartedly, and by My grace be free from fear in all circumstances."[53]

An example of such fearlessness for devotees on the path of spiritual progress is related as follows: Those who are yogis learn how to control their lives so that they pass away from this world at the right moment, and in the right consciousness, so that they will not take birth in this world again. However, Lord Krishna explains this, and concludes that for His devotees there is no reason to be overly concerned about such things. "According to the *Vedas*, there are two ways of passing from this world--one in light and one in darkness. When one passes in light, he does not come back; but when one passes in darkness, he returns..."[54] Those who know the Supreme Brahman pass away from the world during the influence of the fiery god, in the light, at an auspicious moment, during the fortnight of the moon and the six months when the sun travels in the north. The mystic who passes away from this world during the smoke, the night, the moonless fortnight, or in the six months when the sun passes to the south, or who reaches the moon planet, again comes back.[55] However, the devotees who know these two paths, O Arjuna, are never bewildered. Therefore be always fixed in devotion."[56] Thus, for a devotee who is always thinking of Krishna, there is no reason for any other endeavor or concern in the performance of one's spiritual progress.

Krishna further clarifies that whatever mystic perfections can be achieved by good birth, herbs, austerities and mantras can all be achieved by devotional service to Him; indeed one cannot achieve the actual perfection of yoga by any other means.[57] Everything that can be attained through fruitive or karmic activities, penance, knowledge, detachment, mystic yoga, charity, religious duties, or any other means of perfecting life can be easily achieved by His devotee simply through loving service to Him. If for some reason His devotee desires to be promoted to heaven or attain liberation, or a residence in His abode, such benedictions are easily achieved.[58]

A similar point is reiterated by the Lord in His form as Kapiladeva when He explains that because His devotee is completely absorbed in thought of Him, he does not desire such benedictions as going to the higher planetary systems, like Satyaloka, nor any of the eight mystic powers obtained from yoga, nor does he desire to be liberated into the kingdom of God. However, the devotee nonetheless enjoys all offered benedictions even in this life, even without asking for them.[59]

In conclusion, everything that can be accomplished by separate endeavors in other processes are not left out of the path of devotion to the Lord. "A person who accepts the path of devotional service is not bereft of the results derived from studying the *Vedas*, performing austere sacrifices, giving charity, or pursuing philosophical and fruitive activities. At the end he reaches the supreme abode." [60]

HOW TO MEDITATE OR THINK OF LORD KRISHNA

If thinking about or absorbing our consciousness in the Supreme is the highest means of spiritual progress, then what is the best way to do that? How best to think of Lord Krishna? The Lord Himself provides the answers and explains that one should meditate on the Supreme Person as He who knows everything, as He who is the oldest, who is the controller, smaller than the smallest, the maintainer of everything, who is beyond all material conception, inconceivable, always a person, and who is luminous like the sun. Being transcendental, He is beyond this material nature.[61]

"The Supreme Lord said: 'He whose mind is fixed on My personal form, always engaged in worshiping Me with great and transcendental faith, is considered by Me to be most perfect.'" [62]

Engaging in devotional service itself is a form of constantly remembering the Lord because whatever you are doing is being done as an offering to Him. This means it is both the process and the result at the same time. As Lord Krishna explains, "For one who remembers Me without deviation, I am easy to obtain, O son of Pritha [Arjuna], because of his constant engagement in devotional service." [63]

In this way, simply by thinking or remembering Sri Krishna in some way is itself a type of devotional service to Him. We can further ask that if we are to be absorbed in such a way, is there nothing else we can do while thinking of Krishna? And what if it is not so easy for us to do this? Lord Krishna explains to Uddhava in this regard that if you are not able to free your mind from all material disturbances and establish it on the spiritual platform, then simply perform your activities as an offering to Him, without trying to enjoy the results. Narrations of the Lord's pastimes are all-auspicious and purify the universe. So if you are faithful, then just hear, glorify, and constantly remember and relive those transcendental activities through dramatic performances [or in reading about them] and take full shelter of Him. Thus, dedicating your religious, sensual, and occupational activities for His satisfaction, you will obtain devotional service to the Lord, the eternal Supreme Person. If you obtain such pure devotional service through the association of the Lord's devotees and always engage in worshiping Him, you will very easily return to His abode, which is revealed by His pure devotees.[64] Thus, Lord Krishna directly describes how easy it is to engage in His devotional service and focus our thoughts and activities on Him.

CHANTING LORD KRISHNA'S HOLY NAMES

One of the simplest and most recommended ways of meditating on Lord Krishna is by chanting His holy names. In fact, He explains that "... of vibrations I am the transcendental *om*. Of sacrifices, I am the chanting of the holy names [*japa*]." Thus the Lord's holy name is indeed one of the aspects of Lord Krishna Himself. To chant the Lord's holy names for one's own development is called *japa*, or *japa* meditation. Such chanting not only brings our attention to Him in a form of meditation on the Absolute Truth or Supreme Person, but it also brings us into His association through the vibration of His holy names. His holy names, such as Hare Krishna and Hare Rama, contain the same spiritual vibration as Lord Krishna directly, when they are chanted purely. So this should be taken seriously. For this reason we should understand the process and benefits of chanting *japa*, which is also called mantra-yoga.

THE BHAKTI PROCESS ERASES PAST KARMA

Lord Krishna also guides you in explaining that you need to, "Rid yourself of all fruitive activities by devotional service, and surrender fully to that consciousness. Those who want to enjoy the fruits of their work are misers. A man engaged in devotional service rids himself of both good and bad actions even in this life. Therefore strive for yoga, which is the art of all work. The wise, engaged in devotional service, take refuge in the Lord, and free themselves from the cycle of birth and death by renouncing the fruits of action in the material world. In this way, they can attain that state beyond all miseries.[65] One who has renounced the fruits of his action, whose doubts are destroyed by transcendental knowledge, and who is situated firmly in the self, is not bound by works."[66]

So herein we see that the process of bhakti-yoga also accomplishes the same thing as karma-yoga, except more efficiently and easily. Karma, whether good or bad, and no matter whether it leads us to heavenly or hellish destinations, is experienced by another birth. We have to undergo it to work out our karmic reactions from previous lives. But karma clings to the subtle body, which helps determine what our next life will be. However, the process of sincere devotional service to the Lord is so spiritually surcharged that it disintegrates the subtle body and erases our karma so that we become free from enduring any further reactions. In His form as Lord Kapiladeva, the Supreme relates that the process of *bhakti*, devotional service, dissolves the subtle body of the living being [along with its karma] without any separate effort, just as fire in the stomach digests all that we eat.[67]

Furthermore, even if someone who is engaged in devotional service makes some mistake and accidentally does something that could create adverse reactions, or additional karma, the continuation of your service to God is enough to rectify the situation or problems, if it is not overly serious. As it is explained, if a yogi or devotee accidentally commits something abominable because of momentary inattention, the very practice of yoga, or devotional service to the Lord, can burn to ashes the sinful reaction without employing any other process.[68]

Lord Krishna also explains that if His devotee has not fully conquered his or her senses, he may still be troubled by material desires. Nonetheless, because he or she has unflinching devotion for Him, such a devotee will not be defeated by the desire for sense gratification. Just as a blazing fire turns firewood into ashes, devotion to Krishna completely burns to ashes the sins that may be committed by His devotees.[69] Just as a diseased eye gradually regains its power to see with the treatment of proper medicine, a living being cleanses himself of material contamination by hearing and chanting the pious narrations of the Lord's glories, and regains his ability to see Him, the Absolute Truth, in His subtle spiritual form.[70]

Lord Krishna further relates to Uddhava that His devotee should remain happy and worship Him with great faith and conviction. Even though he may sometimes be engaged in sense enjoyment, a sincere devotee knows that all sense gratification leads to a miserable result, and he is sorry for such activities.[71]

EVEN THE WORST OF SINNERS CAN BE DELIVERED AND REACH PEACE

Lord Krishna also explains how, "In this endeavor there is no loss or diminution, and a little advancement on this path can protect one from the most dangerous type of fear.[72] Even if you are considered to be the most sinful of all sinners, when you are situated in the boat of transcendental knowledge, you will be able to cross over the ocean of miseries. As the blazing fire turns firewood into ashes, O Arjuna, so does the fire of [spiritual] knowledge burn to ashes all reactions to material activities. In this world, there is nothing so sublime and pure as transcendental knowledge. Such knowledge is the mature fruit of all mysticism. And one who has achieved this enjoys the self within himself in due course of time. A faithful man who is absorbed in transcendental knowledge and who subdues his senses quickly attains the supreme spiritual peace."[73]

Lord Krishna further reiterates this point: "The sages, knowing Me as the ultimate purpose of all sacrifices and austerities, the Supreme Lord of all planets and demigods and the benefactor and well-wisher of all living entities, attain peace from the pangs of material miseries."[74]

THE CONCLUSIVE DECISION IS UP TO US

As with all things in Vedic culture, this is not a dogma wherein a person has no choice or independent decision in the matter. Everyone can decide for himself or herself what they should do once they have been given the proper spiritual knowledge. No one is forced to act one way or another. Everyone has free will and choice. Even Arjuna in the *Bhagavad-gita* was given the opportunity to make up his own mind regarding what he wanted to do. Similarly we are also given that chance.

In the end, after explaining all this information, Lord Krishna simply advises us in this way: "Thus I have explained to you the most confidential of all knowledge. Deliberate on this fully, and then do what you wish to do. Because you are My very dear friend, I am speaking to you the most confidential part of knowledge. Hear this from Me, for it is for your benefit. Always think of Me and become My devotee. Worship Me and offer your homage unto Me. Thus you will come to Me without fail. I promise you this because you are My very dear friend. Abandon all varieties of religion and just surrender unto Me. I shall protect you from all sinful reactions. Do not fear." [75]

Lord Krishna similarly concludes his conversation to Uddhava, wherein He says, "If you worship Me by your prescribed duties, having no other object of worship, and remain conscious that I am present in all living beings, you will achieve unflinching devotional service to Me. I am the Supreme of all worlds, and, being its ultimate cause, I create and destroy this universe. I am the Absolute Truth, and by worshiping Me with unfailing devotional service, you will come to Me. Once you have purified your existence through your prescribed duties, and fully understand My supreme position with scriptural and realized knowledge, you will very soon achieve Me. I have now described to you the means by which you can come back to Me, the Supreme Personality." [76]

Again He says that persons who seriously follow these methods of achieving Him, which He has personally taught, attain freedom from illusion. Upon reaching the Lord's personal abode they perfectly understand the Absolute Truth.[77]

Lord Krishna simply explains that once you have thought this over, you can make your own choice, but you should very easily and always remember Him and perform all of your duties for Him without being careless. With your mind and intelligence offered to Him, you should fix your mind in attraction to His devotional service.[78] The Lord considers this process of using one's mind, words, and bodily functions for realizing His presence within all living beings to be the best possible method of spiritual enlightenment.[79]

THE NEED TO SPREAD THIS KNOWLEDGE

The need to help spread this spiritual knowledge is also explained by Lord Krishna. But who should receive it is also outlined. It is not meant for everyone, though everyone needs it since we are all, ultimately, spiritual beings in the material atmosphere. "This confidential knowledge may not be explained to those who are not austere, or devoted, or engaged in devotional service, nor to one who is envious of Me. For one who explains this supreme secret to the devotees, devotional service is guaranteed, and at the end he will come back to Me. There is no servant in this world more dear to Me than he, nor will there ever be one more dear." [80] So we can understand how much the Lord appreciates those who take the time and endeavor to help spread this information to others.

This is similar to Lord Kapiladeva's instructions, wherein He says that this knowledge of devotional service is not meant for the envious, agnostics, those who are unclean in their habits, or hypocrites, or those proud of material possessions. It should also not be given to those who are too greedy or overly attached to family life. It is to be given to those who are faithful, who are respectful to the spiritual master, non-envious, friendly to all, and who are eager to render service, and who are detached from material existence. But then Lord Kapiladeva says that anyone who once meditates upon Him with faith and affection, who hears and chants about Him, surely goes back home, back to Godhead.[81] So in spite of the warning about who should be given this knowledge, there is also the importance that anyone fit to receive it should be given that chance.

As Lord Krishna further relates: "And I declare that he who studies this sacred conversation worships Me by his intelligence.

And one who listens with faith and without envy becomes free from sinful reaction and attains the planets where the pious dwell." [82] So here Lord Krishna assures us that even if we are not devotees, by patiently and faithfully listening or reading these instructions of His, then we are still bound to enter into the heavenly planets of the pious after this life. This is a very positive result from such a simple act. Thus, we can only begin to imagine how much more powerful are the results from directly acting in devotional service to the Lord.

"One who liberally disseminates this knowledge among My devotees is the bestower of the Absolute Truth, and to him I give My very own self. He who loudly recites this supreme knowledge, which is most lucid and purifying, becomes purified day by day, for he reveals Me to others with the lamp of transcendental knowledge. Furthermore, anyone who regularly listens to this knowledge with faith and attention, all the while engaging in My pure devotional service, will never become bound by the reactions of material work.[83] However, you should not share this knowledge with anyone who is hypocritical, atheistic or dishonest, or with anyone who will not listen faithfully, who is not a devotee, or who is simply not humble. This knowledge should be taught to those who are free from these bad qualities, who are dedicated to the welfare of the spiritual, and who are saintly and pure. And if any common people are found to have devotion for the Supreme Lord, they can also be accepted as being qualified to listen. When an inquisitive person begins to understand this knowledge, he or she has nothing further to know. After all, one who has drunk the most palatable nectar cannot remain thirsty." [84]

CHAPTER ELEVEN

Those Who Will Remain in Material Bondage

Another thing that is explained is the characteristic of those who are most likely to remain in this material world. Many people often hold high opinions that they are on the path that will surely deliver them to heaven, the promised land, or even to the spiritual world, free from any further cycles of birth and death. However, for those of us who have a genuine spiritual interest, the best thing to do is to find out exactly what it is that would most likely hold us in the material realm. So we find numerous quotes wherein Lord Krishna explains those qualities, however pious or meritorious we may think them to be, that will still keep us bound up in material existence.

One point of consideration is that even when studying the *Vedas*, there are many areas of the Vedic knowledge which do not prescribe the means for spiritual liberation. Instead, they instruct us in the means to advance in material facility. Of course, for the Vedic texts to be complete, they must also contain the means for acquiring material provisions. But Krishna explains how men of small knowledge are very much attached to these flowery words of the *Vedas*. They recommend various means for elevation to heavenly planets, or future good births, power, wealth, blessings from the demigods, or other types of development. Being desirous of this sort of sense gratification and life of opulence, some may say there is nothing more to life than this. In the minds of such people, they are too attached to sense enjoyment and material opulence, and are bewildered by such things so that the determination to engage in devotional service to the Supreme Being does not take place. The early *Vedas* mainly deal with the subjects that are influenced by the three modes of material nature. One must rise above these modes and be transcendental to them, and be established in the Self.[1]

So herein Lord Krishna begins to explain that dealing with the means of working within the modes of nature will not bring about the desired result of being free of them. We must still become established in the Self if we are to actually make any tangible spiritual advancement. We must also be established in genuine spiritual knowledge and vision if we are to expect to become liberated from any more material existence. Merely acting in ways for furthering our facility or development in this world is not enough.

Lord Krishna continues to explain that those who may follow the Vedic path but whose minds are distorted by material desires surrender unto demigods and follow the particular rules and regulations of worship according to their own natures. Men of small intelligence worship the demigods for the temporary fruits and limited blessings they can get. Those who worship the demigods go to the planets of the demigods, but My devotees ultimately reach My supreme planet.[2]

"Those who worship the demigods will take birth among the demigods; those who worship ghosts and spirits will take birth among such beings; those who worship the ancestors go to the ancestors; and those who worship Me will live with Me."[3]

The process of material entanglement is also described by Lord Krishna. When a person contemplates the objects of the senses [those things enjoyed through seeing, hearing, tasting, smelling, and touching], he or she develops attachment for them, and from such attachment lust develops, and from lust anger arises. From anger, which manifests when one does not get what he wants, delusion arises, and from delusion comes bewilderment of memory. When memory is bewildered, then one also loses intelligence, and when intelligence is lost, one falls down again into the material pool of birth and death.[4]

"It is lust only which is born of contact with the material modes of passion and later transformed into wrath, which is the all-devouring, sinful enemy of this world. As fire is covered by smoke, as a mirror is covered by dust, or as the embryo is covered by the womb, similarly, the living entity is covered by different degrees of this lust. Thus a man's pure consciousness is covered by his eternal enemy in the form of lust, which is never satisfied and which burns like fire. The senses, the mind, and the intelligence are sitting places of this lust, which veils the real knowledge of the living entity and bewilders him." [5]

This is how the living being remains attached and bound within the material conception of life. A person's real spiritual identity is covered by the body and remains hidden because of a lack of spiritual knowledge and awareness. Thus, the situation is like a fire which cannot be seen because it is covered by so much smoke.

While discussing this topic with Uddhava, Lord Krishna relates that anyone whose intelligence remains attached to material things has no spiritual knowledge. And anyone who denies the higher authorities such as the demigods, or the existence of the Self and the Supreme Lord, thus ignoring or ruining all religious principles, and is still infected with the six means of contamination or illusion, which consists of lust, anger, greed, false pride, intoxication and agitation, is lost in both this life and the next.[6] Their consciousness does not allow them to be free of the very things that create all of their problems. Thus, they are stuck in material existence like a prisoner who is willingly bound up by the golden chains of illusion.

In the Lord's incarnation as Kapila, He gives additional instructions as to how a person becomes entangled in the continuation of material existence. This can be found in the *Srimad-Bhagavatam* (Third Canto, Chapters 30-32). But in summary, He says that a misguided materialist does not recognize the influence of the time factor. He does not know that his very body is impermanent and that all of his attractions, such as house, home, wife and children, and all his wealth are all temporary. Out of ignorance he thinks he is making a permanent arrangement.[7] He engages in activities that are mostly for counteracting the miseries and anxieties in life. If he can be successful in counteracting such difficulties, he thinks he is happy.[8] For the sake of the body, which is actually a source of constant trouble, and which he has attained because of ties of ignorance and karmic reactions, he engages in various activities that keep him bound in the cycle of birth and death. Thus, if the living being associates with the path of unrighteousness and those who merely engage in the pursuit of satisfying the tongue and sex organs, such a person again enters the regions of darkness.[9] A person whose life is centered around household life may perform religious rituals or other activities in order to fulfill his desires for economic development to attain pleasure for the senses. However, such persons are always bereft of devotional service to the Lord because of such material attachment. Even if such persons can be elevated to the higher planets, they must again return to this planet [when their accumulated good karma has been used up]. At the time of the universal annihilation all the planets of the materialistic persons are vanquished.[10] Such materialists are averse to hearing the nectar of the transcendental pastimes of the Lord and instead indulge in hearing about the abominable activities of other materialists. Thus, they are like stool-eating hogs.[11]

Krishna goes on to explain that the soul who is steadily devoted to Him attains unadulterated peace because he offers the result of all activities to Him; whereas a person who is not in union with the Divine, who is greedy for the fruits of his labor, becomes entangled.[12] And those miscreants who are grossly foolish, lowest among men, whose knowledge is stolen by illusion and are atheistic and demonic, do not surrender to Krishna.[13]

"Those who are thus bewildered are attracted by demonic and atheistic views. In that bewildered condition, their hopes for liberation, their fruitive activities, and their culture of knowledge are all defeated.[14] Arrogance, pride, anger, conceit, harshness, and ignorance--these qualities belong to those of demonic nature."[15]

Sri Krishna continues to relate that those who are intensely materially attached and who exhibit the qualities of the demonic do not know what is to be done or not, nor will you find genuine cleanliness, proper behavior or truth in them. They often view the world as if it is all false, with no value, and without a God in control. The only purpose for the world is sex and enjoyment, and it has no cause other than lust. Following such conclusions they are lost, with no intelligence, and thus they engage in works with no benefit for anyone, and which bring about the destruction of the world. In this way, being illusioned and motivated by insatiable lust, pride and false prestige, they always engage in unclean work, attracted by the temporary material nature. They believe that gratifying their lust at whatever expense is the prime purpose of society. Thus, they are in constant anxiety and intrigue. Being bound to their innumerable desires, lust, and anger, they secure money by illegal means for their temporary pleasure. The demonic are always thinking of gaining more for themselves, at whatever expense it may cost to others. Even if it means they must kill others to get rid of their enemies. Thus perplexed by numerous anxieties, and befooled by a network of illusions, one becomes too strongly attached to sense enjoyment and falls down into hell. Deluded by wealth and false prestige, always self-complacent and impudent, they may perform religious activities but in name only without any rules or regulations. Bewildered by such things as strength, pride, lust and anger, the demoniac become envious and blasphemous even toward the real religion of the Supreme Lord, who is situated in their own bodies. Thus, those who are the lowest of men are cast by Sri Krishna into the ocean of material existence, and into various low and demonic species of life. Entering such repeated births in the demonic species, such living beings [who persist in this materialistic consciousness] can never approach the Supreme

Lord, and gradually sink down to the most abominable type of existence.[16]

Lord Krishna said that those who do not follow the prescribed methods for attaining Him, which include analytical philosophy (jnana-yoga), the execution of prescribed duties (karma-yoga), or direct devotional service to Him (bhakti-yoga), but instead engage in the temporary satisfaction of the senses, being motivated by material desires, will certainly continue in the cycle of birth and death in material existence.[17] By accepting material objects as enticing, one grows attached to them. This attachment leads to lust, which then gives way to quarrel amongst men [who desire the same objects]. This makes way for anger, through which brings dark ignorance [of the true values of life]. This infects a person's consciousness. Such a person is considered to have lost the true perspective and purpose of life, and becomes dull, like someone who is already dead. Even though engaged in all kinds of activities, being absorbed only in sense pleasure, one lives uselessly in ignorance, like a tree, and breathing merely like a bellows.[18] Because one becomes absorbed in attaining sensual happiness, long life, bodily strength, sexual prowess, and friends and family, one misses their actual purpose in life.[19] Bewildered by such illusory goals, they cannot understand or perceive their real identity.[20] Because of this identification with the body, they are blinded by ill-intelligence. Because they think in terms of "this is me" and "that is mine", they wander in perpetual darkness.[21]

Lord Krishna also relates to Uddhava the *Ailo-gita* (in *Srimad-Bhagavatam* 11.26.4-35), otherwise known as the song of King Aila. Herein, King Aila laments his foolishness after realizing how much he had been mislead by his engagement in material activities, all of which were centered around his attraction to a heavenly woman. This is most enlightening. After this story, He further explains that in this way, as long as the embodied spiritual being remains attracted to the body and the satisfaction of the mind and senses, his material existence will continue, though it is ultimately meaningless. Just as in a dream, the conditioned soul encounters all sorts of problems, though his real identity is transcendental to material existence. Such feelings as sadness, material happiness, fear, anger, greed, confusion, and desire, and even the appearance of birth and death, are all experienced by the false ego and not the pure soul who is beyond it all. It is similar to the way one awakens from a dream and is no longer confused by what he had been experiencing in the nightmare. Although the false ego and bodily conception is not real, it can be perceived in the workings of the mind, speech, and functions of the body. However, this ignorance and false identification can be cut asunder with the sword of spiritual knowledge, sharpened with the worship of a genuine spiritual teacher, allowing one to live in this world free from such material misidentification and attachment.[22]

Therefore, as Lord Krishna explains, someone who is intelligent should reject all bad association and begin to take the company of saintly devotees who provide words of wisdom that cut through the excessive material attachment within one's mind.[23] My devotees engage in hearing and chanting about Me, and those who partake in such become purified of all sins. Whoever hears, recites and accepts in their heart topics about Me earns dedicated devotional service to Me. What more is there left to accomplish for a perfect devotee after achieving devotional service to Me, the Supreme Absolute Truth, who am the embodiment of all ecstatic experience? [24]

Lord Krishna concludes this topic with this peace of advice, "A man who does not follow this prescribed Vedic system certainly leads a life of sin, for a person delighting only in the senses lives in vain.[25] And those who, out of envy, disregard these teachings and do not practice them regularly, are to be considered bereft of all knowledge, befooled, and doomed to ignorance and bondage.[26] He who discards scriptural injunctions and acts according to his own whims attains neither perfection, nor happiness, nor the supreme destination." [27]

CHAPTER TWELVE

Those Who are Eligible for Liberation

As presented in the previous chapter, from the instructions of Lord Krishna, we have information on the characteristics of those who are likely to remain bound in the cycles of repeated birth and death in this material realm for many lifetimes. Now let us see what Lord Krishna has to say regarding those who show the most potential for becoming free from this earthly existence.

He first begins to explain to Arjuna in *Bhagavad-gita* (2.15) the basic qualities of those who may indeed be ready for liberation. He relates that those who are not swayed by happiness or distress, but are steady in both, are certainly eligible for liberation. How we become equipoised in such a way is further revealed when He says that the *Vedas* primarily deal with the subject of the modes of material nature. One must rise above these modes and be free from all dualities [of good or bad, hot or cold, happiness or sadness] and from the anxieties for gain and safety by being established in the [true identity of the] Self.[1]

Yet, Arjuna was still not sure what this meant. So he asked Sri Krishna what are the symptoms of one whose consciousness is absorbed in such Transcendence. Lord Krishna answered by explaining that when a man gives up all varieties of desire for sense pleasure, which itself arises from mental concoction, and instead finds pleasure in the Self alone [the spiritual dimension], then he is said to be in pure transcendental consciousness. Such a person will be observed as being free from the disturbance of the threefold miseries [of the body, from natural occurrences, or from other beings] and is not elated when there is happiness. Furthermore, he who is free from material attachments, fear and anger, does not rejoice when he encounters good nor laments when he obtains evil, is called a sage of steady mind, and is fixed in perfect knowledge. One who can withdraw his senses from attractions like a turtle withdraws his limbs within the shell, is understood as situated in knowledge. Even when the embodied soul is restricted from sense enjoyment though the taste for such remains, he can cease such engagements by experiencing a higher taste. The senses are so strong that they can easily and forcibly carry away the mind of a person of discrimination who is trying to control them. Yet, one who can restrain his senses and fix his consciousness on Me in a such a way is a man of steady intelligence.[2]

Krishna further describes how one who can control the senses by practicing the regulated principles of freedom can obtain the mercy of the Lord. With such a blessing, one can become free from all attachment and aversion. When one is situated in such a Divine consciousness, the miseries of material life no longer exist. He is oblivious to them. In such a happy state, one's intelligence becomes steady. However, one who is not in such transcendental consciousness cannot have a controlled mind nor steady intelligence or focus in life. And without that, there is no possibility of peace. And without peace, there is no question of genuine happiness. Such a person is similar to a boat on the water being pushed away by a strong wind. Even one of the senses upon which the mind focuses can create a distraction to carry away a man's intelligence. Therefore, one who can restrain his senses from their attractions can have steady intelligence [and mental equilibrium].[3]

In this way, a person who is not disturbed by the continuous flow of thoughts and desires within the mind can alone achieve peace, and not the man who strives to satisfy all of his desires. Such desires are like the constant flow of rivers into the ocean, which is always filled but still. A person who has given up all desires for gratifying the senses, and who lives free from desires, who also has no sense of ownership and is free from false ego--he alone can attain real peace. That is the way of the spiritual and godly life, after which a man is not bewildered. Being so situated at the time of death, one can enter the kingdom of God.[4]

Krishna goes on to give the process of becoming disentangled from material life. He says, those who are steadily devoted can attain unadulterated peace because they offer all their activities to Me. However, a person who is not united with the Divine, and who is greedy for the fruits of his labor, becomes entangled in material existence.[5] It is spiritual knowledge by which nescience is destroyed and which paves the way for enlightenment. Then one's knowledge will reveal everything, just as the sun reveals everything in the daytime. In this way, when one's intelligence, mind, faith, and refuge are all fixed in the Supreme, then through knowledge one's misgivings and doubts become completely cleansed, and such a person proceeds straight on the path to liberation.[6]

Such an enlightened sage, by virtue of his spiritual knowledge, observes such beings as the learned and gentle brahmana, a cow, an elephant, a dog, and even the dog-eater, with equal vision. Those whose minds are established in such equanimity have already transcended the causes of birth and death. Having a flawless consciousness like Brahman, they are already situated in Brahman [the spiritual dimension]. A person who is not overly swayed by achieving something pleasant or unpleasant, who is unbewildered, and who knows the spiritual science of God, is understood to be already situated in Transcendence. Such a person is liberated, and not attracted to the various material pleasures or external sense objects but is always in trance, enjoying the spiritual pleasure within. This is how the self-realized person experiences unlimited happiness, for he concentrates on the Supreme.[7]

If a person can tolerate the urges of the material senses and curb the force of desire and anger before one gives up the present body, he is a yogi and happy in this world. It is for those whose happiness is within, who is illumined within and active within, they are the perfect mystics, liberated in the Supreme and able to attain the Supreme. Those who are beyond duality and doubt, always busy working for the welfare of all sentient beings, and who is free from sins, they achieve liberation in the Supreme. In this way, those who are free from anger and material desires, self-realized, disciplined, and endeavoring for spiritual perfection, they are assured of liberation in the Supreme in the very near future.[8]

Therefore, "One who is free from illusion, false prestige, and false association, who understands the eternal, who is done with material lust and is freed from the duality of happiness and distress, and who knows how to surrender unto the Supreme Person, attains to that eternal kingdom." [9]

The characteristics of those headed toward liberation are further elaborated by Lord Krishna when He says, "Fearlessness, purification of one's existence, cultivation of spiritual knowledge, charity, self-control, performance of sacrifice, study of the Vedic literature, austerity and simplicity; nonviolence, truthfulness, freedom from anger; renunciation, tranquility, aversion to fault-finding, compassion and freedom from covetousness; gentleness, modesty and steady determination; vigor, forgiveness, fortitude, cleanliness, freedom from envy and the passions for honor--these transcendental qualities belong to godly men endowed with divine nature." [10]

Lord Kapila also describes how those who are intelligent and with a purified consciousness are completely satisfied in spiritual activities. They do not act for satisfying the senses since they are freed from the modes of material nature. When a person engages in his occupational duties of service to the Lord, detached and without a sense of ownership or false ego [bodily consciousness], a person regains his spiritual, constitutional position by dint of complete purification of consciousness, and thus he can easily enter into the kingdom of God. Through this path of illumination, such liberated persons can approach the Supreme Personality.[11]

Lord Vishnu also explained to King Prithu that when a person's heart is cleansed of all material contamination, such a devotee's mind becomes clear and peaceful. At that time he sees things clearly and is situated with Me as *sac-chit-ananda-vigraha*, the eternal form of complete knowledge and bliss. Anyone who clearly knows that the material body is made of the gross elements and the senses for perception and activity, which is supervised by the soul within, is eligible for liberation from material existence.[12]

This is similarly confirmed when Lord Krishna explains to Uddhava that one who has given up the false identification with the products of the modes of nature by spiritual knowledge is freed from the materially conditioned life. Although involved with material items, he avoids entanglement with them because he sees such objects as illusory or temporary.[13] Furthermore, until one has completely eliminated from the mind all contamination of material passion by practicing devotional service to Me, one must carefully avoid the association of the material modes, which are but products of My illusory energy.[14] A wise man whose consciousness is firmly focused on his spiritual identity as the soul within the body, no longer notices his own bodily functions. While standing, sitting, walking, eating, or evacuating, he knows the body is acting according to its own needs. Such a realized soul may sometimes perceive an impure activity or object, but accepts it as part of the illusory energy in the same way that man awakening from sleep views his fading dream.[15]

This is similar to the explanation wherein Lord Krishna further elaborates to Uddhava that an enlightened person sees himself living within yet beyond the body. He sees his body like that seen in a dream. He does not consider himself the performer of bodily activities, but he, as the soul, is above such activities and it is only the senses that come in contact with the objects, all of which are born from the same material energy. But a foolish person sees himself as the body and the one who is motivated to perform various activities, and is thus entangled in such desires, and the results of his actions. But an enlightened person will engage the body in all kinds of functions, such as lying down, walking, sitting, bathing, touching, smelling, eating, etc., but is never entangled. His perception is that he merely is a witness to the functions of his body and does not become entangled or attached to the sensations and actions. Thus, as the sun pervades the atmosphere, it is still not at all affected. Or as the wind blows across all kinds of objects and carries many different aromas, it is never attached to what it carries. Similarly, a self-realized soul is never attached to the material body or the world around it. A person is considered liberated from the physical and subtle bodies when all the functions of the body are performed without any personal desires for its results or sensual benefit. This is how a person, although situated in the body, is not entangled in material existence.[16]

Ultimately, Lord Krishna concludes by instructing Uddhava to control the speaking, regulate the senses, and through the process of purified intelligence bring the mind under control. Thus, you will not fall back into material existence. One who does not do this, though trying to make spiritual progress, will find that his spiritual vows, charity, rituals, or austerities will flow away from him like water out of an unbaked clay pot. Therefore, being surrendered to Me, one should control the mind and senses and through loving devotional intelligence a person can completely fulfill the mission of life.[17]

CHAPTER THIRTEEN

Real Liberation Means Returning to Lord Krishna

If we correctly understand the summary teachings of Lord Krishna, then we should also conclude that real liberation, the real process of freeing ourselves from any further entanglement in material life and the cycle of repeated birth and death, means returning to the spiritual abode of Lord Krishna, which He express multiple time in the *Bhagavad-gita* and other places. That is the ultimate goal, no matter what spiritual process we might accept. And if that is the principal destination, then any spiritual process that leaves that out, or avoids it, must be considered incomplete.

Returning to the supreme abode means that we can fully engage in spiritual activities based on loving devotion to God. Thus, the process of bhakti-yoga gives us the means and the end result at the same time. For in the spiritual abode there are innumerable varieties of activities and recreation, and it is all fun. Nothing to worry about. But the point of all such engagements is that they are centered around pleasing the Lord.

We may all want the facility of the kingdom of God, but how can we have it without God? So we have to center our lives on this Supreme Lover, the Supreme Personality, the ultimate object of all relations, the Absolute Truth. Then we can be happy in every way, and attain the freedom for which we are always looking, and reach the ultimate abode of eternity and divine wisdom and bliss.

How we do this in our busy everyday lives is explained by Sri Krishna Himself when He instructs Arjuna in the *Bhagavad-gita*: "You should always think of Me in the form of Krishna and at the same time carry out your prescribed duty of fighting. With your activities dedicated to Me and your mind and intelligence fixed on Me, you will attain Me without doubt. He who meditates on the Supreme Personality of Godhead, his mind constantly engaged in remembering Me, undeviated from the path, he is sure to reach Me... For one who remembers Me without deviation, O son of Pritha [Arjuna], I am easy to obtain because of his constant engagement in devotional service."[1]

How we should remember or meditate on the Supreme Person is also quite easy, as further explained: "One should meditate upon the Supreme Person as the one who knows everything, as He who is the oldest, who is the controller, who is smaller than the smallest, who is the maintainer of everything, who is beyond all material conception, who is inconceivable, and who is always a person. He is luminous like the sun and, being transcendental, is beyond this material nature."[2]

There are many goals and levels of perfection that religionists, transcendentalists, yogis, and devotees can attain through their spiritual activities, but reaching the Supreme Lord in His personal form is the highest level of success and the ultimate attainment of any spiritual process.

Lord Krishna, in His form as Lord Kapiladeva, also instructed in this regard that when a person ends his service to the modes of material nature, which is the endeavor to find temporary happiness in the illusory energy, and by developing Krishna consciousness, along with knowledge of detachment, one can then engage in yoga. This is the means to keep the mind focused on devotional service unto the Supreme Lord, and then one can achieve His association in this very life, for He is the Supreme Personality, the Absolute Truth.[3]

As Lord Krishna further explains, once the living being is freed from the subtle materialistic conditioning within the mind, and from the modes of nature which is effected by material consciousness, the living being becomes completely satisfied by experiencing the Lord's transcendental form. At that time the living being no longer desires nor seeks enjoyment in the material energy, nor does he even think of or remember such temporary and shallow enjoyments within himself.[4]

This is further verified by Lord Krishna like so: "After attaining Me, the great souls, who are yogis in devotion, never return to this temporary world, which is full of miseries, because they have attained the highest perfection. From the highest planet in the material world down to the lowest, all are places of misery wherein repeated birth and death take place. But one who attains to My abode never takes birth again. There is another nature which is eternal and is transcendental to this manifested and unmanifested matter. It is supreme and is never annihilated. When all in this world is annihilated, that part remains as it is. That supreme abode is called unmanifested and infallible, and it is the supreme destination. When one goes there, he never comes back. That is My supreme abode.[5] That abode of Mine is not illumined by the sun or moon, nor by electricity. One who reaches it never returns to this material world."[6]

Since Lord Krishna is described in various Vedic texts as the Absolute Truth, it is devotion to Him that is the safest way for developing spiritual progress and attaining the path to ultimate and sure liberation from material existence. As Lord Krishna explains to Uddhava, He is the ultimate shelter and way of life for the saintly and liberated persons. Therefore, if one does not engage in the process of loving devotion to Him, which is taught and made available through His pure devotees, then one actually possesses no sure or effective means for escaping from material existence.[7]

As Sri Krishna continues to explain, it is from the association of Krishna's devotees that throughout the many ages of time that living entities, such as the Daityas, Rakshasas, Gandharvas, Apsaras, Nagas, Siddhas, Caranas, Guhyakas, and many different classes of human beings, even birds and beasts, have been able to achieve Lord Krishna's supreme abode. Even such beings as Vritrasura, Prahlada, Bali, Banasura, Maya, Vibhishana, Sugriva, Hanuman, Jambavan, Jatayu, Kubja, the *gopis* of Vrindavana, and others also achieved Lord Krishna's abode through association with the Lord's devotees. None of these people underwent serious studies of the Vedic literature, nor did they worship great saints or undergo severe austerities or vows. Simply by the association with Krishna and His devotees they achieved Him.[8]

Sri Krishna goes on to relate that in Vrindavana even the animals, cows, and living beings with stunted consciousness like the bushes and thickets, or even snakes like Kaliya, all achieved the perfection of life simply by developing unalloyed love for Krishna, and thus achieved Him very easily.[9]

Just as gold gives up all impurities when smelted with fire, and thus returns to its brilliant state, similarly when absorbed in devotional love, bhakti-yoga, the soul is relieved of contamination from all previous fruitive activities and can then return to its original constitutional position of serving the Lord in the spiritual realm.[10]

Lord Krishna also relates that one who has become realized sees everything as being connected with Him, for his knowledge of Krishna destroys the illusory perception of seeing anything separate from the Lord (who is the ultimate cause and source of all manifestations). However, since the material body and mind were conditioned to think and see such illusory separations, it may sometimes appear to recur. Nonetheless, at the time of death the self-realized person will achieve opulences equal to His.[11]

To conclude this topic, Lord Krishna summarizes to Uddhava in this way: "My dear Uddhava, I am the Supreme Lord of all worlds, and I create and destroy this universe, being its ultimate cause. I am thus the Absolute Truth, and one who worships Me with unfailing devotional service comes to Me. Thus, one who has purified his existence by execution of his prescribed duties, who fully understands My supreme position and who is endowed with scriptural and realized knowledge, very soon achieves Me..."[12] Persons who seriously follow these methods of achieving Me, which I have personally taught, attain freedom from illusion, and upon reaching My personal abode they perfectly understand the Absolute Truth."[13]

These methods that have been taught are more fully explained in other books on devotional service, bhakti-yoga, such as my book called *The Bhakti-yoga Handbook: A Guide for Beginning the Essentials of Devotional Yoga*.

CHAPTER FOURTEEN

Krishna--The Ever-Loving God

When it comes to mankind's conception of God, it seems that each religion and culture describe the character of God differently. In some we find God described as an angry and jealous God. Or we find the God of the Old Testament of the Bible with lots of rules but little mercy. Or in other religions we read about a God who is heartless to any nonbelievers, even if they merely lack understanding. In other cultures, God recommends killing all that do not wish to surrender to the local faith. Others may describe that there is a just and loving God watching over you. So what are we to believe?

Naturally God will reveal Himself differently to those who are more devoted. He will reciprocate to the degree in which we love Him. But we are all parts and parcels of Him, so He is our Supreme Father who should have unconditional love for His children, even if we do go astray or get confused. So it makes no sense how a God who is supposed to be all loving and merciful can send His children to an eternal hell or some damnation without the means of retribution or correcting themselves. Of course, we often find mankind projecting his own fears and tendencies into the character of God, without true understanding. However, we find a very different and more loving God in the Vedic tradition in the form of Lord Krishna. So let us find out the nature of this more loving form of the Supreme Being.

Lord Krishna describes His ever-loving nature towards one and all, but especially for those who engage in loving Him. This is not favoritism but a natural reciprocation with those who are filled with loving feelings for Him. Lord Krishna explains Himself this way:

"I envy no one, nor am I partial to anyone. I am equal to all. But whoever renders service unto Me in devotion is a friend, is in Me, and I am also a friend to him. Even if one commits the most abominable actions, if he is engaged in devotional service, he is considered saintly because he is properly situated. He quickly becomes righteous and attains lasting peace. O son of Kunti [Arjuna], declare it boldly that My devotee never perishes. Those who take shelter in Me, even though they be of lower birth, or women, or simple merchants, or ordinary workers, all can approach the supreme destination." [1]

This is further explained by Narada Muni in his talks with Maharaja Yudhisthira. He says that Lord Vishnu, the Supreme Personality, is the supreme controller and Supersoul within all living beings. Because He has no material body, he has no false conception of who He is, or of "I" and "mine." So it is not accurate to think that He feels pain when blasphemed or happy if offered prayers. This is impossible for Him. He has no enemy and no friend in that respect. When He chastises the demons or the envious it is for their own good. When He accepts the prayers of the devotees, it is also for their own good. He is affected neither by prayers or blasphemy. Therefore, by enmity or by devotional service, by fear or affection, or even lusty desires, if the materially conditioned soul can concentrate his mind on the Lord by any method, the result is the same for one's benefit. The Lord, because of His blissful position, is never affected by enmity or friendship.[2]

So if the conditioned souls somehow or other think of Krishna, who is *sac-chit-ananda-vigraha* [the form of eternal knowledge and bliss], they will become free from their sins. Whether thinking of Him as their worshipable Lord or enemy, because of constantly thinking of Him they will regain their spiritual bodies.[3]

In this way, it does not matter how we think or focus our attention on Krishna, He is nonetheless all powerful and purifying. His form alone and any thoughts of Him will uplift our spiritual awareness and purity.

When Akrura was praying to Lord Krishna, he also asked what learned person would approach anyone but Him for shelter, since He was the affectionate, grateful and truthful well-wisher of His devotees. To those who worship Krishna in sincere friendship, He rewards them with everything they desire, even His own self [which is the rarest of attainments].[4]

It is explained by Sri Havir to King Nimi that the Supreme Personality is so kind to the conditioned souls that if they call upon Him by chanting His holy names, even unintentionally or unwillingly, the Lord is willing to destroy innumerable sinful reactions in their hearts. Therefore, when a devotee who has directly taken shelter of the lotus feet of the Lord chants the holy name of Krishna with genuine love, the Supreme Lord will never give up the heart of such a devotee. One who has captured the Supreme Lord within his heart is most exalted, and called a *bhagavata-pradhana* devotee.[5]

Sudama, the garland maker, also prayed to Lords Krishna and Balarama when They went to see him at his house because They are the well-wishing friends and Supreme Soul of the whole universe. They regard everyone with an unbiased vision. Although They reciprocate Their devotees' love and worship, They always remain equally disposed toward all living beings.[6]

As Lord Krishna says in this regard, "To those who are constantly devoted and worship Me with love, I give the understanding by which they can come to Me. Out of compassion for them, I, dwelling in their hearts, destroy with the shining lamp of knowledge the darkness born of ignorance."[7]

Lord Krishna loves His devotees so much that He doesn't descend into this world without them. They all appear in the world to make preparations whenever He is ready to descend. And they all leave this world whenever the Lord again wraps up His pastimes. He gives Himself to them in such a way that no one feels neglected, and they actually feel that they are getting extra and exclusive attention from the Lord.

In His instructions to Durvasa Muni, the Lord explains how much He loves His devotees. He says that He is completely under the control of His devotees. He is not independent of their love. Because His devotees have no material desires, He sits within the core of their hearts. But not only His devotees, but those who are devotees of His devotees are very dear to Him. Without the saintly persons, for whom He is the only destination, He has no desire to enjoy His own transcendental bliss or supreme opulences. Since these devotees give up so much for Him, such as homes, families, even riches and their own lives if need be, how can He give up such devotees at any time? So just as a chaste wife brings their gentle husbands under their control by service, such pure devotees also bring Him under control.

The Lord explains that His devotees are simply satisfied by engaging in service to Him. They are not even interested in liberation, though this is automatically achieved by their service. And they are certainly not interested in the perishable happiness of reaching the heavenly planets that exist within this universe. The pure devotees are always in the core of His heart, and He is always in the heart of His pure devotees. His devotees do not know anything else but Him, and He does not know anything else but them.[8]

When instructing the brahmana ladies who came to render service to Him, Lord Krishna said that those expert personalities who can see their own true interest in life, render unmotivated and uninterrupted devotional service to Him, because He is the most dear to the soul.[9]

In discerning Krishna's love for us in this life, it is said that if Krishna likes us, He will give us everything. But if Krishna loves us, He will take everything away from us. This does not necessarily mean that He leaves us with nothing. But what gets in the way of our devotional life and spiritual advancement may be taken away. As Krishna Himself explained to Indra, the proud King of Heaven, that a man who is blind with the intoxication of power and opulence cannot easily see Him with the rod of punishment in His hand. If He desires someone's real welfare, He will drag such a person down from his materially opulent position.[10] When a person is deprived of unnecessary material benefits, he will at first become morose, but then he will have little else to distract him from understanding his real position in life and the spiritual purpose behind it. This is extremely fortunate, otherwise a person with power and money is often preoccupied with the materialistic aspects of life all the way until the moment of death, at which time a person still loses everything. So it is better to be deprived of such preoccupation before then so that a person can make inquiries into the Self and thus have a chance to prepare oneself for leaving the body. That way one can take care of death before death takes care of him. The joyful process of spiritual advancement is the real benefit that Krishna wishes for everyone, and not the blindness that comes from the preoccupation of a materialistic lifestyle. As Lord Krishna Himself says, "the wealthy hardly ever worship Me."[11]

Krishna continues to explain this aspect of His display of love in His instructions to the *gopis*, the cowherd girls of Vrindavana. He explains that the reason He does not always immediately reciprocate the affection or worship of living beings is that He wants to intensify their loving devotion. Then they become like a poor man who had gained some wealth but then loses it, and who then becomes so anxious about it that he can think of nothing else. This does not mean that Lord Krishna stops loving us, and we should certainly not harbor any bad feelings toward Him.[12] We need to understand that in the broader picture of things, He never stops loving and caring for us, but He understands what is best for us and what we need to learn through the experiences that are sent our way. Our progress toward higher understanding is all that we take with us into the next life, while everything else must be given up or forcibly taken away at the time of death. For most people it is hard to understand this, which is why we sometimes must learn it by force of nature, or the deliberate arrangement of Sri Krishna.

Lord Krishna further explains this point wherein He says that if He especially favors someone, He gradually deprives that person of his wealth, at least if it is getting in the way. Then someone who was wealthy but becomes poverty-stricken will be abandoned by his relatives and friends. So he suffers one distress after another. When he becomes frustrated in his endeavors to make money and instead befriends the Lord's devotees, then the Lord bestows His special mercy on him. Such a person then can become sober and fully realize the Absolute as the highest truth. Realizing the Supreme Truth as the basis of his own existence, he is freed from the cycle of birth and death. However, Krishna admits that because He is difficult to worship, people often avoid worshiping Him and instead worship the other demigods who are more easily satisfied. Then when such people receive rich opulences from these deities, they become arrogant and intoxicated with pride, and then even neglect their own duties. They may even offend those who gave them their blessings.[13]

One point to remember is that Lord Krishna's teachings are for anyone. His love and affection showers down like the sunshine from the sun planet. Yet, if someone persists in living in a cave, or hides in their closet, the sunshine cannot reach that person. Similarly, if someone insists on living in ignorance of the Lord, or without devotion to Him, how can such a person feel the Lord's love?

The Lord showed everyone the path of spiritual progress, which is the way to follow Dharma, the balanced path to righteousness and personal well-being and development. But because people do not understand the depth of His teachings and pastimes, many see only His miracles, while others see His various activities with an eye of criticism. Thus, neither side will reach the real essence. It is for this reason that they have missed the deeper meaning and the value of what the Supreme Being has given us. It is also this sort of misunderstanding, distancing, and even disconnection from the essence of the spiritual path and Vedic culture that has brought such a rapid moral deterioration to India's society. Many people now complain of how rampant is the corruption in society, especially politics and business. But if the

Chapter Fourteen

The Deities of Radha-Govindaji, the devotional center of Jaipur

people could understand the genuine depth of Vedic culture and practice it as it should be, this would help maintain the glorious ways of India's culture. Instead, it has been watered down and polluted with so many other ideas that do not fit well with Bharat anyway, that now India is losing the very culture that at one time made it the center of knowledge, wisdom, and numerous resources.

As far as Lord Krishna is concerned, His every action was rooted in Dharma and an ordinary human mind cannot grasp the depth of all His deeds. For example, Lord Krishna never wanted the war of Kurukshetra, as described in the *Mahabharata*. He had personally gone to the Kauravas to try and negotiate peace, but they would not hear of it. They unfairly persecuted the Pandavas, and it became obvious that the only way to bring justice was through war. There was no other way. If Krishna would have merely tolerated the injustice that had been going on, it would have only encouraged others to do greater violence and harm. So the Lord always acted in ways to suite the particular situations. His main goal was to restore Dharma to society.

If Duryodhana of the Kauravas had offered even one house to the Pandavas, who were warrior kings and used to ruling people, Krishna would have pacified the Pandavas. But no, Duryodhana said he would not even give enough land into which you could drive a pin. So Krishna acted in a way to rid the world of these nefarious rulers so everyone could again live in joy, peace, and social and spiritual progress in Vedic Dharma.

War is acceptable only if there is no other way to uphold Dharma. After having been given ample opportunities, if the enemy refuses to follow the ways of Dharma, then there may be a need to take up arms. To stand by and do nothing but watch evil unfold or grow is an even greater evil. That is why Lord Krishna urged Arjuna to fight, as we read in the *Bhagavad-gita*.

Lord Krishna never exhibited special attachment toward one person over another. When Duryodhana of the Kauravas wanted Krishna's army to fight for him, Krishna gave it to him. And when Arjuna wanted only Krishna on his side, Krishna accepted but told Arjuna He would not take up arms during the battle. He would only act as Arjuna's charioteer. But that was enough for Arjuna.

The same thing goes for the reason why Lord Krishna killed Kamsa, the demon king, even though Kamsa was Krishna's own uncle. Kamsa used everyone for his own agenda and terrorized the area of Vrindavana. He could not stand the thought of the path of righteousness or Dharma. He made so many arrangements in his attempts to kill Krishna until finally Krishna killed him. But, ultimately, only the body was destroyed while Kamsa's soul not only lived on but was purified by Krishna's touch and attained immortality. So this is also Krishna's ultimate level of mercy and care. If Krishna gave His mercy even to the demoniac like Kamsa, then we can understand how much more He will give His love and care to His devotees.

More about the reciprocation between the Lord and His devotees is explained in my book called *Krishna Deities and Their Miracles*.

CHAPTER FIFTEEN

About Other Forms of Religion and Activities

Additional instructions are given by Lord Krishna regarding the type of religious persuasion that a person may have. It is explained that there are many levels of faith that someone may follow, just as there are different ways to get to the top floor of a multi-storey building. You can take the longer and more difficult route of climbing the stairway. Or you can press the button to ride up in the elevator. In the same manner, if a person has come in contact with a higher level of understanding and then acts on that, the individual will reach a superior grade of realization. However, if someone continues to hold an allegiance to a religious path that still perpetuates the material or bodily identity, or that a person belongs to a certain ethnic group or race rather than giving the knowledge of how to rise above such a perception, then that path will take the person to various destinations that remain within material existence. Such a religion is in the lower modes and will give little means for genuine spiritual progress, and is not the real goal of actual spiritual understanding.

This is described in a summarizing fashion by Lord Krishna in the *Srimad-Bhagavatam* (11.25.27), that faith directed toward spiritual life is in the mode of goodness, while faith aimed at fruitive results for mental or bodily development is in the mode of passion. Faith based on irreligious acts is founded in the mode of ignorance. However, faith in Lord Krishna's devotional service is purely transcendental.

This is more fully explained by Lord Krishna in the *Bhagavad-gita* (17.3-6, 11-22). Therein He explains that according to a person's position as influenced under the various modes of nature, one evolves a certain kind of faith or religious inclination. For example, men in the mode of goodness (*sattva-guna*) may worship the demigods; those in the mode of passion (*raja-guna*) worship the demons or follow other materialists; and those in the mode of ignorance (*tama-guna*) worship ghosts and spirits. Those who undergo intense austerities and penances that are not recommended in the scriptures, and who perform them out of pride, egotism, lust and attachment [for temporary enjoyments or positions of power], and who may even torture their bodily organs and the indwelling Supersoul, are known as demoniac. On the other hand, those sacrifices that are performed according to duty and scriptural rules, when no material reward is expected, is of the nature of goodness. Those that are performed for some temporary material gain, benefit, or award out of ostentatious pride, is known to be passionate in nature. Those that are performed in defiance of the scriptural injunctions, wherein there is no spiritual food (*prasada*) that is distributed to the guests, no hymns are chanted, and no remunerations made to the priests, and which are thus faithless, are in the mode of ignorance.

Lord Krishna further relates that one who undergoes voluntary austerities for spiritual merit is of the nature of goodness. These actions consist of worship of the Supreme Lord, the brahmanas or spiritual authorities, the spiritual master, as well as one's superiors like father and mother. Being clean, simple, celibate and nonviolent are also proper austerities of the body. Speaking truthfully and for the benefit of others, avoiding useless talk or offensive words, and reciting the Vedic literature is also austerity of speech. Penances and austerities that are done for show in order to gain respect, honor and reverence are of the mode of passion. Those that are performed foolishly that tortures oneself or to injure others is of the mode of ignorance.

Even among gifts, that which is given out of duty, with proper respect to time and place, to a worthy person, and without expectation of return, is of the mode of goodness. But charity performed with the expectation of some return, or with a desire for particular results, or unwillingly in a grudging mood, is charity in the mode of passion. And that which is given at an improper place and time, given to an unworthy person without respect or with contempt, is charity in the mode of ignorance.

This may all sound a little detailed or technical, but why we should be concerned with this is also explained by Sri Krishna: "Those who leave this world in the mode of goodness go to the heavenly planets, those who pass away in the mode of passion remain amongst the human beings, and those who die in the mode of ignorance must go to hell. But those who are free from the influence of all modes of nature come to Me." [1] Therefore, by understanding what modes of nature various types of actions or faith are situated in can help us determine the result of where they will take us.

A CLOSER LOOK AT THE EFFECTS OF THE MODES OF MATERIAL NATURE

Lord Krishna spends a fair amount of time explaining these modes, called *gunas*, in His conversations. So there is a need to understand them. Yet, we need to take a closer look at what they are and their effects on us if we are going to perceive where they may take us and the results of their association. By understanding this, we can discriminate between what is in the modes of goodness, passion and ignorance, and then adjust our situation and habits toward being situated in the most progressive mode of goodness.

Lord Krishna talks all about these modes to Uddhava in the *Bhagavatam* and begins to explain them in this way: The three modes of material nature, which are the modes of goodness, passion and ignorance, are in connection with the material intelligence and not the spirit soul. By cultivating the aspects of goodness, one can conquer the lower modes of passion and ignorance. Yet by the cultivation of transcendental goodness, which is purely spiritual, one may rise above even material goodness. When a person becomes situated in the mode of material goodness, then we can witness in the person's character the exhibition of religious principles and devotional service to God. By the association with those aspects which are natural to the mode of goodness, that mode will become stronger within the individual. Such religious principles, strengthened by goodness, destroy the influence of the lower modes. When the influence of passion and ignorance is destroyed in this way, their original cause, which is irreligion, will also quickly vanish.

According to the quality of the religious scriptures that one follows, then with whatever one associates, including such things as water, one's children, the type of people, the places, time, activities that one appreciates, his birth, thoughts and meditation, the prayers or mantras that one chants, even the types of purificatory rituals, will all be different due to the nature of whatever material mode is prominent. Great sages of Vedic understanding praise and recommend those items that are in the mode of goodness, criticize and reject those that are in the mode of ignorance, and are indifferent to those in the mode of passion. The point is that until one revives his or her actual perception of being the spirit soul and loses one's illusory identification with the material body and mind, which is actually caused by one's association with these modes of nature, one must enhance those items [and habits and thought patterns] in one's life that are in the mode of goodness. By increasing that, one will automatically understand and practice religious principles which then awaken transcendental knowledge and realizations. It is the competition and interaction of these modes of material nature that generates the different types of gross and subtle material bodies, or species of beings. Yet, if one uses his mind and body to develop one's spiritual knowledge, then such enlightenment can actually destroy the influence of the modes of nature [and the material attachments, ideas and concepts they create] that are the cause of one's own body. Thus, the body and mind become pacified by the progress in dissolving the cause of their birth.[2]

Lord Krishna explains that when one's consciousness is focused on such things as the material body, or house and home, and similar objects for gratifying the senses, one spends his life chasing after these material objects. When one's consciousness is motivated by the mode of passion in such a way, one becomes dedicated to acquiring such things, and thus irreligion, ignorance or delusion, along with attachment and wretchedness arise. Actual religious principles lead one to His devotional service. Real knowledge is the awareness that reveals His all-pervading presence. Genuine detachment is complete disinterest in the material objects for gratifying the senses, while opulence is considered to be the mystic perfections.[3] When one's consciousness is peaceful and strengthened by the mode of goodness, and thus fixed on Him, the Supreme Being, then one achieves these forms of actual religiosity, knowledge, detachment and opulence.[4] From whatever sinful or materialistic activity one can discontinue, one becomes freed from its bondage. This sort of renunciation is the system of religious life for human beings and drives away all suffering, illusion and fear.[5] One who accepts material sense objects as desirable will become attached to them. From this attachment lust arises and expands to create quarrel among men.[6] In this way, one's life becomes spoiled, and, as it spreads, whole societies can become ruined by the improper aim of life.

DIFFERENT QUALITIES IN THE MODES OF NATURE

We can recognize the different qualities that are situated in different modes of nature, and which then give the result of such association, by the description of Lord Krishna to Uddhava. He explains that such qualities as control of the mind and senses, tolerance, discrimination, sticking to one's prescribed duty, truthfulness, mercy, careful study of the past and future, contentment, generosity, renunciation of sense gratification, faith in the spiritual master, charity and simplicity, and humbleness are some of the qualities found in the mode of goodness.

Material desires, great endeavor, pride, praying for material advancement, discontentment even in gain, considering oneself better than others, desires for satisfying the senses, the rash eagerness to fight, a fondness for hearing oneself being praised, advertising one's own expertise, the tendency to ridicule others, and justifying one's actions by strength are qualities in the mode of passion.

Intolerant anger, stinginess, speaking without knowledge, violent hatred, living at the expense of others, hypocrisy, quarrel, lamentation, delusion, unhappiness, depression, laziness, and fear are the major qualities of the mode of ignorance.[7]

OBSERVING THE INTERACTIONS OF THE MODES OF MATERIAL NATURE

Lord Krishna explains that the combination of the material modes is present in the mentality of "I" and "mine". As soon as a person begins thinking of himself in terms of his bodily identity, the interaction of the modes of nature manifest. The ordinary transactions of the world, which are carried out through the agency of the mind, as well as the objects of perception, the senses and the vital airs in the body, are also based on the interaction of the modes of nature. When a person devotes himself to religious principles, or to a certain faith, or economic development and gratification of the senses obtained by his endeavors, these display the interaction of the modes of nature.[8]

In this way, you can recognize a person who exhibits the qualities of self-control, or who worships the Lord in loving devotion, to be predominantly in the mode of goodness. While a person recognized by his lust is in the mode of passion, and one who is angry is in the mode of ignorance.[9]

When the mode of goodness, which is luminous, pure and auspicious, predominates over the other modes of passion and ignorance, then such a person exhibits happiness, virtue, knowledge and good qualities. When the mode of passion dominates, then a person begins to develop attachment for things, and works hard to acquire prestige, power and fortune. Thus he experiences anxiety and struggle. When the mode of ignorance conquers over the other modes, one's consciousness becomes covered over with foolishness and dullness. Such a person falls into lamentation and illusion, sleeps too much and has false hopes, and is often violent toward others.[10]

When one's consciousness becomes clear, and the senses are detached from material objects of enjoyment, one can experience fearlessness within the material body and detachment or an equipoised nature of the mind. This is the predominance of the mode of goodness in which a person can realize God. However, the distortion of the intelligence because of over endeavor, the unsteady nature of a perplexed mind, the inability of the senses to be free from objects of attraction, a diseased condition of the working organs, these are the symptoms of the mode of passion. Then when one's higher awareness is no longer available, and there is a lack of concentration, and the mind exhibits ignorance and depression, this is the predominance of the mode of ignorance--darkness.[11]

It must be understood that different levels of consciousness exhibit the different modes of nature. Alert wakefulness comes from the mode of goodness, sleep with dreaming is in the mode of passion, while dreamless sleep is in the mode of ignorance. Yet that state which pervades and is above all levels of mental activity is transcendental. Furthermore, persons who are learned and dedicated to Vedic culture are elevated by the mode of goodness to increasingly higher positions in life. While those in the mode of ignorance are forced to fall into lower and lower births. And those in the mode of passion continue to transmigrate through the human species.[12]

TYPES OF KNOWLEDGE IN THE MODES

How we can recognize different types of knowledge in the modes of nature is also described by Lord Krishna. He says that absolute knowledge is in the mode of goodness. Knowledge based on the duality found in material nature, such as that which explains what is good and bad, desirable and undesirable, or the basic differences of opposites like hot and cold, is knowledge in the mode of passion. Foolish or materialistic knowledge which perpetuates one's illusion is that in the mode of ignorance. Knowledge which revolves around Lord Krishna is completely transcendental to all other forms of understanding.[13]

TYPES OF FOOD IN THE MODES

Food that is wholesome, pure and obtained without difficulty, meaning that it is fresh and in season, is in the mode of goodness. Food that gives immediate pleasure to the senses is in the mode of passion. And that which is unclean and causes distress or disease is in the mode of ignorance.[14]

The reason why we should understand these differences is because they each give different results. As Sri Krishna explains, food in the mode of goodness increases one's duration of life, purify the existence and give strength, health, happiness, and satisfaction. Such nourishing foods are often sweet, juicy, fattening, and palatable. Foods that are too bitter, too sour, salty, pungent, dry, and hot, are liked by people in the mode of passion. They cause pain, distress and disease. Food that is liked by people in the mode of ignorance is that which is cooked more than three hours before being eaten, or which is tasteless, stale, putrid, decomposed, and unclean.[15]

TYPES OF ACTIONS IN THE MODES

Actions that are performed with regard to duty, without attachment, without love or hate, and by one who has renounced fruitive results, is action in the mode of goodness. Action performed with great effort in hopes of gratifying one's desires, from a sense of false ego, is action in the mode of passion. Action performed without knowledge and in delusion, without consideration of future bondage or consequences, which inflicts injury and is impractical, is action in the mode of ignorance [darkness]. The worker who is free from material attachments and false ego, who is enthusiastic and resolute, and who is indifferent to success or failure, is in the mode of goodness. But one who is attached to the results of his labor, who passionately wants to enjoy them, who is greedy, envious and impure, and moved by happiness and distress, is in the mode of passion. And he who is engaged in activities against the scriptural injunctions, who is materialistic, obstinate, expert in cheating and insulting others, who is lazy, always morose and procrastinating, is in the mode of ignorance.[16]

Lord Krishna further clarifies this in His talk with Uddhava, wherein He says that work performed with personal desire for enjoying the results is in the mode of passion. Work impelled by violence and envy is in the mode of ignorance. But work performed as an offering to Me, without consideration of enjoying the fruits for oneself, is considered work in the mode of goodness.[17] A worker who is free of attachment is in the mode of goodness. A worker who is blinded by personal desire is in the mode of passion, and a worker who has completely forgotten what is right or wrong is in the mode of ignorance. But a worker who has taken shelter of Me is transcendental to all the modes of material nature.[18]

Chapter Fifteen

TYPES OF RESIDENCES IN THE MODES OF NATURE

Even types of residences can be viewed regarding how much they are in the progressive and uplifting or downward modes. Lord Krishna says that a residence in the forest is in the mode of goodness. Residence in the towns or cities is in the mode of passion, and residence in a gambling house, which often contains other things such as drug use and prostitution, is in the mode of ignorance. However, residence in a place where He resides is transcendental to the modes of nature [such a place is a temple, or a spiritual community where the temple is central parts of all activity].[19]

DETERMINATION IN THE MODES

That determination which is unbreakable, sustained with the steadfastness by yoga practice, and controls the mind, life and the activities of the senses, is in the mode of goodness. That determination which clings to the results of fruitive activities, economic development and satisfaction of the senses is of the nature of passion. That determination which does not go beyond dreaming, fearfulness, lamentation, moroseness, and illusion, is in the mode of darkness.[20]

HAPPINESS IN THE MODES

There are three kinds of happiness that the conditioned soul enjoys. That form of happiness which in the beginning may be just like poison but at the end is just like nectar, and which awakens one to self-realization is said to be in the mode of goodness. That happiness which is derived from contact of the senses with their objects of pleasure, and which appears like nectar at first but becomes like poison at the end [which is often the case when something is new and exciting and later becomes old, stale or boring], is said to be of the nature of passion. The kind of happiness which is blind to self-realization, which is delusion from beginning to end and which arises from sleep, laziness and illusion [which can include intoxication and the use of drugs] is said to be in the mode of ignorance.[21]

Lord Krishna clarifies this quite simply in His talk with Uddhava. He says that happiness derived from the soul is in the mode of goodness, happiness based on gratifying the senses is in the mode of passion, happiness based on delusion and degradation of oneself is in the mode of darkness. But happiness centered around Him is transcendental.[22]

THE CONCLUSION AND ULTIMATE PURPOSE OF THE VEDIC SYSTEM--HOW TO BECOME FREE FROM THE MODES OF MATERIAL NATURE

Through the examination of the modes of nature and how they operate we can understand that such things as the material substance, the place, result of the activity, time, knowledge, work, faith, state of consciousness, destination after death and species of life are all based on the three modes of material nature and their interaction with the living beings.[23]

So, ultimately, one must become free from the modes of material nature and all of their effects on us. Though the Vedic literature gives advice and instructions for people on any level of consciousness, still a person must reach that level of practice that frees one from all further material destinations. We need to understand the difference between scripture that induces people to follow its rules due to fear, intimidation or peer pressure, and those that awaken one's perception of his or her real spiritual identity and the natural love for the Supreme Being that is waiting to be revealed. Then the divine love itself is the natural motivator for one's participation in spiritual pursuits. In this way, Lord Krishna also explains:

"Those statements of scripture promising fruitive rewards do not prescribe the ultimate good for men, but are merely enticements for executing beneficial religious duties, like promises of candy spoken to induce a child to take beneficial medicine. Simply by material birth, human beings become attached within their minds to personal sense gratification, long duration of life, sense activities, bodily strength, sexual potency, and friends and family. Their minds are thus absorbed in that which defeats their actual self-interest. Those ignorant of their real self-interest are wandering on the path of material existence, gradually heading toward darkness. Why would the *Vedas* further encourage them in sense gratification if they, although foolish, submissively pay heed to Vedic injunctions? Persons with perverted intelligence do not understand this actual purpose of Vedic knowledge and instead propagate as the highest Vedic truth the flowery statements of the *Vedas* that promise material rewards. Those in actual knowledge of the *Vedas* never speak in that way."[24]

"My dear Uddhava, those who are sworn to sense gratification cannot understand the confidential conclusion of Vedic knowledge as explained by Me. Taking pleasure in violence, they cruelly slaughter innocent animals in sacrifice for their own sense gratification and thus worship demigods, forefathers and leaders among ghostly creatures. Such passion for violence, however, is never encouraged within the process of Vedic sacrifice. Just as a foolish businessman gives up his real wealth in useless business speculation, foolish persons give up all that is actually valuable in life and instead pursue promotion to material heaven, which although pleasing to hear about is actually unreal, like a dream. Such bewildered persons imagine within their hearts that they will achieve all material blessings."[25]

"Those established in material passion, goodness and ignorance worship the particular demigods and other deities, headed by Indra, who manifest the same modes of passion, goodness or ignorance. They fail, however, to properly worship Me.[26] I am the ritualistic sacrifice enjoined by the *Vedas*, and I am the worshipable Deity. It is I who am presented as various philosophical hypotheses, and it is I alone who am then refuted by philosophical analysis. The transcendental sound vibration thus establishes Me as the essential meaning of all Vedic knowledge."[27]

"Therefore, having achieved this human form of life, which allows one to develop full knowledge, those who are intelligent should free themselves from all contamination of the modes of nature and engage exclusively in loving service to Me. A wise person, free from all material association and unbewildered, should subdue his senses and worship Me. He should conquer the modes of passion and ignorance by engaging himself only with things in the mode of goodness. Then being fixed in devotional service, the sage should also conquer the material mode of goodness by indifference toward the modes. Thus pacified within his mind, the spirit soul, freed from all of the modes of nature, gives up the very cause of his conditioned life and attains Me. Freed from the subtle conditioning of the mind and from the modes of nature born of material consciousness, the living entity becomes completely satisfied by experiencing My transcendental form. He no longer searches for enjoyment in the external energy, nor does he contemplate or remember such enjoyment within himself."[28]

"What more remains to be accomplished for the perfect devotee after achieving devotional service unto Me, the Supreme Absolute Truth, whose qualities are innumerable and who am the embodiment of all ecstatic experience?"[29]

CHAPTER SIXTEEN

How to be a Spiritual Person in this Material World

There are so many more instructions and words of advice from Lord Krishna, found in such books as *Bhagavad-gita*, *Srimad-Bhagavatam*, *Mahabharata*, *Vishnu Purana*, and others. And we cannot possibly cover them all here. But I did want to include a few more points regarding what He says about how to conduct ourselves in various situations, many in which we find ourselves on a regular basis. After all, while living in this material world and trying to be spiritually progressive, it may seem like there are so many obstacles, difficulties or distractions with which we are forced to contend. How do we deal with them?

In this regard, Lord Krishna relates a story in *Srimad-Bhagavatam* (Canto Eleven, Chapter Seven and Eight) that contains some most relevant instructions for us to understand how to live in this world while still intent on making spiritual progress. So, while applying to the best of our ability the knowledge that has already been given in the previous chapters, we can also consider the following short summary of some of the relevant points for us to consider.

He explains this to help alleviate the suffering that we tend to experience in this material existence. He says that one who is sober, even when harassed by other living beings, should perceive that his aggressors are acting helplessly under the control of the Lord's material nature. Thus a person should never be distracted from the progress to be made on his path. Just as a mountain provides so many resources for the existence of all kinds of living beings, similarly saintly or spiritual persons should learn from this example on how to devote all one's efforts to the service of others, making the welfare of others the major reason for his existence. Additionally, like the tree, one should learn to dedicate himself to others in a tolerant, non-protesting manner.

A learned person should make his satisfaction in simply maintaining his existence without seeking unnecessary diversion through gratifying the material senses. In this manner, one can care for the body in a simple way while the higher knowledge of spirituality is kept intact, and one's mind and speech remain focused on spiritual advancement. Even one who is a transcendentalist will find him or herself surrounded by so many material objects, all of which possess good and bad qualities. However, one who has risen above the material concept of what is good or evil should not become entangled even when in contact with such material objects; rather he should act like the wind [which may travel through many situations but is never deviated from its main direction]. A spiritually advancing person may live in various material bodies in this world, and will experience the various qualities, functions and circumstances of each body, but still he or she is never entangled, like the wind that may carry many aromas but does not mix with them. The aromas are separate from the wind just as one's bodily situation is different from the soul. The soul or living being is different from the drama that may surround the body.

These understandings are all based on the fact that any spiritually advancing persons will comprehend themselves to be pure spirit souls within a material body, and separate from all of the good or bad material actions that go on around them. In fact, all forms of life, both moving and nonmoving, are actually spirit souls within. Thus, the individual souls are everywhere. A wise person with such a perception should then also see the Supreme Person as the Supersoul, present within all things. The soul is like the wind that may blow clouds or storms across the sky but is not implicated by such a course of events. Or, as the living being enters into a body that is made of varying arrangements of the elements of earth, water and fire, his eternal spiritual nature is not actually affected. In the same way, the eternal position of the soul is not changed or affected by its contact with material nature.

Saintly persons on the spiritual path become powerful by the execution of their austerities [the voluntary simplicity of life for a higher purpose]. Such focus makes their consciousness unshakable because there is little in this material world for which they need to endeavor.

A person needs to recognize that all phases of one's material life, from birth to death, are all properties of the body which do not affect the soul, similar to the waxing and waning of the moon which does not actually affect it, but only the way it appears. These are merely the reactions of the time factor. This time factor, which causes the continued birth, growth and death of innumerable material bodies, is hardly noticed over the short-term by the ordinary living beings.

One also should not indulge in excessive affection or concern for anyone or anything; such attachment leads one to later experience the invariable and great suffering at the loss of the person or object [though spiritual love and compassion for all is always encouraged]. Human life is a great achievement. The doors to liberation from material existence and all the suffering therein are opened to one who has attained the human form. But if a human being merely devotes himself to family life, finding his or her pleasure in the attraction for mundane sex, and works hard to maintain his family for temporary happiness [without any emphasis for spiritual development], such a person is fated to suffer greatly. Such a person is viewed as having attained a high place only to trip and fall all the way back down.

The embodied being, due to one's preoccupation with the body, will automatically experience material happiness or sadness in heavens or hells. Such feelings will also automatically be experienced without trying for it. Therefore, an intelligent person of discrimination does not over endeavor to obtain such material happiness. One follows and performs one's duty but lets whatever blessings come of its own accord, while using his free time for spiritual pursuits. Even though he may possess full sensual, mental and physical strength, a spiritual person should not become active merely for temporary material gain. He or she should always remain focused on one's real spiritual interest.

Such a sage is always happy and pleasing externally, in his appearance, but internally he is always grave and thoughtful. He remains undisturbed by being fixed in his immeasurable spiritual knowledge. Thus, he remains tranquil like the unfathomable waters of the ocean. Such a person does not rejoice in a materially opulent position, nor become sad or despondent when having to do without. It is only a physical consideration from which he or she is detached.

Without cultivating this necessary spiritual knowledge, a man who fails to control his mind and senses will immediately feel attraction towards a woman, who is created from the elements of the Supreme's illusory energy. Such a person is quickly captured when he sees the form of a beautiful woman dressed in fine clothing, decorated with golden ornaments and other cosmetics. He will be immediately aroused with attraction when the woman speaks with enticing words, smiles and moves sensuously. Then he falls blindly into the darkness of material existence, just as a moth attracted to the fire blindly rushes into its flames. The same goes for a woman who has failed to acquire this essential spiritual knowledge and becomes attracted to a well-built, handsome man. Instead of being fixed in one's own self-sufficient, internal and spiritual joy, due to such sensual attraction that develops into attachment, all of one's happiness then depends on the external object of desire and affection. Such relations, being temporary and based on the fleeting disposition of the mind, always guarantee future disappointment in some manner.

In a similar way, a spiritual person should not become absorbed in songs or music that promote material enjoyment. Otherwise, he or she could be captured by the desire and ambition for such sense pleasure, in the same way that a deer becomes captivated by the sweet music of a hunter's horn which then leads to its capture and death. One needs to have the spiritual maturity to discern what is worth working for, and what is best ignored.

When the intelligence of a person is stolen by the mind's attachment for material pleasure, and then by engaging in gratifying the senses, one falls deep into the well of illusion and material existence. Within that well he or she is seized by the deadly serpent of time. It is the imperceptible nature of time that brings one's life to a close, forcing one to give up all that he or she has worked to achieve. This is after wasting away one's life on the pursuits for temporary pleasure without the realization that real happiness, enjoyment and love come from the Supreme Person. This higher form of pleasure is connected with the soul, one's real identity, and is eternal and ever-increasing. The conclusion is that material desire is the cause of the greatest unhappiness and invariable disappointment, while detachment and freedom from such desires paves the way for the greatest happiness, which is in relation to that which is spiritual. For this reason, Lord Krishna gives these instructions to assist us in avoiding suffering and increasing our happiness in reaching the goal of life.

HELPFUL DUTIES FOR WOMEN

The Vedic texts give many instructions for our actions in this life, including those for women. However, Lord Krishna summarizes some of those that are for women. A few are included here. For example, when Lord Krishna was instructing the women of Vraja, He pointed out that the duty of a woman in this world is to sincerely serve her husband and behave well toward his family and take good care of her children. A woman who desires a good destination in her next life should never abandon her husband who has not fallen from his religious standards, even if he is obnoxious, unfortunate, old, unintelligent, sickly or poor. For a woman with a respectable family who engages in adulterous affairs, such manners are always condemned. They will keep her from reaching heaven and will cause ruin for her reputation and bring difficulty and fear. (*Bhag.*10.29.24-26)

Of course, this also implies that a woman should first make sure she marries a qualified husband. Not one who lacks spiritual understanding or fails to treat her properly or with little or no respect. Husband and wife are partners, and the most important part of this partnership is the assistance and consideration each one gives to the other for spiritual progress. Otherwise, the arrangement is for little more than economic and sensual enhancement and the outgrowths of such activity, all of which are temporary and yield little spiritual development. Such activities dedicated solely for the development of the body and mind do not help bring one to the higher dimensions of life, but instead keep one entangled in the pursuit to increase one's material happiness and in trying to avoid problems in the continual ups and downs of material existence.

This is the way Lord Krishna instructed Rukmini, the goddess of fortune Herself, before answering Her prayers that He marry Her. He said that women are usually destined to suffer when they stay with men whose behavior is uncertain and who take to activities that are not approved by society... Proper marriage and friendship between people are those in which wealth, birth, influence, physical appearance or beauty, and the capacity for progeny are equal, but never between two people who are superior and inferior. (*Bhag.* 10.60.13, 15) Such determinations need to be made before any marriage vows or commitments are made.

A further consideration, as explained elsewhere, is that Kali-yuga is an age of reversals. Where in the earlier ages, such as in Satya, Treta and Dvapara-yugas, men were responsible, strong and focused, now in Kali-yuga many men show a real lack in these qualities. Thus, women may be forced to increasingly exhibit the necessary strength and intelligence that was once expected from men. These days the foundation and strength of many families is increasingly seen to be the mother rather than the father. So women should also be prepared and educated so, when necessary, they can take care of themselves without any assistance from men. This is unfortunate, but a sign of the times. If they have a husband who falls from the proper spiritual standard, or no longer maintains responsibility, or is violent toward them, then she may very well be forced to leave him. In this case, she will need to take care of herself and should have the ability to do so. Furthermore, if a rare woman is so spiritually motivated that she feels no need for family life or the association of men, then she can devote herself to the higher cause of spiritual development without the need for being married.

ON SERVING PARENTS

Lord Krishna, in a conversation with His father, Vasudeva, spoke on the importance of parents. He said it is one's parents who give to one's body its birth and sustenance. Through this body one can acquire all the goals of life. Thus, no mortal man can repay his debt to his parents, even if he should serve them for a full lifetime of a hundred years. Therefore, a son who fails to take care of his parents with his physical resources and wealth, especially if he has the means to do so, is forced into a situation after death wherein he must eat his own flesh. Though he is able, a man who fails to support his elderly parents, chaste wife, young child or spiritual master, or who neglects a brahmana [a spiritually progressive person or priest] or anyone who comes to him for shelter, is considered dead, though breathing. (*Bhag.*10.45.5-7)
Lord Krishna also points out that the real father and mother of a child are those who care for children as if they were their own, even those children who may have been abandoned by relatives who are unable to maintain and protect them. (*Bhag.*10.45.22) Thus, the real father and mother of a child is exhibited by their display of love, care and protection, not merely by birth.

CRITICIZING OTHERS

Lord Krishna once explained to Uddhava that people should not praise nor criticize the conditioned nature and activities of others. Instead, they should see this world as simply the combination of the material energy and the enjoying souls all based on the one Absolute Truth. Whoever takes part in praising or criticizing the qualities or activities of others will quickly become deviated from what is best for himself and entangled in the same illusory dualities [for which he criticizes others]... One who understands the process of becoming firmly fixed in theoretical and realized knowledge does not take part in criticism or praise. He wanders freely in the world, like the sun. (*Bhag.*11.28.1-2, 8)

DUTIES OF A RULER

Lord Vishnu tells King Prithu that a king or ruler must provide protection for the general society who are citizens of the country. Such a ruler in his next life will then share one-sixth of the results of all pious activities of the people. However, the king or head of state who merely collects taxes from the people and does not provide the correct protection to them, loses all the credit for whatever pious or good activities he has performed, and he must then accept responsibility and suffer for the impious or sinful acts of the citizens over which he rules. He is punishable for the crimes of the citizens. (*Bhag.*4.20.14)

This also means that protection for the human beings includes providing them with the proper spiritual knowledge that will protect them from ignorance and the improper aims of life. If such knowledge is kept from the people, or purposely criticized and ridiculed so that people do not give it the necessary respect for inquiry, or are left with mere blind faith in a less than complete religious doctrine, then society will run amuck with crime and numerous forms of sinful activity. Then there will not be peace amongst the people in the country, and society will become attracted to so many dangerous habits and addictions. A leader that fails in this way to lead society will be forced to accept the consequences for the crimes committed by the mass of society. The *Manu-samhita* (8.304-309) explains that such a leader is forced to accept as much as one-sixth of all the sinful activities committed by the people in his land. That is why in Kali-yuga only the most qualified person should run for a political position, otherwise, if he cannot lead the people properly and establish a peaceful society, his future after death becomes extremely dark.

Furthermore, when the citizens serve a wicked king or ruler, someone who takes pleasure in violence and cannot control his senses, addicted to pleasures of the mind and flesh, they are doomed to suffer misery and poverty. (*Bhag.*10.89.24)

This is why Lord Krishna instructed the kings in the *Srimad-Bhagavatam* (10.73.21) that by understanding that they are not this body, that it and everything connected with it has a beginning and end, they should worship Him, God, by Vedic principles and with a clear intelligence protect their subjects in accordance with the established religious principles.

Lord Krishna further explains that a king who properly attends to the welfare of the citizens, and not merely makes false promises and assurances, but honestly keeps the citizens happy and protected both spiritually and materially, is very dear to Him. (*Bhag.*10.52.34)

* * *

These are only a few more of the instructions that are given by Lord Krishna to assist those of us who are living in this material world while trying to maintain our spiritual progress. Combine these with the instructions and knowledge that has already been given in the previous chapters, and we have a complete path that will take us to the ultimate goal.

CONCLUSION

So herein we have been fortunate enough to come in contact with the information that explains who is Lord Krishna, and the direct instructions from God, in the form of Lord Krishna, that explains the purpose of life and what to do now that we are in this human form. This knowledge and these explanations are most rare and is a great opportunity for us.

This information gives us the insights to understand how we got in our present situation, where we are going, and how to use it for our best advantage. It especially explains what is the purpose of material existence, but most importantly how to become free from it, and the best process to use to accomplish this and attain our natural spiritual identity.

Naturally, it is up to us to decide how to use this information, but Lord Krishna advises us to take it seriously for our own progress, and to reach our highest potential both materially and spiritually. This is also the mercy of Lord Krishna and the beauty of the Vedic system–all the tools and information are supplied to us, but nothing is forced. We can decide how serious we want to take it.

Nonetheless, any intelligent person will study it carefully and then use it to one's best ability, at least if he or she understands the great fortune one has attained by finally coming in contact with this rare and exceptional information and secrets of life. Good luck. More information can be found in my other books and website.

APPENDIX ONE

The Importance of Bhagavad-gita in This Day and Age

Most everyone at some point hears about the *Bhagavad-gita*, but do they know what it really contains, or how profound and deep is the knowledge that it provides?

Besides being the classic Eastern text that it is, and the summary of most Upanishadic information, it is the core of the deepest levels of spiritual knowledge. It is also like a handbook for life. Just as when you purchase an appliance of some kind, like a refrigerator, television or computer, you get a manual that teaches you how to use it. So in the same way, if God created this world and put us here, doesn't it seem that He should also tell us what is the purpose of this life and how to use it accordingly? The *Bhagavad-gita* is such an instruction manual for anyone. It provides the basic answers that most people have about life, and the universal spiritual truths that can be used by anyone, anywhere, and at any time in history. In this way it is timeless.

So let me explain a little of its importance and why we should take it seriously. I will not go into all of the details of what the *Bhagavad-gita* teaches, but I will provide a quick overview and summary of each chapter to give you an idea of the information you can discover and the benefits if you read it.

Of course, we know it was spoken on the battlefield at Kurukshetra as the forces prepared for war, a war meant to uphold the Dharmic principles against those who were bereft of them and before things became more evil then they already were, so there was little time in which to speak the *Bhagavad-gita*. Therefore, it was a brief conversation between Arjuna and Lord Krishna.

So, once the scene is set in the first chapter, from the second chapter it begins to explain some of the highest spiritual realizations known to humanity. It begins to explain exactly who and what we really are as spiritual beings. Without this knowledge in a person's life, the Vedic literature says that humans are little better than polished animals.

The reason for this conclusion is that the human life is especially meant for spiritual inquiry because in no other species of life here on earth does the living being have the faculty, such as the intelligence and the means to understand spiritual knowledge. Otherwise, this implies that there is little difference in the purpose of life between humans and animals who are mostly interested in merely eating, sleeping, mating, and defending what they think is theirs.

However, human life is not merely the means to acquire knowledge from the teachings and explanations of others, but it also offers the facility to realize it within oneself by practice. It is a matter of uplifting one's consciousness so that one can perceive the higher dimensions that exist all around us. This is more than merely accepting something on faith alone, but it is a matter of attaining direct perception of what the Vedic literature discusses.

So, from the second chapter of the *Bhagavad-gita*, we begin to learn our real identity as the soul within these bodies. The *Bhagavad-gita* explains the size and nature of the soul, and how it is completely transcendental or beyond the body itself. It is beyond time and beyond the effects of the three dimensional world. It is beyond the limitations of the body and mind.

This teaches us many things. It shows that regardless of our physical limitations, we can rise above them because, spiritually, we are already above them. We simply have to realize that. What does it mean to realize it? It means to directly perceive that truth, to see it as plain as day. And then live according to that realization. This teaches us that regardless of our situation, socially or physically or economically, we can rise to higher levels of existence, both in this world and in the next.

This teaches us that no matter what kind of pressures we may feel from our classmates at school, or what good or bad biases that may come from our fellow workers, or what kind of labels they put on us, or how much they may purposefully demean or criticize us, or even how great we think we are, we can be grounded, fixed in understanding who and what we really are as a spiritual being inside the limited material body. That is how we should see ourselves. And then we can be confident that regardless of what others may say, we know who we are and can go through life fixed in perceiving our real identity and our purpose in this life and what really is our higher potential. As an old saying points out, it is better to see yourself truly than to care how others see you.

When you are spiritually grounded, it is no longer necessary to always try to convince others of your self-worth, or of your social status, or of trying to make it into the right clique or group of people. We become convinced of who we are. We work in our own way to provide a contribution to society, to make something of ourselves that has meaning, beyond the typical superficialities and meaningless and worldly gossip that occupy the minds of most youth and adults today. We know that as long as we keep working in our own way, both intellectually and spiritually, attaining the skills that will enable us to do something significant, that our time will come when we can make a mark on this world in our own sphere of influence, which may continue to expand from there.

So we may be popular in school or not, or recognized in our career or not, but by our spiritual knowledge, as provided in the *Bhagavad-gita*, and by the confidence it gives us, we work to always become better, more uplifted, more refined, and more realized than we are, always making ourselves into a better person. Then we can help ourselves and others in more effective ways. This is just some of what the second chapter of the *Bhagavad-gita* can provide if we look into it carefully and understand who we really are and what is our greater potential.

As we proceed through the *Bhagavad-gita*, in Chapter Three, Lord Krishna discusses Karma-yoga, the knowledge of how every action creates an opposite and equal reaction. Fifty years ago in this country of the USA, hardly anyone spoke of karma, unless they were students of yoga or Eastern philosophy. Now everyone talks of karma, it is a part of the vocabulary, whether they really understand it or not. But the point is, where do you think that came from? How do you think they started to know about karma, or yoga for that matter, except for the fact that the teachings of the East and yoga, which are centered around the *Bhagavad-gita*, continued to spread throughout the West.

Similarly, considering all the knowledge that the *Bhagavad-gita* has within it, do you think that you will learn such things in the colleges or university courses? Hardly. You have to go beyond that. You have to take separate or alternative studies, like in studying the *Bhagavad-gita* or other Vedic texts, or listening to those who know about it. Then you can also begin to learn the basic laws of the universe as outlined in the *Bhagavad-gita*, as in the laws of karma. Otherwise, how will you begin to understand that your present circumstances and tendencies may be carry-overs from a previous existence? Or even from many previous existences that we have experienced. You only begin to understand these things by studying the *Bhagavad-gita*, the teachings of which are also expanded in the *Upanishads*, and then even more elaborated in the *Puranas* and other Vedic texts and commentaries.

In Chapter Four, called Transcendental Knowledge, it is explained to Arjuna how this knowledge was given down through the *parampara*, or disciplic succession. Lord Krishna explains the purpose and the transcendental nature of His appearance in this world. Also how to perform one's actions so they are spiritual activities, which can then enable a person to reach the spiritual abode.

Appendix One

In Chapter Five, Karma-yoga, Action in Krishna Consciousness, it is explained how to perform one's actions in the right consciousness of bhakti-yoga, and the way to focus on the natural, self-sufficient happiness within.

In Chapter Six, Sankhya-yoga, we find the instructions on how to conquer the mind to attain the natural inner happiness–beyond the senses–and become established in self-realization, the perception of one's real identity. And then to see all else, all things around you with a steady mind, free from desires and possessiveness.

Then Lord Krishna gives instructions on how to practice yoga and meditation so that we can eventually perceive the spiritual dimension all around us, of which we are a part. Then we can enter and experience boundless transcendental joy and bliss, free from maya or illusion, and in touch with the Supreme Consciousness. Then such a person can see God everywhere and every being in God. Thus, he is never lost.

In Chapter Seven, Knowledge of the Absolute, we have the instructions on how to know God, and how to see that everything rests and depends on God, like pearls strung on a thread. Also, how to recognize the power of God in all the powerful aspects of nature. Thus, we become aware of God and His potencies in all things around us until we reach the abode of God.

Chapter Eight, Attaining the Supreme. This chapter gives more specific information about the ways of material nature, how to get free of it, and how our consciousness at the time of death, developed by our thoughts, words and deeds, determines our next life, our next destination. Therefore, if we are remembering God, Krishna, then we can attain Him. So the instructions include how to think of Lord Krishna and attain Him through devotional yoga. Also, there are instructions in how to understand the higher and eternal nature, beyond all matter, which is the ultimate destination of us all.

In Chapter Nine, The Most Confidential Knowledge, Lord Krishna gives advice that this spiritual knowledge is the king of all knowledge, the most secret of all secrets, and by following it we can attain direct perception of the self by realization. Lord Krishna goes on to explain how everything is working under Him, but fools will never be able to recognize this. But by engaging in devotional yoga, the mind becomes spiritualized enough to understand God as He is by realization, far beyond any mental speculation. Lord Krishna goes on to explain that He is impartial to all, but becomes a friend to those who offer loving service. By engaging in this process systematically, you can reach the highest abode.

In Chapter Ten, The Opulence of the Absolute, we find explanations on how everything, all spiritual and material worlds, emanate from the Absolute Truth–God. Those who know this engage in devotional yoga to God, and with that love, Lord Krishna gives them the understanding by which they can come to Him.

Then Lord Krishna tells Arjuna how He is situated in all the powers and powerful things throughout the universe, whether it is the radiant sun, the tranquil moon, the water of the ocean, the transcendental Om, the chanting of the holy names as in japa meditation, and in the immovable Himalayas, and much more. But it is only with a single fragment of His energy does Lord Krishna pervade and support this entire universe. This leads to...

Chapter Eleven, The Universal Form. It is in this chapter wherein Lord Krishna shows Arjuna, by giving Arjuna divine eyes, how He is spread throughout the entire universe by His energies and expansions. Some of what Arjuna sees is beautiful beyond compare, and other things that he sees in this universal form are terrible and frightening. Some are hundreds of thousands of multicolored divine forms, as well as demigods, planets, past and future events, and a splendor so bright it would equal hundreds of thousands of suns. Both birth and death could be seen within this amazing universal form that spread in all directions, both near and far throughout the universe.

This made Arjuna humble, who then requested Krishna to relieve him of this view and show him His four-armed form, and then again His more familiar and lovable two-armed form.

Appendix One

Now Arjuna was convinced that Lord Krishna was the Supreme and everything both within and beyond this material manifestation, as well as the father and creator of this material manifestation.

Then in Chapter Twelve, Devotional Service, Lord Krishna explains the ultimate goal of life, and the essence of how to practice bhakti-yoga, focusing especially on how to serve and fix our mind and intelligence on the Supreme as Lord Krishna in all our activities and undertakings.

Then we have Chapter Thirteen, Nature, The Enjoyer, and Consciousness. This explains how the body is the center of the field of material activities, and how we should understand the body as the vehicle in which both the soul and Supersoul–Paramatma–reside. Also, that the body is not our real identity, but we should see through the body to recognize the living being within. The soul is beyond the body and illuminates the body by consciousness. This is the symptom of the soul within. Now we merely have to spiritualize our consciousness to directly perceive the soul, and then see the difference between the body and soul.

The field of activities also includes the five elements, ego, intelligence, the senses, mind, and various emotions that project from the mind, along with all moving and non-moving things. Aside from all this, Lord Krishna explains the characteristics of His expansion as the Supersoul and how to perceive Him within.

In Chapter Fourteen, The Three Modes of Material Nature, Lord Krishna describes the three modes or *gunas* and their characteristics as goodness (*sattva*), passion (*rajas*) and ignorance (*tamas*), and the nature of those according to how they are situated in each of these modes of nature. This also determines if one is progressing upward while acting in the mode of goodness, or simply maintaining while in the mode of passion, or regressing downward in ignorance or darkness. This analysis will also reveal the condition of one's next birth. As explained in verses 14 and 15 in this chapter: "When one dies in the mode of goodness, he attains the pure higher planets. When one dies in the mode of passion, he takes birth among those engaged in fruitive activities; and when he dies in the mode of ignorance, he takes birth in the animal kingdom."

So the goal is to know how to act in order to rise above these three modes, which Lord Krishna clearly explains as being the process of devotional yoga.

Chapter Fifteen, The Yoga of the Supreme Person. Here Lord Krishna emphasizes how to engage in that yoga process which can elevate you to rise above all material inebriates and limitations, and material happiness and distress, in order to reach the spiritual abode.

Even though the living beings are all parts of the Lord, they are struggling very hard with the mind and the mental interpretations of our experiences within this material field of activities and the way we see ourselves in this world. Furthermore, until these conceptions are purified, they are carried from one body to the next, one life to the next, just as air carries aromas. One who is spiritually ignorant cannot understand how this takes place. But the progressing transcendentalist can clearly see all of this. Krishna also explains that one who knows Him as the Supreme Being knows everything and engages in devotional yoga to Him, and his endeavors will know perfection.

Chapter Sixteen, The Divine and Demoniac Natures. Here Lord Krishna makes it clear how to recognize the Divine qualities and actions, as well as the demoniac, both of which are in ourselves and in those around us. It is only the divine qualities that are conducive to spiritual progress and liberation, whereas the demoniac actions and qualities will keep you bound in material existence for many lifetimes. So the next step is to associate with those of a divine nature and develop such qualities in ourselves, and avoid the demoniac. The demoniac can never approach God nor the spiritual world, but reach progressively lower forms of existence.

Chapter Seventeen, The Divisions of Faith. In this chapter Lord Krishna explains that there are different kinds of faith and religions depending on what level of the modes of material nature are displayed by the living being, such as goodness, passion or ignorance. Therefore, some religions will be more materialistic, based on ego, or the bodily identification and attachment and pride, while others will be more spiritual. So there is a difference between various religions, as explained in this chapter. They are not all the same, which sometimes people like to say. Lord Krishna describes the difference herein in a way we can clearly see the varieties and categories to which they belong. It is up to us to study this carefully to understand this.

So as we go along in our study of these chapters, we begin to see a pattern or repetition in these teachings. There is much knowledge on various aspects of life and spiritual understanding, but time and again Lord Krishna expresses that it is He who is the Supreme Being, the creator of the universe, and it is He who should be the center of our worship and meditation. Furthermore, all of this knowledge is meant to raise our consciousness so we can return to the spiritual world. That is what this is for. Lord Krishna repeats this in several chapters herein. This is not some kind of philosophy to contemplate, but it is an action plan for the benefit of humanity so we can directly attain a spiritual vision and perceive the spiritual reality all around us, up to the point in which we can enter that spiritual domain, which is our real home. The material world is temporary and can never give the joy we are seeking. This is why Lord Krishna is explaining all of this, to motivate us to act according to His directions and attain the realm of eternal happiness and bliss, which is our eternal and constitutional nature. And He summarizes this in the final chapter of *Bhagavad-gita*.

Chapter Eighteen, The Conclusion, The Perfection of Renunciation, or Yoga of Renunciation for Moksha–Liberation from Material Existence. Herein Lord Krishna explains the way to become spiritually perfect through the proper means of renunciation or detachment from activities, but also how to continue with prescribed duties. Yet, out of all we may do or practice, Lord Krishna finally concludes with the instructions on the ultimate way of perfecting one's spiritual life and realize the highest truth, which is by performing devotional service, bhakti-yoga, and in this way rekindle one's relationship with God and then reach the eternal and imperishable spiritual abode.

In this way, a person can cross over all obstacles of conditional life by Lord Krishna's grace. Otherwise, a person will remain lost in the whirlpool of material existence. By surrendering unto Him, and then by His grace you can attain peace and the supreme abode. Lord Krishna then concludes that this is the most confidential of all knowledge given for your benefit. He instructs that if you think of Him, become His devotee, worship Him, just surrender unto Him, then you will be free from all sinful reactions and come to Him without fail.

It is further concluded that anyone who studies this conversation between Lord Krishna and Arjuna worships Lord Krishna with his or her intelligence. And simply by listening with faith to this conversation a person becomes free from sinful reaction and at least attains the planets of the pious.

So these are the basic instructions that are related in the *Bhagavad-gita*, and some of the benefits of studying it. So, in this way, a person can acquire proper direction in life, a deeper realization of one's true identity, and attain a level of self-confidence and peace by inward reflection and realization that can never be reached through ordinary, materialistic studies or endeavors. Furthermore, these can be applied to assist us in all aspects of life to help bring us to our higher potential in everything we do, materially or spiritually. This is the power and the importance of the *Bhagavad-gita* and the instructions of Lord Krishna found within it.

CHAPTER NOTES

CHAPTER ONE
1. *Bhagavad-gita* 13.8-12
2. Ibid., 18.20-22
3. Ibid., 18.30-32
4. *Srimad-Bhagavatam* 11.28.18
5. Ibid., 11.7.10
6. Ibid., 11.19.3-5
7. *Bhagavad-gita* 4.1-3
8. Ibid., 4.4-6
9. *Srimad-Bhagavatam* 11.14.3-8)
10. Ibid., 12.13.19

CHAPTER TWO
1. *Srimad-Bhagavatam* 8.22.25
2. Ibid., 11.9.29
3. Ibid., 11.20.17
4. Ibid., 11.20.12-14
5. Ibid., 11.23.22-23
6. Ibid., 11.25.33
7. Ibid., 11.26.1
8. Ibid., 11.7.22-23

CHAPTER THREE
1. *Bhagavad-gita* 2.14
2. *Srimad-Bhagavatam* 11.11.15
3. *Bhagavad-gita* 2.16
4. Ibid., 5.22

5. *Srimad-Bhagavatam* 6.16.69
6. Ibid., 11.10.17
7. Ibid., 11.10.18-20, 22
8. Ibid., 11.10.23-25
9. *Bhagavad-gita* 8.16
10. Ibid., 9.8
11. *Srimad-Bhagavatam* 11.19.18
12. Ibid., 2.9.34
13. Ibid., 4.20.12
14. *Srimad-Bhagavatam* 10.54.41
15. Ibid., 10.28.13
16. Ibid., 10.54.44-45
17. Ibid., 11.7.7-8
18. Ibid., 11.10.2-3
19. Ibid., 11.10.7
20. Ibid., 11.11.2
21. Ibid., 11.28.3
22. Ibid., 11.10.11
23. Ibid., 11.11.23
24. Ibid., 11.13.34
25. Ibid., 11.13.34
26. Ibid., 11.13.34-37
27. Ibid., 11.19.16-17
28. Ibid., 11.28.9
29. Ibid., 11.20.14, 16

CHAPTER FOUR
1. *Bhagavad-gita* 2.17-21

2. Ibid., 2.22
3. Ibid., 2.23-25
4. Ibid., 2.30
5. Ibid., 4.35
6. Ibid., 6.9
7. Ibid., 2.29
8. Ibid., 13.20-21
9. Ibid., 15.7
10. Ibid., 15.16
11. Ibid., 13.30-35
12. *Srimad-Bhagavatam* 6.16.57
13. Ibid., 11.10.10
14. *Bhagavad-gita* 13.22
15. *Srimad-Bhagavatam* 3.26.1-5
16. Ibid., 4.20.3-9
17. Ibid., 10.23.27
18. Ibid., 10.54.45-49
19. Ibid., 11.10.8
20. Ibid., 11.11.4-9
21. Ibid., 11.13.9-12
22. Ibid., 11.13.25
23. Ibid., 11.13.31-32
24. Ibid., 11.28.23-24
25. Ibid., 12.5.8

CHAPTER FIVE
1. *Bhagavad-gita* 2.22
2. Ibid., 2.25-27
3. Ibid., 8.6
4. Ibid., 15.8-9
5. Ibid., 15.10-11
6. *Srimad-Bhagavatam* 11.10.32

7. Ibid., 11.11.10-11
8. Ibid., 11.12.21
9. Ibid., 11.13.37
10. Ibid., 11.22.37-42
11. Ibid., 11.22.43-48
12. Ibid., 11.22.49-59

CHAPTER SIX
1. *Srimad-Bhagavatam* 11.20.6-12
2. Ibid., 11.28.1-4
3. Ibid., 11.28.8-9
4. Ibid., 11.28.12-13
5. Ibid., 11.28.15
6. Ibid., 11.28.17
7. Ibid., 11.28.18
8. Ibid., 11.28.23-24
9. Ibid., 11.28.31-34
10. Ibid., 11.28.27
11. Ibid., 11.19.15
12. Ibid., 3.32.32
13. Ibid., 10.24.13-17
14. Ibid., 10.54.38
15. *Bhagavad-gita* 4.15-24
16. Ibid., 3.3-8
17. Ibid., 3.9-15
18. Ibid., 3.16
19. Ibid., 3.17-19
20. Ibid., 3.20-21
21. Ibid., 3.25-26
22. Ibid., 3.28-33
23. Ibid., 3.41
24. Ibid., 3.42-43
25. Ibid., 4.14-15
26. Ibid., 17.5

Chapter Notes

27. Ibid., 5.7
28. *Srimad-Bhagavatam* 11.14.19

CHAPTER SEVEN
1. *Bhagavad-gita* 12.3-7
2. Ibid., 14.27
3. Ibid., 6.1-9
4. Ibid., 5.27-28
5. Ibid., 6.10-19
6. Ibid., 6.20-25
7. Ibid., 6.26-32
8. Ibid., 8.10-13
9. *Srimad-Bhagavatam* 11.15.24
10. *Bhagavad-gita* 6.33-4
11. Ibid., 6.35-36
12. Ibid., 6.37-38
13. Ibid., 6.40-46
14. Ibid., 6.47
15. *Srimad-Bhagavatam* 11.29.1-3
16. Ibid., 11.28.29
17. Ibid., 11.28.38-41
18. Ibid., 11.28.42-44
19. Ibid., 11.23.45-46
20. Ibid., 10.51.60
21. *Bhagavad-gita* 8.14-15
22. *Srimad-Bhagavatam* 11.14.20
23. Ibid., 11.11.46
24. Ibid., 3.25.13
25. Ibid., 3.25.19
26. Ibid., 11.9.22
27. Ibid., 11.14.27-28
28. Ibid., 3.9.30-33
29. *Bhagavad-gita* 9.1-2
30. Ibid., 4.35
31. Ibid., 6.29-31
32. *Srimad-Bhagavatam* 6.16.63
33. Ibid., 11.15.3-9
34. Ibid., 11.9.11-13

CHAPTER EIGHT
1. *Bhagavad-gita* 15.12-14
2. Ibid., 8.4
3. Ibid., 9.6
4. Ibid., 9.17-19
5. Ibid., 10.19-39
6. Ibid., 10.40-42
7. Ibid., 10.3-8
8. *Srimad-Bhagavatam* 11.2.48
9. Ibid., 11.12.21
10. *Bhagavad-gita* 8.22
11. *Srimad-Bhagavatam* 11.13.24

CHAPTER NINE
1. *Bhagavad-gita* 15.15
2. Ibid., 13.23
3. Ibid., 13.25
4. Ibid., 13.28-29
5. *Srimad-Bhagavatam* 11.16.9
6. Ibid., 11.7.12
7. *Bhagavad-gita* 13.14-18
8. *Srimad-Bhagavatam* 7.10.12

CHAPTER TEN
1. *Bhagavad-gita* 9.2
2. Ibid., 4.10-11
3. Ibid., 4.24
4. Ibid., 5.2, 6-7
5. Ibid., 5.10-12
6. Ibid., 9.26
7. Ibid., 9.27-28
8. Ibid., 9.34
9. Ibid., 18.56-58
10. Ibid., 12.6-12
11. Ibid., 12.13-20
12. *Srimad-Bhagavatam* 3.21.24
13. Ibid., 7.9.54
14. Ibid., 11.11.33
15. Ibid., 11.19.33-35
16. Ibid., 11.19.36-39
17. Ibid., 11.19.40-45
18. Ibid., 10.23.33 & 10.29.27
19. Ibid., 10.73.22-23
20. Ibid., 11.19.19-24
21. Ibid., 3.29.17-20
22. Ibid., 3.29.11-12
23. Ibid., 11.11.34-41
24. Ibid., 11.11.47
25. Ibid., 3.27.28-29
26. Ibid., 3.29.33
27. Ibid., 3.33.10-11
28. *Bhagavad-gita* 3.9
29. Ibid., 7.30
30. Ibid., 8.5-7
31. Ibid., 11.53-55
32. Ibid., 18.55
33. *Srimad-Bhagavatam* 11.20.12
34. Ibid., 11.14.12-13
35. Ibid., 11.14.17
36. *Bhagavad-gita* 7.16-19
37. Ibid., 7.28-29
38. Ibid., 9.13-15
39. Ibid., 9.22
40. Ibid., 15.19-20
41. Ibid., 4.40
42. Ibid., 7.20
43. Ibid., 9.23-24
44. Ibid., 7.15
45. Ibid., 9.3
46. *Srimad-Bhagavatam* 11.11.18-20
47. *Bhagavad-gita* 2.64
48. Ibid., 6.47
49. Ibid., 8.8, 10
50. Ibid., 8.15
51. *Srimad-Bhagavatam* 11.12.1-2
52. Ibid., 11.12.9
53. Ibid., 11.12.9-15
54. *Bhagavad-gita* 8.26
55. Ibid., 8.24-25
56. Ibid., 8.27
57. *Srimad-Bhagavatam* 11.15.34
58. Ibid., 11.20.32-33
59. Ibid., 3.25.37
60. *Bhagavad-gita* 8.28
61. Ibid., 8.9
62. Ibid., 12.2
63. Ibid., 8.14

64. *Srimad-Bhagavatam* 11.11.22-25
65. *Bhagavad-gita* 2.49-51
66. Ibid., 4.41
67. *Srimad-Bhagavatam* 3.25.33
68. Ibid., 11.20.25
69. Ibid., 11.14.18-19
70. Ibid., 11.14.26
71. Ibid., 11.20.28
72. *Bhagavad-gita* 2.40
73. Ibid., 4.36-9
74. Ibid., 5.29
75. Ibid., 18.63-66
76. *Srimad-Bhagavatam* 1.18.44-46, 48
77. Ibid., 11.20.37
78. Ibid., 11.29.9
79. Ibid., 11.29.19
80. *Bhagavad-gita* 18.67-69
81. *Srimad-Bhagavatam* 3.32.39-43
82. *Bhagavad-gita* 18.70-71
83. *Srimad-Bhagavatam* 11.29.26-28
84. Ibid., 11.29.30-32

CHAPTER ELEVEN
1. *Bhagavad-gita* 2.42-45
2. Ibid., 7.20, 23
3. Ibid., 9.25
4. Ibid., 2.62-63
5. Ibid., 3.37-40
6. *Srimad-Bhagavatam* 11.18.40-41

7. Ibid., 3.30.1-3
8. Ibid., 3.30.9
9. Ibid., 3.31.32-33
10. Ibid., 3.32.1-4
11. Ibid., 3.32.19
12. *Bhagavad-gita* 5.12
13. Ibid., 7.15
14. Ibid., 9.12
15. Ibid., 16.4
16. Ibid., 16.7-20
17. *Srimad-Bhagavatam* 11.21.1
18. Ibid., 11.21.19-22
19. Ibid., 11.21.24
20. Ibid., 11.21.27
21. Ibid., 11.23.49
22. Ibid., 11.28.12-17
23. Ibid., 11.26.26
24. Ibid., 11.26.28-30
25. *Bhagavad-gita* 3.16
26. Ibid., 3.32
27. Ibid., 16.23

CHAPTER TWELVE
1. *Bhagavad-gita* 2.45
2. Ibid., 2.54-61
3. Ibid., 2.64-68
4. Ibid., 2.70-72
5. Ibid., 5.12
6. Ibid., 5.16-18
7. Ibid., 5.19-21
8. Ibid., 5.23-26
9. Ibid., 15.5
10. Ibid., 16.1-3, this is similar to *Bg*.18.51-53

11. *Srimad-Bhagavatam*
    3.32.5-7
12. Ibid., 4.20.10-11
13. Ibid., 11.26.2
14. Ibid., 11.28.27
15. Ibid., 11.28.31-32
16. Ibid., 11.11.8-14
17. Ibid., 11.16.42-44

CHAPTER THIRTEEN
1. *Bhagavad-gita* 8.7-8, 14
2. Ibid., 8.9
3. *Srimad-Bhagavatam*
   3.25.27
4. Ibid., 11.25.36
5. *Bhagavad-gita* 8.15-16, 20-21
6. Ibid., 15.6
7. *Srimad-Bhagavatam*
   11.11.48
8. Ibid., 11.12.3-7
9. Ibid., 11.12.8
10. Ibid., 11.14.25
11. Ibid., 11.18.37
12. Ibid., 11.18.45-46
13. Ibid., 11.20.37

CHAPTER FOURTEEN
1. *Bhagavad-gita* 9.29-32
2. *Srimad-Bhagavatam*
   7.1.25-26
3. Ibid., 7.1.28-29
4. Ibid., 10.48.26
5. Ibid., 11.2.55
6. Ibid., 10.41.47

7. *Bhagavad-gita* 10.10-11
8. *Srimad-Bhagavatam*
   9.4.63-68
9. Ibid., 10.23.26
10. Ibid., 10.27.16
11. Ibid., 10.60.14
12. Ibid., 10.32.20-21
13. Ibid., 10.88.8-11

CHAPTER FIFTEEN
1. *Srimad-Bhagavatam*
   11.25.22
2. Ibid., 11.31.1-7
3. Ibid., 11.19.26-27
4. Ibid., 11.19.25
5. Ibid., 11.21.18
6. Ibid., 11.21.19
7. Ibid., 11.25.2-5
8. Ibid., 11.25.6-7
9. Ibid., 11.25.9
10. Ibid., 11.25.13-15
11. Ibid., 11.25.16-18
12. Ibid., 11.25.20-21
13. Ibid., 11.25.24
14. Ibid., 11.25.28
15. *Bhagavad-gita* 17.8-10
16. Ibid., 18.23-28
17. *Srimad-Bhagavatam*
    11.25.23
18. Ibid., 11.25.26
19. Ibid., 11.25.25
20. *Bhagavad-gita* 18.33-35
21. Ibid., 18.36-39
22. *Srimad-Bhagavatam*
    11.25.29

23. Ibid., 11.25.30
24. Ibid., 11.21.23-26
25. Ibid., 11.21.29-31
26. Ibid., 11.21.34
27. Ibid., 11.21.43
28. Ibid., 11.25.33-36
29. Ibid., 11.26.30

REFERENCES

The following is a list of all the authentic Vedic and religious texts that were used, researched, referred to or directly quoted to explain or verify all the knowledge and information presented in this book.

Agni Purana, translated by N. Gangadharan, Motilal Banarsidass, Delhi, 1984

Atharva-veda, translated by Devi Chand, Munshiram Manoharlal, Delhi, 1980

Bhagavad-gita As It Is, translated by A. C. Bhaktivedanta Swami, Bhaktivedanta Book Trust, New York/Los Angeles, 1972

Bhagavad-gita, translated by Swami Chidbhavananda, Sri Ramakrishna Tapovanam, Tiruchirappalli, India, 1991

The Song of God, Bhagavad-gita, translated by Swami Prabhavananda and Christopher Isherwood, New America Library, New York, 1972,

Bhagavad-gita, translated by Winthrop Sargeant, State University of New York Press, Albany, 1984

Bhakti-rasamrita-sindhu, (Nectar of Devotion), translated by A. C. Bhaktivedanta Swami, Bhaktivedanta Book Trust, New York/Los Angeles, 1970

Bible, New York International Bible Society, 1981

Brahma Purana, edited by J.L.Shastri, Motilal Banarsidass, Delhi 1985

Brahmanda Purana, edited by J.L.Shastri, Motilal Banarsidass, 1983

Brahma-samhita, translated by Bhaktisiddhanta Sarasvati Gosvami Thakur, Bhaktivedanta Book Trust, New York/Los Angeles,

Brahma-Sutras, translated by Swami Vireswarananda and Adidevananda, Advaita Ashram, Calcutta, 1978

Brahma-vaivarta Purana

Brihad-vishnu Purana

References

Brihan-naradiya Purana
Brihadaranyaka Upanishad
Caitanya-caritamrita, translated by A. C. Bhaktivedanta Swami, Bhaktivedanta Book Trust, Los Angeles, 1974
Caitanya Upanisad, translated by Kusakratha dasa, Bala Books, New York, 1970
Chandogya Upanishad
Garbha Upanishad
Garuda Purana, edited by J. L. Shastri, Motilal Barnasidass, Delhi, 1985
Gautamiya Tantra
Kali-santarana Upanishad
Katha Upanishad
Kaushitaki Upanishad
Kurma Purana, edited by J. L. Shastri, Motilal Banarsidass, Delhi, 1981
Linga Purana, edited by J. L. Shastri, Motilal Banarsidass, Delhi, 1973
Mahabharata, translated by C. Rajagopalachari, Bharatiya Vidya Bhavan, New Delhi, 1972
Mahabharata, Kamala Subramaniam, Bharatiya Vidya Bhavan, Bombay, 1982
Matsya Purana
The Law of Manu, [*Manu-samhita*], translated by Georg Buhlerg, Motilal Banarsidass, Delhi, 1970
Minor Upanishads, translated by Swami Madhavananda, Advaita Ashram, Calcutta, 1980; contains Paramahamsopanishad, Atmopanishad, Amritabindupanishad, Tejabindupanishad, Sarvopanishad, Brahmopanisad, Aruneyi Upanishad, Kaivalyopanishad.
Mukunda-mala-stotra
Mundaka Upanishad
Narada-pancaratra
Narada Purana, tr. by Ganesh Vasudeo Tagare, Banarsidass, Delhi, 1980

Narada Sutras, translated by Hari Prasad Shastri, Shanti Sadan, London, 1963

Narada-Bhakti-Sutra, A. C. Bhaktivedanta Swami, Bhaktivedanta Book Trust, Los Angeles, 1991

Padma Purana, tr. by S. Venkitasubramonia Iyer, Banarsidass, Delhi, 1988

Ramayana of Valmiki, tr. by Makhan Lal Sen, Oriental Publishing Co., Calcutta

Hymns of the Rig-veda, tr. by Griffith, Motilal Banarsidass, Delhi, 1973

Rig-veda Brahmanas: The Aitareya and Kausitaki Brahmanas of the Rigveda, translated by Arthur Keith, Motilal Banarsidass, Delhi, 1971

Samnyasa Upanisads, translated by Prof. A. A. Ramanathan, Adyar Library, Madras, India, 1978; contains Avadhutopanisad, Arunyupanisad, Katharudropanisad, Kundikopanisad, Jabalopanisad, Turiyatitopanisad, Narada-parivrajakopanisad, Nirvanopanisad, Parabrahmopanisad, Paramahamsa-parivrajakopanisad, Paramahamsopanisad, Brahmopanisad, Bhiksukopanisad, Maitreyopanisad, Yajnavalkyopanisad, Satyayaniyopanisad, and Samnyasopanisad.

Shiva Purana, edited by Professor J. L. Shastri, Banarsidass, Delhi, 1970

Siksastaka, of Sri Caitanya Mahaprabhu.

Sixty Upanisads of the Vedas, by Paul Deussen, translated from German by V. M. Bedekar and G. B. Palsule, Motilal Banarsidass, Delhi, 1980; contains Upanishads of the Rigveda: Aitareya and Kausitaki. Upanisads of the Samaveda: Chandogya and Kena. Upanisads of the Black Yajurveda: Taittiriya, Mahanarayan, Kathaka, Svetasvatara, and Maitrayana. Upanisads of the White Yajurveda: Brihadaranyaka and Isa. Upanisads of the Atharvaveda: Mundaka, Prasna, Mandukya, Garbha, Pranagnihotra, Pinda, Atma, Sarva, Garuda; (Yoga Upanisads): Brahmavidya, Ksurika, Culik,

Nadabindu, Brahma-bindu, Amrtabindu, Dhyanabindu, Tejobindu, Yoga-sikha, Yogatattva, Hamsa; (Samnyasa Upanisads): Brahma, Samnyasa, Aruneya, Kantha-sruti, Paramahamsa, Jabala, Asrama; (Shiva Upanisads): Atharvasira, Atharva-sikha, Nilarudra, Kalagnirudra, Kaivalya; (Vishnu Upanisads): Maha, Narayana, Atmabodha, Nrisimhapurvatapaniya, Nrisimhottara-tapaniya, Ramapurvatapaniya, Ramottaratapaniya. (Supplemental Upanisads): Purusasuktam, Tadeva, Shiva-samkalpa, Baskala, Chagaleya, Paingala, Mrtyu-langala, Arseya, Pranava, and Saunaka Upanisad.

Skanda Purana

Sri Brihat Bhagavatamritam, by Sri Srila Sanatana Gosvami, Sree Gaudiya Math, Madras, India, 1987

Sri Caitanya Bhagavat, by Sri Vrindavan dasa Thakura

Sri Caitanya Shikshamritam, Thakura Bhakti Vinode, Sree Gaudiya Math, Madras, 1983

Sri Isopanisad, translated by A. C. Bhaktivedanta Swami, Bhaktivedanta Book Trust, New York/Los Angeles, 1969

Srimad-Bhagavatam, translated by A. C. Bhaktivedanta Swami, Bhaktivedanta Book trust, New York/Los Angeles, 1972

Srimad-Bhagavatam, translated by N. Raghunathan, Vighneswar Publishing House, Madras, 1976

Srimad-Bhagavatam MahaPurana, translated by C. L. Goswami, M. A., Sastri, Motilal Jalan at Gita Press, Gorkhapur, India, 1982

Svetasvatara Upanishad

Taittiriya Upanishad

Twelve Essential Upanishads, Tridandi Sri Bhakti Prajnan Yati, Sree Gaudiya Math, Madras, 1982. Includes the *Isha, Kena, Katha, Prashna, Mundaka, Mandukya, Taittiriya, Aitareya, Chandogya, Brihadaranyaka, Svetasvatara,*and *Gopalatapani Upanishad* of the Pippalada section of the *Atharva-veda.*

Upadesamrta (Nectar of Instruction), translated by A. C. Bhaktivedanta Swami, Bhaktivedanta Book Trust, New

York/Los Angeles, 1975

The Upanishads, translated by Swami Prabhavananda and Frederick Manchester, New American Library, New York, 1957; contains Katha, Isha, Kena, Prasna, Mundaka, Mandukya, Taittiriya, Aitareya, Chandogya, Brihadaranyaka, Kaivalya, and Svetasvatara Upanishads.

The Upanisads, translated by F. Max Muller, Dover Publications; contains Chandogya, Kena, Aitareya, Kausitaki, Vajasaneyi (Isa), Katha, Mundaka, Taittiriya, Brihadaranyaka, Svetasvatara, Prasna, and Maitrayani Upanisads.

Varaha Purana, tr. by S.Venkitasubramonia Iyer, Banarsidass, Delhi, 1985

Vayu Purana, translated by G. V. Tagare, Banarsidass, Delhi, India, 1987

Vishnu Purana, translated by H. H. Wilson, Nag Publishers, Delhi

Vedanta-Sutras of Badarayana with Commentary of Baladeva Vidyabhusana, translated by Rai Bahadur Srisa Chandra Vasu, Munshiram Manoharlal, New Delhi, 1979

White Yajurveda, translated by Griffith, The Chowkhamba Sanskrit Series Office, Varanasi, 1976

Yajurveda, translated by Devi Chand, Munshiram Manoharlal, Delhi, 1980

Yoga Sutras of Patanjali

GLOSSARY

Acharya--the spiritual master who sets the proper standard by his own example.

Acintya-bhedabheda-tattva--simultaneously one and different. The doctrine Lord Sri Caitanya taught referring to the Absolute as being both personal and impersonal.

Advaita--nondual, meaning that the Absolute is one with the infinitesimal souls with no individuality between them. The philosophy of Sankaracharya.

Agni--fire, or Agni the demigod of fire.

Ahankara--false ego, identification with matter.

Ahimsa--nonviolence.

Akarma--actions which cause no *karmic* reactions.

Akasha--the ether, or etheric plane; a subtle material element in which sound travels.

Ananda--spiritual bliss.

Ananta--unlimited.

Arati--the ceremony of worship when incense and ghee lamps are offered to the Deities.

Arca-vigraha--the worshipable Deity form of the Lord made of stone, wood, etc. Aryan--a noble person, one who is on the path of spiritual advancement.

Asana--postures for meditation, or exercises for developing the body into a fit instrument for spiritual advancement.

Asat--that which is temporary.

Ashrama--one of the four orders of spiritual life, such as *brahmachari* (celibate student), *grihastha* (married householder), *vanaprastha* (retired stage), and *sannyasa* (renunciate); or the abode of a spiritual teacher or *sadhu*.

Astanga-yoga--the eightfold path of mystic yoga.

Asura--one who is ungodly or a demon.

Atma--the self or soul. Sometimes means the body, mind, and senses.

Atman--usually referred to as the Supreme Self.

Avatara--an incarnation of the Lord who descends from the spiritual world.
Avidya--ignorance or nescience.
Aum--*om* or *pranava*
Ayurveda--the original holistic form of medicine as described in the Vedic literature.
Babaji--wandering mendicant holy man.
Badrinatha--one of the holy places of pilgrimage in the Himalayas, and home of the Deity Sri Badrinatha along with many sages and hermits.
Bhagavan--one who possesses all opulences, God.
Bhajan--song of worship.
Bhakta--a devotee of the Lord who is engaged in *bhakti-yoga*.
Bhakti--love and devotion for God.
Bhakti-yoga--the path of offering pure devotional service to the Supreme.
Brahma--the demigod of creation who was born from Lord Vishnu, the first created living being and the engineer of the secondary stage of creation of the universe when all the living entities were manifested.
Brahmachari--a celebate student who is trained by the spiritual master. One of the four divisions or ashramas of spiritual life.
Brahmajyoti--the great white light or effulgence which emanates from the body of the Lord.
Brahmaloka--the highest planet or plane of existence in the universe; the planet where Lord Brahma lives.
Brahman--the spiritual energy; the all-pervading impersonal aspect of the Lord; or the Supreme Lord Himself.
Brahmana or brahmin--one of the four orders of society; the intellectual class of men who have been trained in the knowledge of the *Vedas* and initiated by a spiritual master.
Brahmana--the supplemental books of the four primary *Vedas*. They usually contained instructions for performing Vedic *agnihotras*, chanting the *mantras*, the purpose of the rituals, etc. The *Aitareya* and *Kaushitaki Brahmanas* belong to the *Rig-*

Glossary

veda, the *Satapatha Brahmana* belongs to the *White Yajur-veda*, and the *Taittiriya Brahmana* belongs to the *Black Yajur-veda*. The *Praudha* and *Shadvinsa Brahmanas* are two of the eight *Brahmanas* belonging to the *Atharva-veda*.

Brahminical--to be clean and upstanding, both outwardly and inwardly, like a brahmana should be.

Buddha--Lord Buddha or a learned man.

Caitanya-caritamrita--the scripture by Krishnadasa Kaviraja which explains the teachings and pastimes of Lord Caitanya Mahaprabhu.

Caitanya Mahaprabhu--the most recent incarnation of the Lord who appeared in the 15th century in Bengal and who originally started the *sankirtana* movement, based on congregational chanting of the holy names.

Causal Ocean or Karana Ocean--is the corner of the spiritual sky where Maha-Vishnu lies down to create the material manifestation.

Cit--eternal knowledge.

Chakra--a wheel, disk, or psychic energy center situated along the spinal column in the subtle body of the physical shell.

Darshan--the devotional act of seeing and being seen by the Deity in the temple.

Deity--the *arca-vigraha*, or worshipful form of the Supreme in the temple, or deity as the worshipful image of the demigod.

Devas--demigods or heavenly beings from higher levels of material existence, or a godly person.

Devaki--the devotee who acted as Lord Krishna's mother.

Dham--a holy place.

Dharma--the essential nature or duty of the living being.

Dharmashala--a shelter or guesthouse for pilgrims at temples or holy towns.

Dualism--as related in this book refers to the Supreme as both an impersonal force as well as a person.

Dvapara-yuga--the third age which lasts 864,000 years.

Dwaita--dualism, the principle that the Absolute Truth consists of the infinite Supreme Being and the infinitesimal individual souls.

Ganesh--a son of Shiva, said to destroy obstacles (as Vinayaka) and offer good luck to those who petition him.

Ganges--the sacred and spiritual river which, according to the *Vedas*, runs throughout the universe, a portion of which is seen in India. The reason the river is considered holy is that it is said to be a drop of the Karana Ocean that leaked in when Lord Vishnu, in His incarnation as Vamanadeva, kicked a small hole in the universal shell with His toe. Thus, the water is spiritual as well as being purified by the touch of Lord Vishnu.

Gangapuja--the arati ceremony for worshiping the Ganges.

Gangotri--the source of the Ganges River in the Himalayas.

Garbhodakasayi Vishnu--the expansion of Lord Vishnu who enters into each universe.

Gayatri--the spiritual vibration or *mantra* from which the other *Vedas* were expanded and which is chanted by those who are initiated as *brahmanas* and given the spiritual understanding of Vedic philosophy.

Goloka Vrindavana--the name of Lord Krishna's spiritual planet.

Gosvami--one who is master of the senses.

Govinda--a name of Krishna which means one who gives pleasure to the cows and senses.

Grihastha--the householder order of life. One of the four *ashramas* in spiritual life.

Gunas--the modes of material nature of which there is *sattva* (goodness), *rajas* (passion), and *tamas* (ignorance).

Guru--a spiritual master.

Hare--the Lord's pleasure potency, Radharani, who is approached for accessibility to the Lord.

Hari--a name of Krishna as the one who takes away one's obstacles on the spiritual path.

Hatha-yoga--a part of the yoga system which stresses various sitting postures and exercises.

Hiranyagarbha--another name of Brahma who was born of Vishnu

Glossary

in the primordial waters within the egg of the universe.

Hrishikesa--a name for Krishna which means the master of the senses.

Impersonalism--the view that God has no personality or form, but is only an impersonal force.

Impersonalist--those who believe God has no personality or form.

Incarnation--the taking on of a body or form.

Indra--the King of heaven and controller of rain, who by his great power conquers the forces of darkness.

ISKCON--International Society for Krishna Consciousness.

Jai or *Jaya*--a term meaning victory, all glories.

Japa--the chanting one performs, usually softly, for one's own meditation.

Japa-mala--the string of beads one uses for chanting.

Jiva--the individual soul or living being.

Jivanmukta--a liberated soul, though still in the material body and universe.

Jiva-shakti--the living force.

Jnana--knowledge which may be material or spiritual.

Jnana-yoga--the process of linking with the Supreme through empirical knowledge and mental speculation.

Kali--the demigoddess who is the fierce form of the wife of Lord Shiva. The word *kali* comes from *kala*, the Sanskrit word for time: the power that dissolves or destroys everything.

Kali-yuga--the fourth and present age, the age of quarrel and confusion, which lasts 432,000 years and began 5,000 years ago.

Kalpa--a day in the life of Lord Brahma which lasts a thousand cycles of the four *yugas*.

Kama--lust or inordinate desire.

Kama sutra--a treatise on sex enjoyment.

Kapila--an incarnation of Lord Krishna who propagated the Sankhya philosophy.

Karanodakasayi Vishnu (Maha-Vishnu)--the expansion of Lord Krishna who created all the material universes.

Karma--material actions performed in regard to developing one's position or for future results which produce *karmic* reactions. It is also the reactions one endures from such fruitive activities.

Karma-yoga--the system of yoga for dovetailing one's activities for spiritual advancement.

Kirtana--chanting or singing the glories of the Lord.

Krishna--the name of the original Supreme Personality of Godhead which means the most attractive and greatest pleasure. He is the source of all other incarnations, such as Vishnu, Rama, Narasimha, Narayana, Buddha, Parashurama, Vamanadeva, Kalki at the end of Kali-yuga, etc.

Krishnaloka--the spiritual planet where Lord Krishna resides.

Kshatriya--the second class of *varna* of society, or occupation of administrative or protective service, such as warrior or military personel.

Ksirodakasayi Vishnu--the Supersoul expansion of the Lord who enters into each atom and the heart of each individual.

Kuruksetra--the place of battle 5,000 years ago between the Pandavas and the Kauravas ninety miles north of New Delhi, where Krishna spoke the *Bhagavad-gita*.

Lakshmi--the goddess of fortune and wife of Lord Vishnu.

Lila--pastimes.

Lilavataras--the many incarnations of God who appear to display various spiritual pastimes to attract the conditioned souls in the material world.

Linga--the shapeless form of Lord Shiva.

Mahabhagavata--a great devotee of the Lord.

Mahabharata--the great epic of the Pandavas, which includes the *Bhagavad-gita*, by Vyasadeva.

Maha-mantra--the best mantra for self-realization in this age, called the Hare Krishna mantra.

Mahatma--a great soul or devotee.

Mahat-tattva--the total material energy.

Maha-Vishnu or Karanodakasayi Vishnu--the Vishnu expansion of Lord Krishna from whom all the material universes emanate.

Glossary

Mandir--a temple.

Mantra--a sound vibration which prepares the mind for spiritual realization and delivers the mind from material inclinations. In some cases a mantra is chanted for specific material benefits.

Martya-loka--the earth planet, the place of death.

Maya--illusion, or anything that appears to not be connected with the eternal Absolute Truth.

Mayavadi--the impersonalist or voidist who believes that the Supreme has no form.

Moksha--liberation from material existence.

Murti--a Deity of the Lord or spiritual master that is worshiped.

Murugan--means the divine child, the Tamil name for Subramaniya, one of the sons of Shiva and Parvati, especially worshiped in South India.

Narayana--the four-handed form of the Supreme Lord.

Nirguna--without material qualities.

Nirvana--the state of no material miseries, usually the goal of the Buddhists or voidists.

Om or *Omkara*--*pranava*, the transcendental *om mantra*, generally referring to the attributeless or impersonal aspects of the Absolute.

Paramahamsa--the highest level of self-realized devotees of the Lord.

Paramatma--the Supersoul, or localized expansion of the Lord.

Parampara--the system of disciplic succession through which transcendental knowledge descends.

Pradhana--the total material energy in its unmanifest state.

Prajapati--deity presiding over procreation.

Prakriti--matter in its primordial state, the material nature.

Prana--the life air or cosmic energy.

Pranayama--control of the breathing process as in astanga or raja-yoga.

Prasada--food or other articles that have been offered to the Deity in the temple and then distributed amongst people as the blessings or mercy of the Deity.

Prema--matured love for Krishna.
Puja--the worship offered to the Deity.
Pujari--the priest who performs worship, *puja*, to the Deity.
Purusha or *Purusham*--the supreme enjoyer.
Raja-yoga--the eightfold yoga system.
Rajo-guna--the material mode of passion.
Ramachandra--an incarnation of Krishna as He appeared as the greatest of kings.
Ramayana--the great epic of the incarnation of Lord Ramachandra.
Rasa--an enjoyable taste or feeling, a relationship with God.
Rishi--saintly person who knows the Vedic knowledge.
Sacrifice--in this book it in no way pertains to human sacrifice, as many people tend to think when this word is used. But it means to engage in an austerity of some kind for a higher, spiritual purpose.
Shabda-brahma--the original spiritual vibration or energy of which the *Vedas* are composed.
Sac-cid-ananda-vigraha--the transcendental form of the Lord or of the living entity which is eternal, full of knowledge and bliss.
Sadhana--a specific practice or discipline for attaining God realization.
Sadhu--Indian holy man or devotee.
Saguna Brahman--the aspect of the Absolute with form and qualities.
Samadhi--trance, the perfection of being absorbed in the Absolute.
Samsara--rounds of life; cycles of birth and death; reincarnation.
Sanatana-dharma--the eternal nature of the living being, to love and render service to the supreme lovable object, the Lord.
Sangam--the confluence of two or more rivers.
Sankhya--analytical understanding of material nature, the body, and the soul.
Sankirtana-yajna--the prescribed sacrifice for this age: congregational chanting of the holy names of God.
Sannyasa--the renounced order of life, the highest of the four *ashramas* on the spiritual path.

Glossary

Sarasvati--the goddess of knowledge and intelligence.
Sattva-guna--the material mode of goodness.
Satya-yuga--the first of the four ages which lasts 1,728,000 years.
Shaivites--worshipers of Lord Shiva.
Shakti--energy, potency or power, the active principle in creation. Also the active power or wife of a deity, such as Shiva/Shakti.
Shastra--the authentic revealed scripture.
Shiva--the benevolent one, the demigod who is in charge of the material mode of ignorance and the destruction of the universe. Part of the triad of Brahma, Vishnu, and Shiva who continually create, maintain, and destroy the universe. He is known as Rudra when displaying his destructive aspect.
Sikha--a tuft of hair on the back of the head signifying that one is a Vaishnava.
Smaranam--remembering the Lord.
Smriti--the traditional Vedic knowledge "that is remembered" from what was directly heard by or revealed to the *rishis*.
Sravanam--hearing about the Lord.
Srimad-Bhagavatam--the most ripened fruit of the tree of Vedic knowledge compiled by Vyasadeva. Also called the *Bhagavata Purana*.
Sruti--scriptures that were received directly from God and transmitted orally by brahmanas or *rishis* down through succeeding generations. Traditionally, it is considered the four primary *Vedas*.
Sudra--the working class of society, the fourth of the *varnas*.
Svami--one who can control his mind and senses.
Tamo-guna--the material mode of ignorance.
Tapasya--voluntary austerity for spiritual advancement.
Tilok--the clay markings that signify a person's body as a temple, and the sect or school of thought of the person.
Tirtha--a holy place of pilgrimage.
Treta-yuga--the second of the four ages which lasts 1,296,000 years.

Tulasi--the small tree that grows where worship to Krishna is found. It is called the embodiment of devotion, and the incarnation of Vrinda-devi.

Upanishads--the portions of the *Vedas* which primarily explain philosophically the Absolute Truth. It is knowledge of Brahman which releases one from the world and allows one to attain self-realization when received from a qualified teacher. Except for the *Isa Upanishad*, which is the 40th chapter of the *Vajasaneyi Samhita* of the *Sukla* (*White*) *Yajur-veda*, the *Upanishads* are connected to the four primary *Vedas*, generally found in the *Brahmanas*.

Vaikunthas--the planets located in the spiritual sky.

Vaishnava--a worshiper of the Supreme Lord Vishnu or Krishna and His expansions or incarnations.

Vaishnava-aparadha--an offense against a Vaisnava or devotee, which can negate all of one's spiritual progress.

Vaisya--the third class of society engaged in business or farming.

Vanaprastha--the third of the four *ashramas* of spiritual life in which one retires from family life in preparation for the renounced order.

Varna--sometimes referred to as caste, a division of society, such as brahmana (a priestly intellectual), a kshatriya (ruler or manager), vaishya (a merchant, banker, or farmer), and sudra (common laborer).

Varnashrama--the system of four divisions of society and four orders of spiritual life.

Vedanta-sutras--the philosophical conclusion of the four *Vedas*.

Vedas--generally means the four primary *samhitas;* the *Rig, Yajur, Sama,* and *Atharva*.

Vidya--knowledge.

Vikarma--sinful activities performed without scriptural authority and which produce sinful reactions.

Virajanadi or *Viraja River*--the space that separates the material creation from the spiritual sky.

Vishnu--the expansion of Lord Krishna who enters into the

material energy to create and maintain the cosmic world.

Vrindavana--the place where Lord Krishna displayed His village pastimes 5,000 years ago, and is considered to be part of the spiritual abode.

Vyasadeva--the incarnation of God who appeared as the greatest philosopher who compiled all the *Vedas* into written form.

Yajna--a ritual or austerity that is done as a sacrifice for spiritual merit, or ritual worship of a demigod for good *karmic* reactions.

Yamaraja--the demigod and lord of death who directs the living entities to various punishments according to their activities.

Yantra--a machine, instrument, or mystical diagram used in ritual worship.

Yoga--linking up with the Absolute.

Yoga-*siddhi*--mystic perfection.

Yuga-avataras--the incarnations of God who appear in each of the four *yugas* to explain the authorized system of self-realization in that age.

INDEX

Absolute Truth
    all there was before creation.......... 92
Actions in the modes.... 202
Ailo-gita............. 172
Arjuna
    wanted only Krishna on his side......... 192
Asanas
    promotes better health.275
Astanga-yoga.......... 102
Austerities
    for spiritual merit.... 195
Being spiritual........ 275
Bhagavan.......... 19, 104
    the Supreme Person. . 136
Bhakti-yoga.... 90, 101, 136
    can deliver the worst of sinners......... 163
    gives both the means and end result of yoga. 180
    gives fearlessness.... 158
    how to meditate on Krishna......... 159
    king of education.... 136
    knowledge must be spread 165
    the primary principles. 146
    why it should be done. 151
Birth.................. 87
Body, created by material nature........... 75

does material activities. 75
Brahmaloka........... 125
Brahman.......... 102, 103
Brahman realization...... 45
Brahmayoti........... 103
Charity
    of different types..... 195
Consciousness
    developed through life. 85
Cosmic creation
    under Krishna........ 67
Criticism............. 214
Death................. 87
Demonic views......... 171
Determination in the modes
    203
Devotional service...... 173
    brings Krishna under control......... 113
Divine Love............ 81
Divinity in each of us..... 81
Duryodhana........... 192
Faith
    different types....... 194
Food
    offered to Krishna.... 138
Foods in the modes..... 201
Gifts
    of different types..... 195
God
    seeing God everywhere.127
Goloka Vrindavana...... 50

Index

Happiness in the modes.. 203
Human birth
    is rare. 62
India
    why a rapid deterioration
    190
Intelligence
    when stolen by the minds attachment for material pleasure
    211
Jnana-yoga. 90, 91
Kali-yuga
    began in 3102 BC. 60
    when the age began.. . . 30
Kamsa
    why Krishna killed him.93
Karma.. 86
    is erased by bhakti. . . 161
Karma-yoga. 90, 94
Knowledge
    types of. 56
Krishna
    accepts only vegetarian foods.. 138
    basis of the Brahman. 103
    better than Brahman realization.. 45
    cause of all causes.. . . . 43
    descends into this world27
    description of His form in the heart. 120
    easy to obtain through devotion. 112
    explanation of the name. 7
    failing to know Him. . . 48
    His appearance on this planet. 30
    His beauty. 38
    His devotees are simply satisfied in service.188
    His eternal abode. 50
    His instructions.. 207
    how to attain Him.. . . 181
    how to understand Him.44
    instructions on liberation
    174
    left this world in 3102 BC
    60
    never manifest to the foolish. 46
    no Truth superior to Him
    115
    not a representation.. . . 18
    pastimes full of meaning and purpose. 36
    perceived by different people in different ways. 38
    returning to Him is real liberation. 180
    source of all other incarnations of God 24
    source of all power and beauty. 128
    source of all spiritual and material worlds.. . . 20
    teachings on jnana-yoga91
    teachings on karma-yoga
    94

teachings on yoga 102, 105
the Absolute Truth. . . 183
the ever-loving God. . . 185
thoughts of Him uplift our spiritual awareness 186
who is dear to Him. . . 141
who is He?. 5
Krishnaloka 50
Kuruksetra war
   near 3143 BC. 60
Liberation. 174
   returning to Krishna. . 180
Lust
   dangers of it. 169
Maharloka. 125
Mantra-yoga
   especially for this age. 278
Material attachment
   based on lack of spiritual knowledge. 169
Material Bondage. 167
Material emotions
   are all creations of the illusory energy. . . . 69
Material existence
   and its purpose. 65
   continues with false aim of life. 76
   destroyed only by real knowledge. 76
   like a dream. 78
Materialistic workers
   are often unhappy. 66
Maya
   makes men forget their real selves. 68
Meditation. 102
Krishna's instructions
. . . . 102, 118
   on Krishna. 159
   on the Supreme Person 181
   the ultimate goal. 113
Modes of material nature
. . . . 196, 198
Mystic powers. 117
Paramatma. 104
   Supersoul within. 133
Parents
   serving them. 213
Philosophical research culminates in understanding the Supreme. 94
Prasada. 138
Raja-yoga. 102
Real fulfillment. 69
Reincarnation. 84
Religion
   various persuasions. . . 194
Religious scriptures. 204
   different types. 197
Residences in the modes. 203
Ruler
   accepts one-sixth of all sinful activities. . . 215
   duties to people. 214
Saintly persons. 209
Satyaloka. 125
Self
   realization is the supreme

Index

goal of life. 75
separate from material activities. 75
Sense pleasures
   have a beginning and end 66
Senses
   how they can be controlled. 175
   withdrawn from sense objects. 175
Soul
   is eternal. 84
   separate from the material body. 78
Spiritual knowledge
   must be spread. 165
Supersoul. 104, 133
Supreme abode
   has innumerable activities and recreation. . . . 180
Time factor. 209
Transcendence
   symptoms of one in it. 174
Truth
   the highest truth. 116
Vedas
   primarily deal with modes of material nature. 174
Vedic culture
   practice it as it should be 192
Vedic knowledge

first spoken to Brahma 60
how it descends down through time. 59
its appearance. 60
offers many Vedic rituals, mantras, and rewards 61
Vedic literature
   provides details about our spiritual identity. . . 72
Vegetarian foods. 138
Vishnu
   the supreme controller. 186
Women
   helpful duties. 211
Yoga. 102
   an unsuccessful yogi. . 110
   benefits. 275
   best of yogis. 110
   easiest is remembering Krishna. 112
   leaving the body. 123
   overcoming disturbances 111
   the difficulties. 109
   the goal. 108
   the highest yoga system 113
   the ultimate goal. 114
   ultimate goal. 113
Yugas
   their timing. 60

ABOUT THE AUTHOR

Stephen Knapp grew up in a Christian family, during which time he seriously studied the Bible to understand its teachings. In his late teenage years, however, he sought answers to questions not easily explained in Christian theology. So he began to search through other religions and philosophies from around the world and started to find the answers for which he was looking. He also studied a variety of occult sciences, ancient mythology, mysticism, yoga, and the spiritual teachings of the East. After his first reading of the *Bhagavad-gita*, he felt he had found the last piece of the puzzle he had been putting together through all of his research. Therefore, he continued to study all of the major Vedic texts of India to gain a better understanding of the Vedic science.

It is known amongst all Eastern mystics that anyone, regardless of qualifications, academic or otherwise, who does not engage in the spiritual practices described in the Vedic texts cannot actually enter into understanding the depths of the Vedic spiritual science, nor acquire the realizations that should accompany it. So, rather than pursuing his research in an academic atmosphere at a university, Stephen directly engaged in the spiritual disciplines that have been recommended for hundreds of years. He continued his study of Vedic knowledge and spiritual practice under the guidance of a spiritual master. Through this process, and with the sanction of His Divine Grace A. C. Bhaktivedanta Swami Prabhupada, he became initiated into the genuine and authorized spiritual line of the Brahma-Madhava-Gaudiya *sampradaya*, which is a disciplic succession that descends back through Sri Chaitanya Mahaprabhu and Sri Vyasadeva, the compiler of Vedic literature, and further back to Sri Krishna. At that time he was given the spiritual name of Sri Nandanandana dasa. In this way, he has been practicing yoga, especially bhakti-yoga, for forty plus years, and has attained many insights and realizations through this means. Besides being *brahminically* initiated, Stephen has also been to India several times and traveled extensively throughout the country, visiting

About the Author

most of the major holy places and gaining a wide variety of spiritual experiences that only such places can give. He has also spent nearly 40 years in the management of various temples.

Stephen has put the culmination of over forty years of continuous research and travel experience into his books in an effort to share it with those who are also looking for spiritual understanding. More books are forthcoming, so stay in touch through his website to find out further developments.

More information about Stephen, his projects, books, free ebooks, and numerous articles and videos can be found on his website at: www.stephen-knapp.com or http://stephenknapp.info or his blog at http://stephenknapp.wordpress.com.

Stephen has continued to write books that include in *The Eastern Answers ot the Mysteries of Life* series:
1. *The Secret Teachings of the Vedas: The Eastern Answers to the Mysteries of Life*
2. *The Universal Path to Enlightenment*
3. *The Vedic Prophecies: A New Look into the Future*
4. *How the Universe was Created and Our Purpose In It*
   He has also written:
5. *Toward World Peace: Seeing the Unity Between Us All*
6. *Facing Death: Welcoming the Afterlife*
7. *The Key to Real Happiness*
8. *Proof of Vedic Culture's Global Existence*
9. *The Heart of Hinduism: The Eastern Path to Freedom, Enlightenment and Illumination*
10. *The Power of the Dharma: An Introduction to Hinduism and Vedic Culture*
11. *Vedic Culture: The Difference it can Make in Your Life*
12. *Reincarnation & Karma: How They Really Affect Us*
13. *The Eleventh Commandment: The Next Step for Social Spiritual Development*
14. *Seeing Spiritual India: A Guide to Temples, Holy Sites, Festivals and Traditions*

15. *Crimes Against India: And the Need to Protect its Ancient Vedic Tradition*
16. *Yoga and Meditation: Their Real Purpose and How to Get Started*
17. *Avatars, Gods and Goddesses of Vedic Culture: Understanding the Characteristics, Powers and Positions of the Hindu Divinities*
18. *The Soul: Understanding Our Real Identity*
19. *Prayers, Mantras and Gayatris: A Collection for Insights, Protection, Spiritual Growth, and Many Other Blessings*
20. *Krishna Deities and Their Miracles: How the Images of Lord Krishna Interact with Their Devotees*
21. *Defending Vedic Dharma: Tackling the Issues to Make a Difference*
22. *Advancements of the Ancient Vedic Culture*
23. *Spreading Vedic Traditions Through Temples*
24. *The Bhakti-Yoga Handbook*
25. *Destined for Infinity,* an exciting novel for those who prefer lighter reading, or learning spiritual knowledge in the context of an action oriented, spiritual adventure.

If you have enjoyed this book, or if you are serious about finding higher levels of real spiritual Truth, and learning more about the mysteries of India's Vedic culture, then you will also want to get other books written by Stephen Knapp, which include:

The Secret Teachings of the Vedas
The Eastern Answers to the Mysteries of Life

This book presents the essence of the ancient Eastern philosophy and summarizes some of the most elevated and important of all spiritual knowledge. This enlightening information is explained in a clear and concise way and is essential for all who want to increase their spiritual understanding, regardless of what their religious background may be. If you are looking for a book to give you an in-depth introduction to the Vedic spiritual knowledge, and to get you started in real spiritual understanding, this is the book!

The topics include: What is your real spiritual identity; the Vedic explanation of the soul; scientific evidence that consciousness is separate from but interacts with the body; the real unity between us all; how to attain the highest happiness and freedom from the cause of suffering; the law of karma and reincarnation; the karma of a nation; where you are really going in life; the real process of progressive evolution; life after death—heaven, hell, or beyond; a description of the spiritual realm; the nature of the Absolute Truth—personal God or impersonal force; recognizing the existence of the Supreme; the reason why we exist at all; and much more. This book provides the answers to questions not found in other religions or philosophies, and condenses information from a wide variety of sources that would take a person years to assemble. It also contains many quotations from the Vedic texts to let the texts speak for themselves, and to show the knowledge the Vedas have held for thousands of years. It also explains the history and origins of the Vedic literature. This book has been called one of the best reviews of Eastern philosophy available.

Trim size 6"x9", 320 pages, ISBN: 0-9617410-1-5, $19.95.

The Universal Path to Enlightenment
The Way to Spiritual Success for Everyone

This book brings together the easy and joyful principles and practices that are common to all major religions of the world. These are what can be used by all people from any culture or tradition for the highest spiritual progress, and to bring about a united, one world religion. This is a happy process of spiritual success for everyone. This is much easier to recognize than most people think, and is a way to bring down the differences, barriers and separations that seem to exist between religions. This book also presents:

- A most interesting and revealing survey of the major spiritual paths of the world, describing their histories, goals, and how they developed, which are not always what we would expect of a religion;
- The philosophical basis of Christianity, Judaism, Islam, Hinduism, Buddhism, Zoroastrianism, Jainism, Sikhism, etc., and the types of spiritual knowledge they contain;
- How Christianity and Judaism were greatly influenced by the early pre-Christian or "pagan" religions and adopted many of their legends, holidays, and rituals that are still accepted and practiced today;
- The essential teachings of Jesus;
- Benefits of spiritual advancement that affect all aspects of a person's life, and the world in which we live;
- How spiritual enlightenment is the real cure for social ills;
- And, most importantly, how to attain the real purpose of a spiritual process to be truly successful, and how to practice the path that is especially recommended as the easiest and most effective for the people of this age.

This book is 6"x9" trim size, 340 pages, ISBN: 1453644660, $19.95.

The Vedic Prophecies:
A New Look into the Future

The Vedic prophecies take you to the end of time! This is the first book ever to present the unique predictions found in the ancient Vedic texts of India. These prophecies are like no others and will provide you with a very different view of the future and how things fit together in the plan for the universe.

Now you can discover the amazing secrets that are hidden in the oldest spiritual writings on the planet. Find out what they say about the distant future, and what the seers of long ago saw in their visions of the destiny of the world.

This book will reveal predictions of deteriorating social changes and how to avoid them; future droughts and famines; low-class rulers and evil governments; whether there will be another appearance (second coming) of God; and predictions of a new spiritual awareness and how it will spread around the world. You will also learn the answers to such questions as:

- Does the future get worse or better?
- Will there be future world wars or global disasters?
- What lies beyond the predictions of Nostradamus, the Mayan prophecies, or the Biblical apocalypse?
- Are we in the end times? How to recognize them if we are.
- Does the world come to an end? If so, when and how?

Now you can find out what the future holds. The Vedic Prophecies carry an important message and warning for all humanity, which needs to be understood now!

Trim size 6"x9", 325 pages, ISBN:0-9617410-4-X, $20.95.

How the Universe was Created And Our Purpose In It

This book provides answers and details about the process of creation that are not available in any other traditions, religions, or areas of science. It offers the oldest rendition of the creation and presents insights into the spiritual purpose of it and what we are really meant to do here.

Every culture in the world and most religions have their own descriptions of the creation, and ideas about from where we came and what we should do. Unfortunately, these are often short and generalized versions that lack details. Thus, they are often given no better regard than myths. However, there are descriptions that give more elaborate explanations of how the cosmic creation fully manifested which are found in the ancient Vedic *Puranas* of India, some of the oldest spiritual writings on the planet. These descriptions provide the details and answers that other versions leave out. Furthermore, these Vedic descriptions often agree, and sometimes disagree, with the modern scientific theories of creation, and offer some factors that science has yet to consider.

Now, with this book, we can get a clearer understanding of how this universe appears, what is its real purpose, from where we really came, how we fit into the plan for the universe, and if there is a way out of here. Some of the many topics included are:

- Comparisons between other creation legends.
- Detailed descriptions of the dawn of creation and how the material energy developed and caused the formation of the cosmos.
- What is the primary source of the material and spiritual elements.
- Insights into the primal questions of, "Who am I? Why am I here? Where have I come from? What is the purpose of this universe and my life?"
- An alternative description of the evolutionary development of the various forms of life.
- Seeing beyond the temporary nature of the material worlds, and more.

This book will provide some of the most profound insights into these questions and topics. It will also give any theist more information and understanding about how the universe is indeed a creation of God.

This book is 6" x 9" trim size, $19.95, 308 pages, ISBN: 1456460455.

Proof of Vedic Culture's Global Existence

This book provides evidence which makes it clear that the ancient Vedic culture was once a global society. Even today we can see its influence in any part of the world. Thus, it becomes obvious that before the world became full of distinct and separate cultures, religions and countries, it was once united in a common brotherhood of Vedic culture, with common standards, principles, and representations of God.

No matter what we may consider our present religion, society or country, we are all descendants of this ancient global civilization. Thus, the Vedic culture is the parent of all humanity and the original ancestor of all religions. In this way, we all share a common heritage.

This book is an attempt to allow humanity to see more clearly its universal roots. This book provides a look into:

- How Vedic knowledge was given to humanity by the Supreme.
- The history and traditional source of the Vedas and Vedic Aryan society.
- Who were the original Vedic Aryans. How Vedic society was a global influence and what shattered this world-wide society. How Sanskrit faded from being a global language.
- Many scientific discoveries over the past several centuries are only rediscoveries of what the Vedic literature already knew.
- How the origins of world literature are found in India and Sanskrit.
- The links between the Vedic and other ancient cultures, such as the Sumerians, Persians, Egyptians, Romans, Greeks, and others.
- Links between the Vedic tradition and Judaism, Christianity, Islam, and Buddhism.
- How many of the western holy sites, churches, and mosques were once the sites of Vedic holy places and sacred shrines.
- The Vedic influence presently found in such countries as Britain, France, Russia, Greece, Israel, Arabia, China, Japan, and in areas of Scandinavia, the Middle East, Africa, the South Pacific, and the Americas.
- Uncovering the truth of India's history: Powerful evidence that shows how many mosques and Muslim buildings were once opulent Vedic temples, including the Taj Mahal, Delhi's Jama Masjid, Kutab Minar, as well as buildings in many other cities, such as Agra, Ahmedabad, Bijapur, etc.
- How there is presently a need to plan for the survival of Vedic culture.

This book is sure to provide some amazing facts and evidence about the truth of world history and the ancient, global Vedic Culture. This book has enough startling information and historical evidence to cause a major shift in the way we view religious history and the basis of world traditions.

This book is 6"x9" trim size, 431 pages, ISBN: 978-1-4392-4648-1, $20.99.

Toward World Peace: Seeing the Unity Between Us All

This book points out the essential reasons why peace in the world and cooperation amongst people, communities, and nations have been so difficult to establish. It also advises the only way real peace and harmony amongst humanity can be achieved.

In order for peace and unity to exist we must first realize what barriers and divisions keep us apart. Only then can we break through those barriers to see the unity that naturally exists between us all. Then, rather than focus on our differences, it is easier to recognize our similarities and common goals. With a common goal established, all of humanity can work together to help each other reach that destiny.

This book is short and to the point. It is a thought provoking book and will provide inspiration for anyone. It is especially useful for those working in politics, religion, interfaith, race relations, the media, the United Nations, teaching, or who have a position of leadership in any capacity. It is also for those of us who simply want to spread the insights needed for bringing greater levels of peace, acceptance, unity, and equality between friends, neighbours, and communities. Such insights include:

- The factors that keep us apart.
- Breaking down cultural distinctions.
- Breaking down the religious differences.
- Seeing through bodily distinctions.
- We are all working to attain the same things.
- Our real identity: The basis for common ground.
- Seeing the Divinity within each of us.
- What we can do to bring unity between everyone we meet.

This book carries an important message and plan of action that we must incorporate into our lives and plans for the future if we intend to ever bring peace and unity between us.

This book is $6.95, 90 pages, 6" x 9" trim size, ISBN: 1452813744.

Facing Death
Welcoming the Afterlife

Many people are afraid of death, or do not know how to prepare for it nor what to expect. So this book is provided to relieve anyone of the fear that often accompanies the thought of death, and to supply a means to more clearly understand the purpose of it and how we can use it to our advantage. It will also help the survivors of the departed souls to better understand what has happened and how to cope with it. Furthermore, it shows that death is not a tragedy, but a natural course of events meant to help us reach our destiny.

This book is easy to read, with soothing and comforting wisdom, along with stories of people who have been with departing souls and what they have experienced. It is written especially for those who have given death little thought beforehand, but now would like to have some preparedness for what may need to be done regarding the many levels of the experience and what might take place during this transition.

To assist you in preparing for your own death, or that of a loved one, you will find guidelines for making one's final days as peaceful and as smooth as possible, both physically and spiritually. Preparing for deathcan transform your whole outlook in a positive way, if understood properly. Some of the topics in the book include:

- The fear of death and learning to let go.
- The opportunity of death: The portal into the next life.
- This earth and this body are no one's real home, so death is natural.
- Being practical and dealing with the final responsibilities.
- Forgiving yourself and others before you go.
- Being the assistant of one leaving this life.
- Connecting with the person inside the disease.
- Surviving the death of a loved one.
- Stories of being with dying, and an amazing near-death-experience.
- Connecting to the spiritual side of death.
- What happens while leaving the body.
- What difference the consciousness makes during death, and how to attain the best level of awareness to carry you through it, or what death will be like and how to prepare for it, this book will help you.

Published by iUniverse.com, $13.95, 135 pages, ISBN: 978-1-4401-1344-4

Destined for Infinity

Deep within the mystical and spiritual practices of India are doors that lead to various levels of both higher and lower planes of existence. Few people from the outside are ever able to enter into the depths of these practices to experience such levels of reality.

This is the story of the mystical adventure of a man, Roman West, who entered deep into the secrets of India where few other Westerners have been able to penetrate. While living with a master in the Himalayan foothills and traveling the mystical path that leads to the Infinite, he witnesses the amazing powers the mystics can achieve and undergoes some of the most unusual experiences of his life. Under the guidance of a master that he meets in the mountains, he gradually develops mystic abilities of his own and attains the sacred vision of the enlightened sages and enters the unfathomable realm of Infinity. However, his peaceful life in the hills comes to an abrupt end when he is unexpectedly forced to confront the powerful forces of darkness that have been unleashed by an evil Tantric priest to kill both Roman and his master. His only chance to defeat the intense forces of darkness depends on whatever spiritual strength he has been able to develop.

This story includes traditions and legends that have existed for hundreds and thousands of years. All of the philosophy, rituals, mystic powers, forms of meditation, and descriptions of the Absolute are authentic and taken from narrations found in many of the sacred books of the East, or gathered by the author from his own experiences in India and information from various sages themselves.

This book will will prepare you to perceive the multi-dimensional realities that exist all around us, outside our sense perception. This is a book that will give you many insights into the broad possibilities of our life and purpose in this world.

Published by iUniverse.com, 255 pages, 6" x 9" trim size, $16.95, ISBN: 0-595-33959-X.

Reincarnation and Karma: How They Really Affect Us

Everyone may know a little about reincarnation, but few understand the complexities and how it actually works. Now you can find out how reincarnation and karma really affect us. Herein all of the details are provided on how a person is implicated for better or worse by their own actions. You will understand why particular situations in life happen, and how to make improvements for one's future. You will see why it appears that bad things happen to good people, or even why good things happen to bad people, and what can be done about it. Other topics include:

- Reincarnation recognized throughout the world
- The most ancient teachings on reincarnation
- Reincarnation in Christianity
- How we transmigrate from one body to another
- Life between lives
- Going to heaven or hell
- The reason for reincarnation
- Free will and choice
- Karma of the nation
- How we determine our own destiny
- What our next life may be like
- Becoming free from all karma and how to prepare to make our next life the best possible.

Combine this with modern research into past life memories and experiences and you will have a complete view of how reincarnation and karma really operate.

Published by iUniverse.com, 135 pages, 6" x 9" trim size, $13.95, ISBN: 0-595-34199-3.

Vedic Culture
The Difference It Can Make In Your Life

The Vedic culture of India is rooted in Sanatana-dharma, the eternal and universal truths that are beneficial to everyone. It includes many avenues of self-development that an increasing number of people from the West are starting to investigate and use, including:

- Yoga
- Meditation and spiritual practice
- Vedic astrology
- Ayurveda
- Vedic gemology
- Vastu or home arrangement
- Environmental awareness
- Vegetarianism
- Social cooperation and arrangement
- The means for global peace
- And much more

Vedic Culture: The Difference It Can Make In Your Life shows the advantages of the Vedic paths of improvement and self-discovery that you can use in your life to attain higher personal awareness, happiness, and fulfillment. It also provides a new view of what these avenues have to offer from some of the most prominent writers on Vedic culture in the West, who discovered how it has affected and benefited their own lives. They write about what it has done for them and then explain how their particular area of interest can assist others. The noted authors include, David Frawley, Subhash Kak, Chakrapani Ullal, Michael Cremo, Jeffrey Armstrong, Robert Talyor, Howard Beckman, Andy Fraenkel, George Vutetakis, Pratichi Mathur, Dhan Rousse, Arun Naik, Parama Karuna Devi, and Stephen Knapp, all of whom have numerous authored books or articles of their own.

For the benefit of individuals and social progress, the Vedic system is as relevant today as it was in ancient times. Discover why there is a growing renaissance in what the Vedic tradition has to offer in *Vedic Culture*.

Published by iUniverse.com, 300 pages, 6"x 9" trim size, $22.95, ISBN: 0-595-37120-5.

The Heart of Hinduism:
The Eastern Path to Freedom, Empowerment and Illumination

This is a definitive and easy to understand guide to the essential as well as devotional heart of the Vedic/Hindu philosophy. You will see the depths of wisdom and insights that are contained within this profound spiritual knowledge. It is especially good for anyone who lacks the time to research the many topics that are contained within the numerous Vedic manuscripts and to see the advantages of knowing them. This also provides you with a complete process for progressing on the spiritual path, making way for individual empowerment, freedom, and spiritual illumination. All the information is now at your fingertips.

Some of the topics you will find include:
- A complete review of all the Vedic texts and the wide range of topics they contain. This also presents the traditional origins of the Vedic philosophy and how it was developed, and their philosophical conclusion.
- The uniqueness and freedom of the Vedic system.
- A description of the main yoga processes and their effectiveness.
- A review of the Vedic Gods, such as Krishna, Shiva, Durga, Ganesh, and others. You will learn the identity and purpose of each.
- You will have the essential teachings of Lord Krishna who has given some of the most direct and insightful of all spiritual messages known to humanity, and the key to direct spiritual perception.
- The real purpose of yoga and the religious systems.
- What is the most effective spiritual path for this modern age and what it can do for you, with practical instructions for deep realizations.
- The universal path of devotion, the one world religion.
- How Vedic culture is the last bastion of deep spiritual truth.
- Plus many more topics and information for your enlightenment.

So to dive deep into what is Hinduism and the Vedic path to freedom and spiritual perception, this book will give you a jump start. Knowledge is the process of personal empowerment, and no knowledge will give you more power than deep spiritual understanding. And those realizations described in the Vedic culture are the oldest and some of the most profound that humanity has ever known.

Published by iUniverse.com, 650 pages, $35.95, 6" x 9" trim size, ISBN: 0-595-35075-5.

The Power of the Dharma
An Introduction to Hinduism and Vedic Culture

The Power of the Dharma offers you a concise and easy-to-understand overview of the essential principles and customs of Hinduism and the reasons for them. It provides many insights into the depth and value of the timeless wisdom of Vedic spirituality and why the Dharmic path has survived for so many hundreds of years. It reveals why the Dharma is presently enjoying a renaissance of an increasing number of interested people who are exploring its teachings and seeing what its many techniques of Self-discovery have to offer.

Herein you will find:
- Quotes by noteworthy people on the unique qualities of Hinduism
- Essential principles of the Vedic spiritual path
- Particular traits and customs of Hindu worship and explanations of them
- Descriptions of the main Yoga systems
- The significance and legends of the colorful Hindu festivals
- Benefits of Ayurveda, Vastu, Vedic astrology and gemology,
- Important insights of Dharmic life and how to begin.

The Dharmic path can provide you the means for attaining your own spiritual realizations and experiences. In this way it is as relevant today as it was thousands of years ago. This is the power of the Dharma since its universal teachings have something to offer anyone.

Published by iUniverse.com, 170 pages, 6" x 9" trim size, $16.95, ISBN: 0-595-39352-7.

Seeing Spiritual India
A Guide to Temples, Holy Sites, Festivals and Traditions

This book is for anyone who wants to know of the many holy sites that you can visit while traveling within India, how to reach them, and what is the history and significance of these most spiritual of sacred sites, temples, and festivals. It also provides a deeper understanding of the mysteries and spiritual traditions of India.

This book includes:
- Descriptions of the temples and their architecture, and what you will see at each place.
- Explanations of holy places of Hindus, Buddhists, Sikhs, Jains, Parsis, and Muslims.
- The spiritual benefits a person acquires by visiting them.
- Convenient itineraries to take to see the most of each area of India, which is divided into East, Central, South, North, West, the Far Northeast, and Nepal.
- Packing list suggestions and how to prepare for your trip, and problems to avoid.
- How to get the best experience you can from your visit to India.
- How the spiritual side of India can positively change you forever.

This book goes beyond the usual descriptions of the typical tourist attractions and opens up the spiritual venue waiting to be revealed for a far deeper experience on every level.

Published by iUniverse.com, 592 pages, $33.95, ISBN: 978-0-595-50291-2.

Crimes Against India:
And the Need to Protect its Ancient Vedic

1000 Years of Attacks Against Hinduism and What to Do about It

India has one of the oldest and most dynamic cultures of the world. Yet, many people do not know of the many attacks, wars, atrocities and sacrifices that Indian people have had to undergo to protect and preserve their country and spiritual tradition over the centuries. Many people also do not know of the many ways in which this profound heritage is being attacked and threatened today, and what we can do about it.

Therefore, some of the topics included are:
- How there is a war against Hinduism and its yoga culture.
- The weaknesses of India that allowed invaders to conquer her.
- Lessons from India's real history that should not be forgotten.
- The atrocities committed by the Muslim invaders, and how they tried to destroy Vedic culture and its many temples, and slaughtered thousands of Indian Hindus.
- How the British viciously exploited India and its people for its resources.
- How the cruelest of all Christian Inquisitions in Goa tortured and killed thousands of Hindus.
- Action plans for preserving and strengthening Vedic India.
- How all Hindus must stand up and be strong for Sanatana-dharma, and promote the cooperation and unity for a Global Vedic Community.

India is a most resilient country, and is presently becoming a great economic power in the world. It also has one of the oldest and dynamic cultures the world has ever known, but few people seem to understand the many trials and difficulties that the country has faced, or the present problems India is still forced to deal with in preserving the culture of the majority Hindus who live in the country. This is described in the real history of the country, which a decreasing number of people seem to recall.

Therefore, this book is to honor the efforts that have been shown by those in the past who fought and worked to protect India and its culture, and to help preserve India as the homeland of a living and dynamic Vedic tradition of Sanatana-dharma (the eternal path of duty and wisdom).

Available from iUniverse.com. 370 pages, $24.95, ISBN: 978-1-4401-1158-7.

The Eleventh Commandment
The Next Step in Social Spiritual Development

A New Code to Bring Humanity to a Higher Level of Spiritual Consciousness

This is some of Stephen's boldest and most direct writing. Based on the Universal Spiritual Truths, or the deeper levels of spiritual understanding, it presents a new code in a completely nonsectarian way that anyone should be able and willing to follow. Herein is the next step for consideration, which can be used as a tool for guidance, and for setting a higher standard in our society today. This new commandment expects and directs us toward a change in our social awareness and spiritual consciousness. It is conceived, formulated, and now provided to assist humanity in reaching its true destiny, and to bring a new spiritual dimension into the basic fabric of our ordinary every day life. It is a key that unlocks the doors of perception, and opens up a whole new aspect of spiritual understanding for all of us to view. It is the commandment which precepts us to gain the knowledge of the hidden mysteries, which have for so long remained an enigma to the confused and misdirected men of this world. It holds the key which unlocks the answers to man's quest for peace and happiness, and the next step for spiritual growth on a dynamic and all-inclusive social level.

This 11th Commandment and the explanations provided show the means for curing social ills, reducing racial prejudices, and create more harmony between the races and cultures. It shows how to recognize the Divine within yourself and all beings around you. It shows how we can bring some of the spiritual atmosphere into this earthly existence, especially if we expect to reach the higher domain after death. It also explains how to:

- Identify our real Self and distinguish it from our false self.
- Open our hearts to one another and view others with greater appreciation.
- Utilize higher consciousness in everyday life.
- Find inner contentment and joy.
- Attain a higher spiritual awareness and perception.
- Manifest God's plan for the world.
- Be a reflection of God's love toward everyone.
- Attain the Great Realization of perceiving the Divine in all beings.

The world is in need of a new direction in its spiritual development, and this 11th Commandment is given as the next phase to manifest humanity's most elevated potentials.

This book is $13.95, Size: 6" x 9", Pages: 128, ISBN: 0-595-46741-5.

Yoga and Meditation
Their Real Purpose and How to Get Started

Yoga is a nonsectarian spiritual science that has been practiced and developed over thousands of years. The benefits of yoga are numerous. On the mental level it strengthens concentration, determination, and builds a stronger character that can more easily sustain various tensions in our lives for peace of mind. The assortment of *asanas* or postures also provide stronger health and keeps various diseases in check. They improve physical strength, endurance and flexibility. These are some of the goals of yoga.

Its ultimate purpose is to raise our consciousness to directly perceive the spiritual dimension. Then we can have our own spiritual experiences. The point is that the more spiritual we become, the more we can perceive that which is spiritual. As we develop and grow in this way through yoga, the questions about spiritual life are no longer a mystery to solve, but become a reality to experience. It becomes a practical part of our lives. This book will show you how to do that. Some of the topics include:

- Benefits of yoga
- The real purpose of yoga
- The types of yoga, such as Hatha yoga, Karma yoga, Raja and Astanga yogas, Kundalini yoga, Bhakti yoga, Mudra yoga, Mantra yoga, and others.
- The Chakras and Koshas
- Asanas and postures, and the Surya Namaskar
- Pranayama and breathing techniques for inner changes
- Deep meditation and how to proceed
- The methods for using mantras
- Attaining spiritual enlightenment, and much more

This book is 6"x9" trim size, $17.95, 240 pages, 32 illustration, ISBN: 1451553269.

Avatars, Gods and Goddesses of Vedic Culture

The Characteristics, Powers and Positions of the Hindu Divinities

Understanding the assorted Divinities or gods and goddesses of the Vedic or Hindu pantheon is not so difficult as some people may think when it is presented simply and effectively. And that is what you will find in this book. This will open you to many of the possibilities and potentials of the Vedic tradition, and show how it has been able to cater to and fulfill the spiritual needs and development of so many people since time immemorial. Here you will find there is something for everyone.

This takes you into the heart of the deep, Vedic spiritual knowledge of how to perceive the Absolute Truth, the Supreme and the various powers and agents of the universal creation. This explains the characteristics and nature of the Vedic Divinities and their purposes, powers, and the ways they influence and affect the natural energies of the universe. It also shows how they can assist us and that blessings from them can help our own spiritual and material development and potentialities, depending on what we need.

Some of the Vedic Divinities that will be explained include Lord Krishna, Vishnu, Their main avatars and expansions, along with Brahma, Shiva, Ganesh, Murugan, Surya, Hanuman, as well as the goddesses of Sri Radha, Durga, Sarasvati, Lakshmi, and others. This also presents explanations of their names, attributes, dress, weapons, instruments, the meaning of the Shiva lingam, and some of the legends and stories that are connected with them. This will certainly give you a new insight into the expansive nature of the Vedic tradition.

This book is: $17.95 retail, 230 pages, 11 black & white photos, ISBN: 1453613765, EAN: 9781453613764.

The Soul
Understanding Our Real Identity
The Key to Spiritual Awakening

This book provides a summarization of the most essential spiritual knowledge that will give you the key to spiritual awakening. The descriptions will give you greater insights and a new look at who and what you really are as a spiritual being.

The idea that we are more than merely these material bodies is pervasive. It is established in every religion and spiritual path in this world. However, many religions only hint at the details of this knowledge, but if we look around we will find that practically the deepest and clearest descriptions of the soul and its characteristics are found in the ancient Vedic texts of India.

Herein you will find some of the most insightful spiritual knowledge and wisdom known to mankind. Some of the topics include:

- How you are more than your body
- The purpose of life
- Spiritual ignorance of the soul is the basis of illusion and suffering
- The path of spiritual realization
- How the soul is eternal
- The unbounded nature of the soul
- What is the Supersoul
- Attaining direct spiritual perception and experience of our real identity

This book will give you a deeper look into the ancient wisdom of India's Vedic, spiritual culture, and the means to recognize your real identity.

This book is 5 1/2"x8 1/2" trim size, 130 pages, $7.95, ISBN: 1453733833.

Prayers, Mantras and Gayatris
A Collection for Insights, Spiritual Growth, Protection, and Many Other Blessings

Using mantras or prayers can help us do many things, depending on our intention. First of all, it is an ancient method that has been used successfully to raise our consciousness, our attitude, aim of life, and outlook, and prepare ourselves for perceiving higher states of being.

The Sanskrit mantras within this volume offer such things as the knowledge and insights for spiritual progress, including higher perceptions and understandings of the Absolute or God, as well as the sound vibrations for awakening our higher awareness, invoking the positive energies to help us overcome obstacles and oppositions, or to assist in healing our minds and bodies from disease or negativity. They can provide the means for requesting protection on our spiritual path, or from enemies, ghosts, demons, or for receiving many other benefits. In this way, they offer a process for acquiring blessings of all kinds, both material and spiritual. There is something for every need. Some of what you will find includes:

- The most highly recommended mantras for spiritual realization in this age.
- A variety of prayers and gayatris to Krishna, Vishnu and other avatars, Goddess Lakshmi for financial well-being, Shiva, Durga, Ganesh, Devi, Indra, Sarasvati, etc., and Surya the Sun-god, the planets, and for all the days of the week.
- Powerful prayers of spiritual insight in Shiva's Song, along with the Bhaja Govindam by Sri Adi Shankaracharya, the Purusha Sukta, Brahma-samhita, Isha Upanishad, Narayana Suktam, and Hanuman Chalisa.
- Prayers and mantras to Sri Chaitanya and Nityananda.
- Strong prayers for protection from Lord Narasimha. The protective shield from Lord Narayana.
- Lists of the 108 names of Lord Krishna, Radhika, Goddess Devi, Shiva, and Sri Rama.
- The Vishnu-Sahasranama or thousand names of Vishnu, Balarama, Gopala, Radharani, and additional lists of the sacred names of the Vedic Divinities;
- And many other prayers, mantras and stotras for an assortment of blessings and benefits.

This book is 6"x9" trim size, 760 pages, ISBN:1456545906, $31.95.

Krishna Deities and Their Miracles
How the Images of Lord Krishna Interact with Their Devotees

This book helps reveal how the Deities of Krishna in the temple are but another channel through which the Divine can be better understood and perceived. In fact, the Deities Themselves can exhibit what some would call miracles in the way They reveal how the Divine accepts the Deity form. These miracles between the Deities of Krishna and His devotees happen in many different ways, and all the time. This is one process through which Krishna, or the Supreme Being, reveals Himself and the reality of His existence. Stories of such miracles or occurrences extend through the ages up to modern times, and all around the world. This book relates an assortment of these events to show how the images in the temples have manifested Their personality and character in various ways in Their pastimes with Their devotees, whether it be for developing their devotion, instructing them, or simply giving them His kindness, mercy or inspiration.

This book helps show that the Supreme Reality is a person who plays and exhibits His pastimes in any manner He likes. This is also why worship of the Deity in the temple has been and remains a primary means of increasing one's devotion and connection with the Supreme Being.

Besides presenting stories of the reciprocation that can exist between Krishna in His Deity form and the ordinary living beings, other topics include:

- The antiquity of devotion to the Deity in the Vedic tradition.
- Historical sites of ancient Deity worship.
- Scriptural instructions and references to Deity veneration.
- The difference between idols and Deities.
- What is darshan and the significance of Deities.
- Why God would even take the initiative to reveal Himself to His devotees and accept the position of being a Deity.

This book will give deeper insight into the unlimited personality and causeless benevolence of the Supreme, especially to those who become devoted to Him.

This book is 6"x9" trim size, 210 pages, $14.95, ISBN: 1463734298.

Defending Vedic Dharma
Tackling the Issues to Make a Difference

The Vedic culture and its philosophy is one of the most deeply spiritual and all encompassing traditions in the world, and has been a major contributor to philosophical thought and the development of civilization. It does not take that long to understand, but it can take some serious consideration. Until then, there can be some aspects of it that are misunderstood or misinterpreted.

Therefore, this book takes some of the issues of the day and describes what they are and the remedies for dealing with them in order to make a difference in how we participate in Vedic culture, how we can make it more effective in our lives, and how it can be perceived in a more positive way. All of this makes a difference in the objectives of preserving, protecting, promoting, and perpetuating the Vedic spiritual path.

So this book shows some of the many uplifting and insightful qualities we can find in the Vedic tradition, of which everyone should be aware and can appreciate. Some of the important issues discussed within include:

- Why it is important to use the proper vocabulary to express Vedic concepts.
- Why all religions really are not the same, though many Hindus and gurus like to think they are. Time to wake up to reality.
- The power of a united Vedic community, and how it could rapidly change things if Hindus actually became more united and worked together.
- The importance of becoming a Dharmic leader and to do your part, and the danger of Hindu teachers who really do not lead in a way they should.
- The long-term but realistic cure for the corruption in India.
- The importance of Vedic temples as centers of sacred knowledge, and why temples should be open to everyone.
- How and why the Vedic texts say that the knowledge within them must be shared with everyone.
- The real purpose of the natural Vedic way of social arrangement, but why the present caste system in India should be changed or thrown out completely.
- An eight point action plan for how Hindus in America can best use the freedoms they have, which often exceed the decreasing freedoms in India, to cultivate their tradition to its fullest extent while they have the means to do so.

The clarity with which these and other issues are addressed make this an important book for consideration.

This book is 6" x 9" trim size, $12.95, 214 pages, ISBN: 1466342277.

Advancements of Ancient India's Vedic Culture
The Planet's Earliest Civilization and How it Influenced the World

This book shows how the planet's earliest civilization lead the world in both material and spiritual progress. From the Vedic culture of ancient India thousands of years ago, we find for example the origins of mathematics, especially algebra and geometry, as well as early astronomy and planetary observations, many instances of which can be read in the historical Vedic texts. Medicine in Ayurveda was the first to prescribe herbs for the remedy of disease, surgical instruments for operations, and more.

Other developments that were far superior and ahead of the rest of the world included:
- Writing and language, especially the development of sophisticated Sanskrit;
- Metallurgy and making the best known steel at the time;
- Ship building and global maritime trade;
- Textiles and the dying of fabric for which India was known all over the world;
- Agricultural and botanical achievements;
- Precise Vedic arts in painting, dance and music;
- The educational systems and the most famous of the early universities, like Nalanda and Takshashila;
- The source of individual freedom and fair government, and the character and actions of rulers;
- Military and the earliest of martial arts;
- Along with some of the most intricate, deep and profound of all philosophies and spiritual paths, which became the basis of many religions that followed later around the world.

These and more are the developments that came from India, much of which has been forgotten, but should again be recognized as the heritage of the ancient Indian Vedic tradition that continues to inspire humanity.

This book is 6"x9" trim size, 350 pages, $20.95, ISBN: 1477607897.

Spreading Vedic Traditions Through Temples
Proven Strategies that Make them More Effective

After forty years of managing Vedic temples or Mandirs in many different ways, as well as traveling all over India and seeing how others utilize successful plans, Stephen Knapp has put together a book that explains the most important programs that any temple can use for more effectively protecting and perpetuating the Vedic traditions. In a non-sectarian way, he lists and describes how the Dharmic temples of all kinds can increase their congregations as well as engage their members in service to help in maintaining the temples and traditions, and expanding their influence. Some of what is included are:

- The primary mission of the temple.
- Services the guests can easily offer in seva to the temple or deity.
- Giving Vedic culture to the next generation.
- Temple classes, the Sunday program and children's schools and youth camps.
- Vedic temples as centers of sacred knowledge.
- The power of adult study groups, cultural and outreach programs, and festivals.
- Utilizing temple restaurants, gift shops, exhibits, and support groups.
- Ways of reaching more people, both in India and the USA.
- The need and ways for promotion, and radio, television, and newspapers.
- An action plan on how to cultivate Vedic culture in America.
- Attracting and welcoming non-Indians and Western seekers for more support.
- Starting a spiritual revolution in India and elsewhere.
- Working with priests, rituals, and teaching the culture and traditions.
- Unifying and organizing the Vedic community.

This book covers many more methods that are not merely ideas, but are already being used in practical and successful ways to help preserve, promote and spread what is the last bastion of deep spiritual truth. As more temples are built in Western countries, these strategies will become increasingly important. Using these techniques as the basis of your ideas, your temple cannot help but be successful.

This book is 6"x9" trim size, 186 pages, $11.95, ISBN: 1478222999.

The Bhakti-yoga Handbook

A Guide for Beginning the Essentials of Devotional Yoga

This book is a guide for anyone who wants to begin the practice of bhakti-yoga in a practical and effective way. This supplies the information, the principles, the regular activities or *sadhana*, and how to have the right attitude in applying ourselves to attain success on the path of bhakti-yoga, which is uniting with God through love and devotion.

This outlines a general schedule for our daily spiritual activities and a typical morning program as found in most Krishna temples that are centered around devotional yoga. In this way, you will find the explanations on how to begin our day and set our mind, what meditations to do, which spiritual texts are best to study, and how we can make most everything we do as part of bhakti-yoga. All of these can be adjusted in a way that can be practiced and applied by anyone by anyone regardless of whether you are in a temple ashrama or in your own home or apartment.

Such topics include:
- The secret of bhakti-yoga and its potency in this day and age,
- The essential morning practice, the best time for meditation,
- The standard songs and mantras that we can use, as applied in most Krishna temples,
- Understanding the basics of the Vedic spiritual philosophy, such as karma, reincarnation, the Vedic description of the soul, etc.,
- How Vedic culture is still as relevant today as ever,
- Who is Sri Krishna,
- How to chant the Hare Krishna mantra,
- Standards for temple etiquette,
- The nine processes of bhakti-yoga, a variety of activities from which anyone can utilize,
- How to make our career a part of the yoga process,
- How to turn our cooking into bhakti-yoga,
- How to set up a home altar or temple room, depending on what standard you wish to establish,
- How to take care of deities in our home, if we have Them,
- How to perform the basic ceremonies like arati,
- How to take care of the Tulasi plant if you have one,
- And the spiritual results you can expect to attain through this yoga.

All of the basics and effective applications to get started and continue with your practice of bhakti-yoga is supplied so you can progress in a steady way, from beginner to advanced.

This book is 278 pages, $14.95, ISBN: 149030228X.

www.Stephen-Knapp.com
http://stephenknapp.info
http://stephenknapp.wordpress.com

Be sure to visit Stephen's web site. It provides lots of information on many spiritual aspects of Vedic and spiritual philosophy, and Indian culture for both beginners and the scholarly. You will find:

- All the descriptions and contents of Stephen's books, how to order them, and keep up with any new books or articles that he has written.
- Reviews and unsolicited letters from readers who have expressed their appreciation for his books, as well as his website.
- Free online booklets are also available for your use or distribution on meditation, why be a Hindu, how to start yoga, meditation, etc.
- Helpful prayers, mantras, gayatris, and devotional songs.
- Over a hundred enlightening articles that can help answer many questions about life, the process of spiritual development, the basics of the Vedic path, or how to broaden our spiritual awareness. Many of these are emailed among friends or posted on other web sites.
- Over 150 color photos taken by Stephen during his travels through India. There are also descriptions and 40 photos of the huge and amazing Kumbha Mela festival.
- Directories of many Krishna and Hindu temples around the world to help you locate one near you, where you can continue your experience along the Eastern path.
- Postings of the recent archeological discoveries that confirm the Vedic version of history.
- Photographic exhibit of the Vedic influence in the Taj Mahal, questioning whether it was built by Shah Jahan or a pre-existing Vedic building.
- A large list of links to additional websites to help you continue your exploration of Eastern philosophy, or provide more information and news about India, Hinduism, ancient Vedic culture, Vaishnavism, Hare Krishna sites, travel, visas, catalogs for books and paraphernalia, holy places, etc.
- A large resource for vegetarian recipes, information on its benefits, how to get started, ethnic stores, or non-meat ingredients and supplies.
- A large "Krishna Darshan Art Gallery" of photos and prints of Krishna and Vedic divinities. You can also find a large collection of previously unpublished photos of His Divine Grace A. C. Bhaktivedanta Swami.

This site is made as a practical resource for your use and is continually being updated and expanded with more articles, resources, and information. Be sure to check it out.

Printed in Great Britain
by Amazon